IMAGES
of America

DOVER

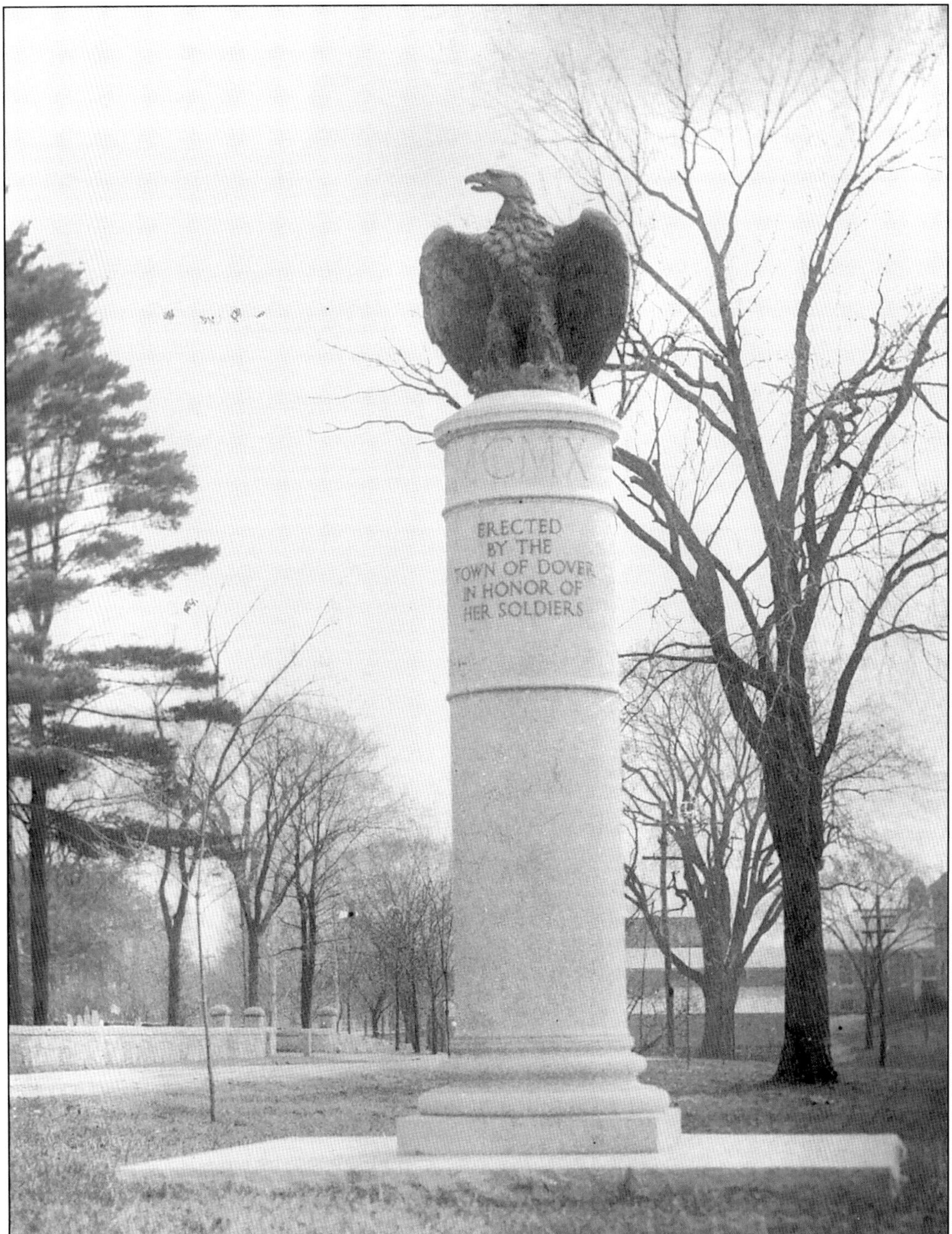

The Dover Soldiers' Monument—designed by Richardson, Barott & Richardson at a cost of $2,500—was dedicated on June 18, 1910, by Gov. Eden S. Draper. The monument dominates the Old Training Field and can be seen by those coming into town from Needham or Dedham. The dates of the ten wars in which Dover soldiers participated are inscribed on the opposite side of the 14 foot-high, circular, granite shaft. The Powisset Garden Club maintains the garden and plantings for the memorial.

IMAGES
of America

DOVER

Paul H. Tedesco

ARCADIA
PUBLISHING

ISBN 978-0-7385-0424-7

Published by Arcadia Publishing
Charleston, South Carolina

Printed in the United States of America

Library of Congress Catalog Card Number: 00106411

For all general information contact Arcadia Publishing at:
Telephone 843-853-2070
Fax 843-853-0044
E-mail sales@arcadiapublishing.com
For customer service and orders:
Toll-Free 1-888-313-2665

Visit us on the Internet at www.arcadiapublishing.com

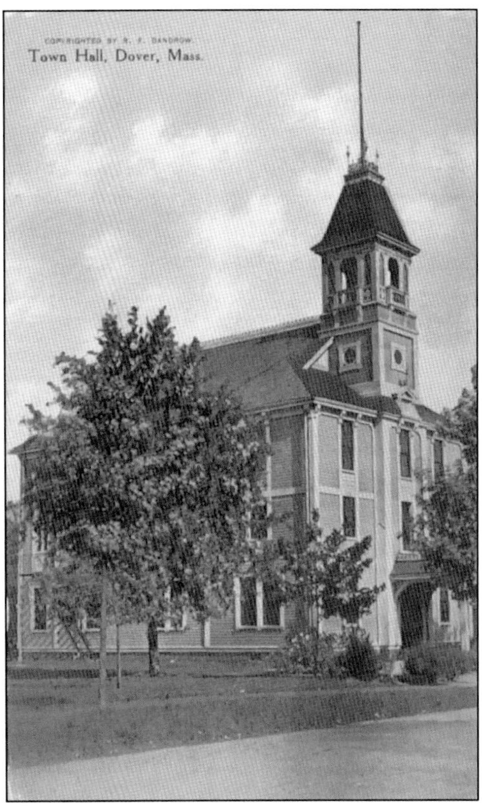

The March 1879 town meeting voted to spend $3,000 to build a town hall. As work neared completion, a cyclone blew the building down on July 19, 1879. To avoid calamity again, the town hired Thomas W. Silloway, a Boston architect and designer of the Vermont state capitol. The new town hall was dedicated on June 17, 1880, and cost $4,499. (Hope Hynes scrapbook.)

Contents

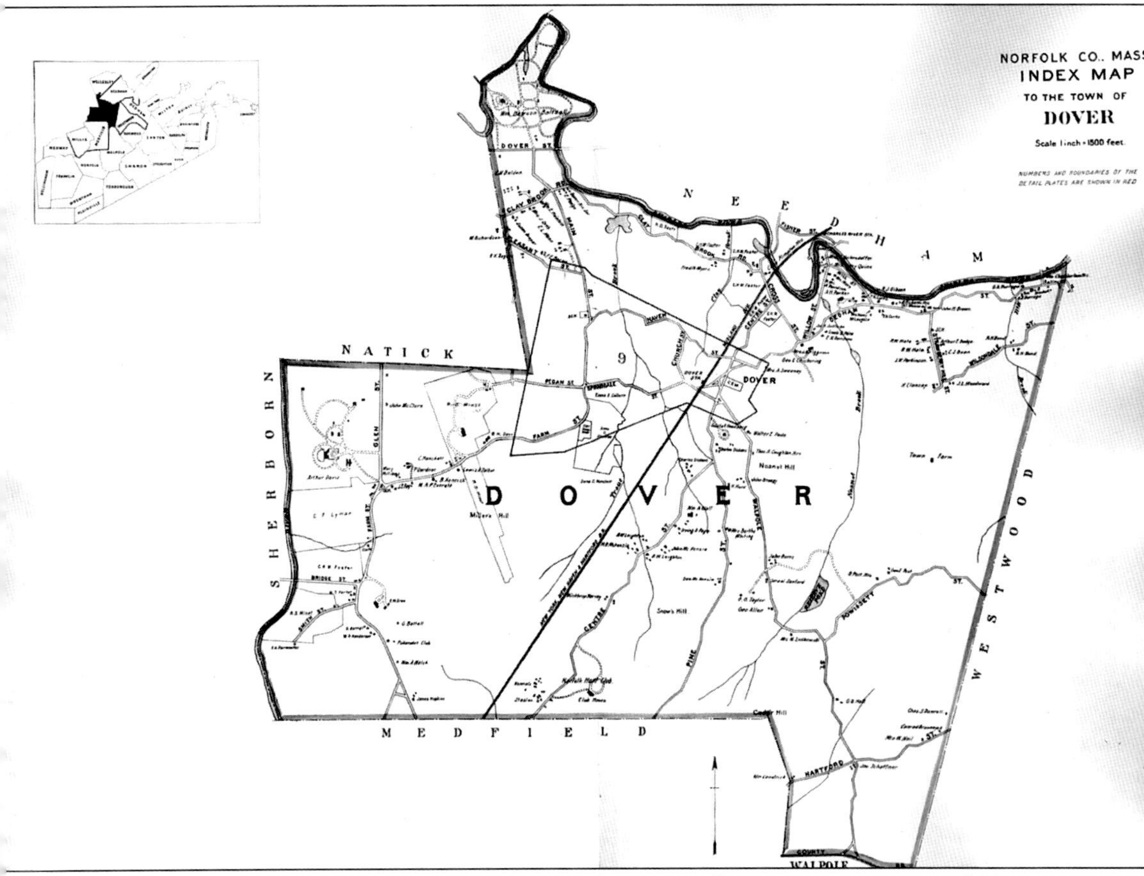

The Norfolk County map of Dover was created in 1909. (By permission, Harvard University Map Collection.)

Introduction

Dover, Massachusetts—a rural suburb tucked away in the southwestern corner of the Boston metropolitan area—was originally part of the Dedham Grant of 1635. Although there is no clear date of settlement, there were enough tax-paying families by 1729 to form Dedham's Fourth Precinct. This became the Springfield Parish of Dedham in 1748 and the District of Dover in 1784, before incorporation as a town by the Commonwealth of Massachusetts in 1836.

From its beginnings, Dover was a farming community that "relied on agriculture and grazing as the basis of its colonial economy although the ruggedness of its terrain plus the relative lack of water power limited its early growth. The damming of the Charles River in the late 18th century provided some power and allowed the development of mills which made nails and rolled iron." (Massachusetts Historical Commission.) In the 19th century, dairy farming became a good business for many residents.

The railroad came to Dover in the 1850s, making it easier for farmers to transport their products to surrounding markets and allowing residents access to the opportunities in Boston. Dover's commercial center, Bliss' Corners, developed where Springdale Avenue meets Farm and Main Streets. Here, a variety of small businesses-grew in support of the agricultural base: a whip factory; a straw business; a brush factory; a shoe business; a manufacturer of plows, hoops, paper, and cigars; two blacksmiths; and a wheelwright. However, the future of the community was not industrial. In 1876, a fire destroyed much of this area, and the commercial center shifted toward the railroad.

However, two businesses that began as small, home-based ventures expanded rapidly, employing many Dover residents and marketing their products worldwide by the late 19th century. Dr. William Porter started the Harvard Apparatus Company on his farm at the corner of Farm and Smith Streets; the company manufactured instruments needed to teach Harvard Medical School students their craft. In 1896, E.F. Hodgson, a manufacturer of portable prefabricated buildings, began his Peep-O-Day chicken brooder business on his father's farm on Farm Street.

Hodgson's business developed an ingenious method of bolting factory-made building sections together, which could be transported, broken down, and reassembled easily. The business grew and moved to a site closer to the center of town, prospering until the building was leveled by a fire in 1911. Hodgson rebuilt the firm near the railroad to take advantage of cheaper and easier transportation. After World War II, Hodgson buildings were shipped all over the world via Logan International Airport. Many of the houses still exist, especially on Meetinghouse Hill Road and elsewhere in Dover, as well as on Cape Cod and the Maine coast. The business flourished until it was sold and moved to Millis, Massachusetts, in 1961. Most of the factory buildings were dismantled, but some served as the office and garage for the Dover Highway Department until they were destroyed by a snowstorm on March 31 and April 1, 1997. The new Phillip S. Luttazi town garage now occupies the site.

By 1900, Dover was starting to become a residential community on the outer edge of the "new suburbs" of Boston. Wealthy Bostonians discovered Dover's open fields and established summer cottages as their neighbors had done in Wellesley and Needham. The Norfolk Hunt Club, founded with a nucleus from the neighboring Dedham Polo Club, rivaled the North Shore's Myopia Hunt Club. Between 1900 and 1914, wealthy Bostonians built at least 18 estates, mainly in the Farm Street and Strawberry Hill Street areas. Some of these estates were as large as 300 and 400 acres.

In 1908, the Edison Electric Illuminating Company pointed out, "During the recent years there have been erected in Dover several important dwellings and there can be no doubt that the establishment will follow of other home estates or summer residences. Several localities for these are yet available and presenting the same advantages of a fine climate, quiet rural charm and surroundings of scenic beauty together with unusual opportunities for out of door recreation. At the same time there are in Dover many appropriate sites for building of less expensive houses removed from the noisy and restricted city streets, but yet within convenient traveling distance of Boston with its business interests."

From 1900 to 1950, Dover slowly evolved. The railroad and the automobile made it possible for people to live in the community and work outside, a pattern associated with the development of Boston and the surrounding areas. The population was 656 in 1900; 867 in 1920; 1,195 in 1930; and 1,374 in 1940. WWII saw population adjustments, while the peacetime impact continued the upward movement. There were 2,846 residents in 1960; 4,529 in 1970; 4,703 in 1980; 4,915 in 1990; and 5,420 in 1995.

On July 7, 1909 (Old Home Day), townsman George D. Hall declared, "I feel that Dover's greatest future lies in her developing as a community of country homes—free from the noise and the turmoil of the city; developing but not changing the character of the place or the charms of her individuality; cherishing the sentiments of the past, and rejoicing in the natural picturesqueness of our township which already has attracted so many in our town. I, for one, hope to see Dover develop, but always in the spirit of simplicity and on those lines which will maker her remarkable as *the ideal community of ideal homes*."

Over the past 40 years or so, the town has grown appreciably. It has also maintained the character that Hall described and has made the transition from a rural town to a bedroom community. Until the last 10 to 15 years, that growth has been generally inconspicuous. Despite its restricted pattern of expansion, Dover has retained a far greater diversity than generally is recognized. The hills, streams, woods, and fields are still used, appreciated, and guarded by residents.

As Neil R. Pierce has pointed out, "the dynamic that initiates and primarily determines land use will continue to be the developers in pursuit of profit." Mansionization has come again to Dover. Urban sprawl has put increased pressure on the community to build. How much longer the residents can resist is an urgent question that has great importance for the future of the community and its people. Today, the town is a community of professionals—academic, artistic, business, legal, and medical—and townspeople who volunteer their time to contribute to the well being of the town, the Commonwealth of Massachusetts, New England, the nation, and the world. Dover has always been a special place, part of the world around it, but slightly out of the mainstream. May it so remain.

One

THE LAND

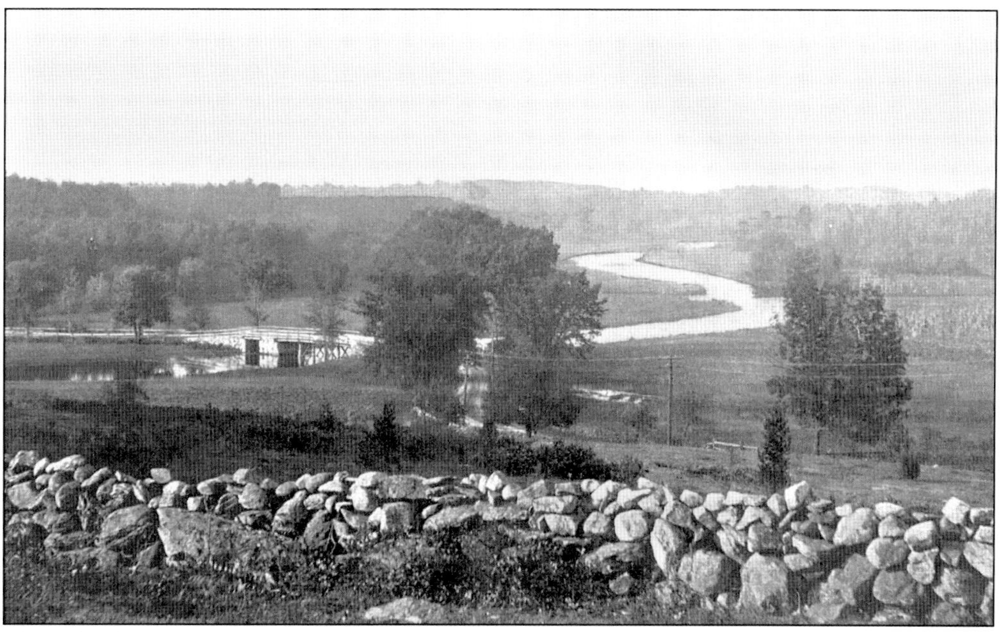

The Charles River separates Dover, Sherborn, Natick, Wellesley, and Needham. In this 1890s view, the Bridge Street Bridge connects Dover and Sherborn. The bridge has just been completely renovated. The old granite posts from the Dover side were removed and placed at the entrance to the Sawin Museum, home of the Dover Historical Society. One post has 1935 engraved on it, the date of the last renovation.

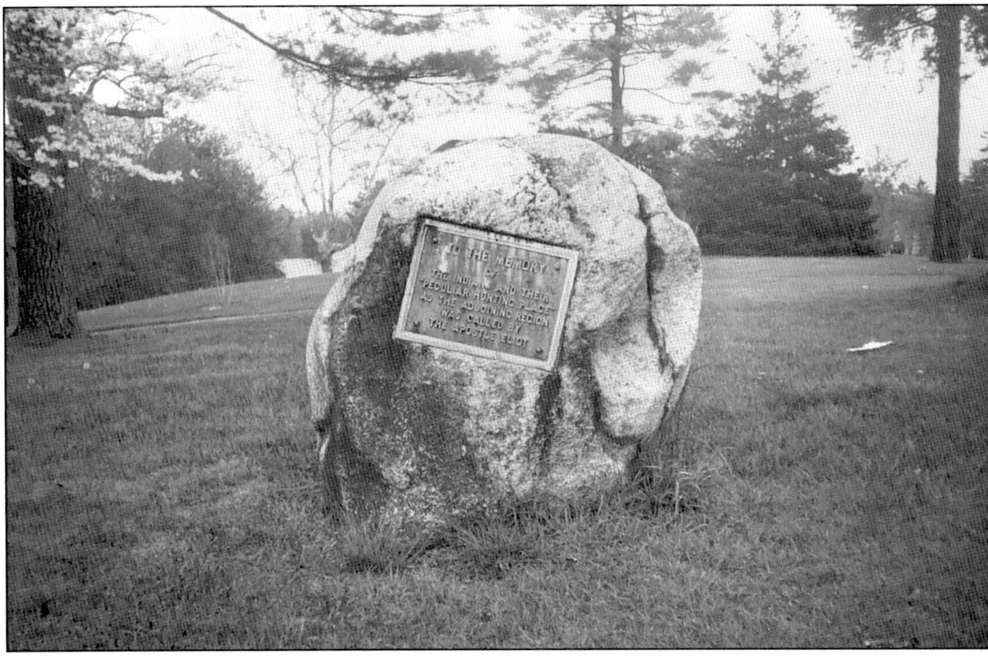

This bronze tablet on Dover Common was dedicated on January 13, 1912: "To the memory of the Indians and their 'peculiar hunting place' as the adjoining region was called by the apostle Eliot." Rev. John Eliot's Indian Village was not in Dover, but he most likely had to cross town land to get from Dedham to South Natick.

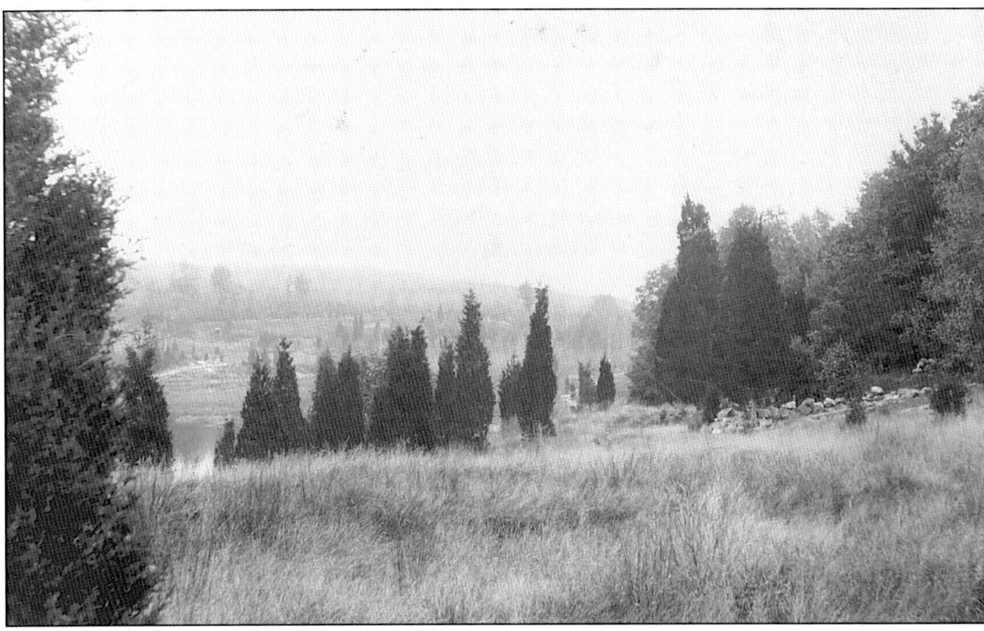

In 1909, the Edison Electric Illuminating Company of Boston noted, "Practically all of Dover lies on its hills, but among these are many interspersing broad meadows and fertile level fields, while further diversity is given the landscape of frequent bits of woodland and by occasional water courses flowing from never-failing springs." This quote remains good advertisement copy, even today.

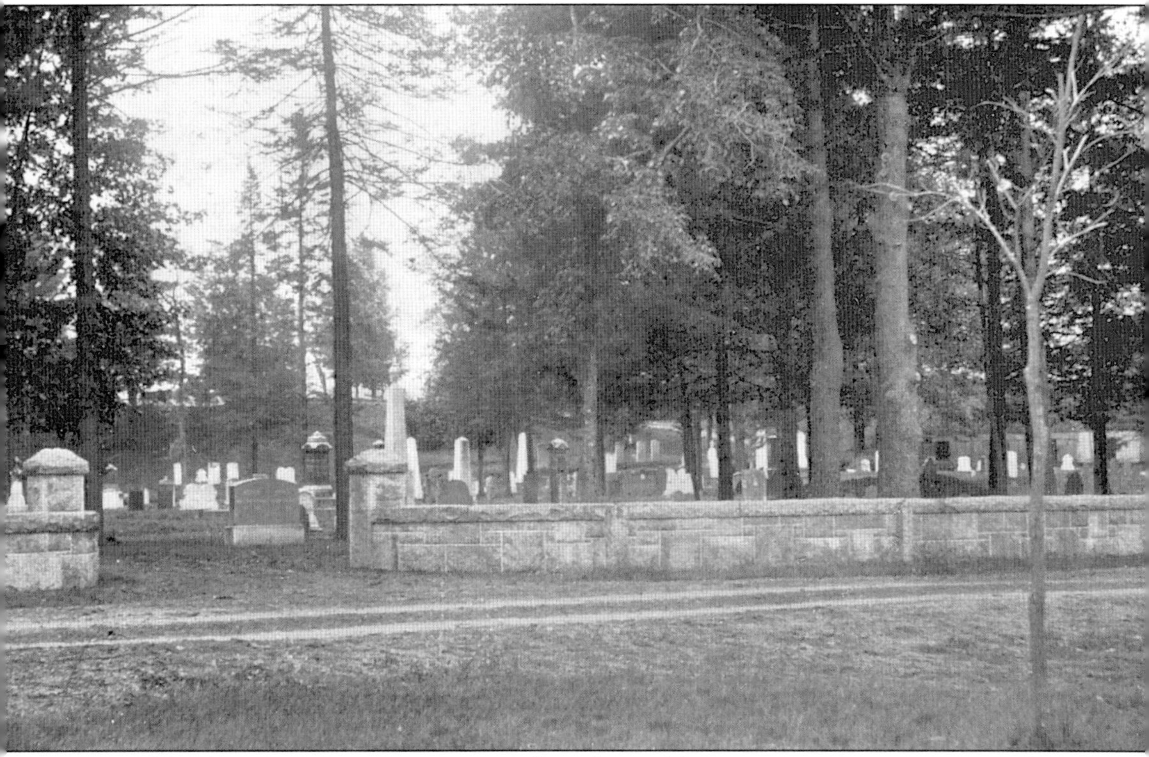

The Highland Cemetery on Centre Street offers a beautiful green space in Dover Center. John Battle was the first person to be buried here in 1729. The original 1746 burial ground and its additions, bequeathed by Nathaniel Chickering, were separated from the street by a stone wall in 1892. Soldier's graves dating to the French and Indian War constitute the first rank of graves.

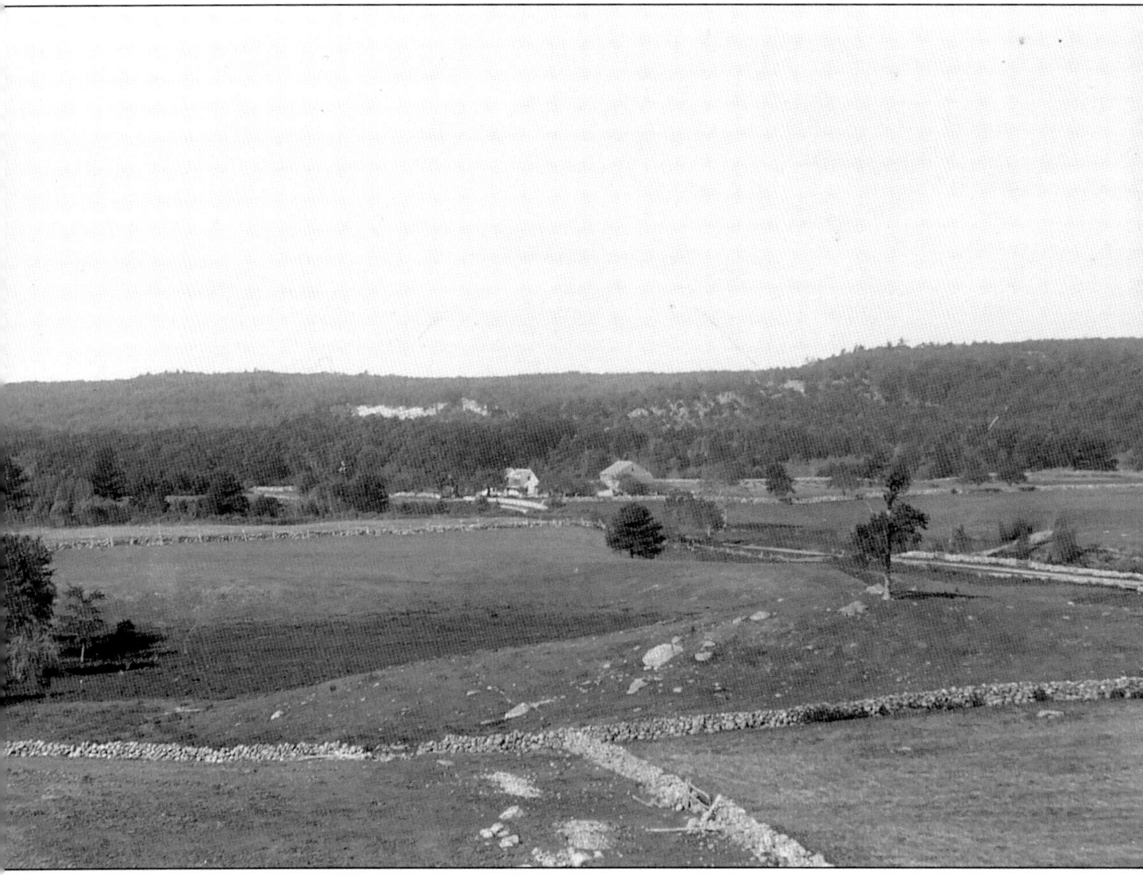

Hurd's *History of Norfolk County* concludes, "It is not difficult to imagine why Dover was called Springfield Parish more than a century ago, when at present time sixty buildings are supplied with pure spring water, which gushes forth from Pegan and the neighboring hills." Rev. Ralph Sanger noted that Dover had an advantage over many towns in the Commonwealth of Massachusetts in regard to climate and air.

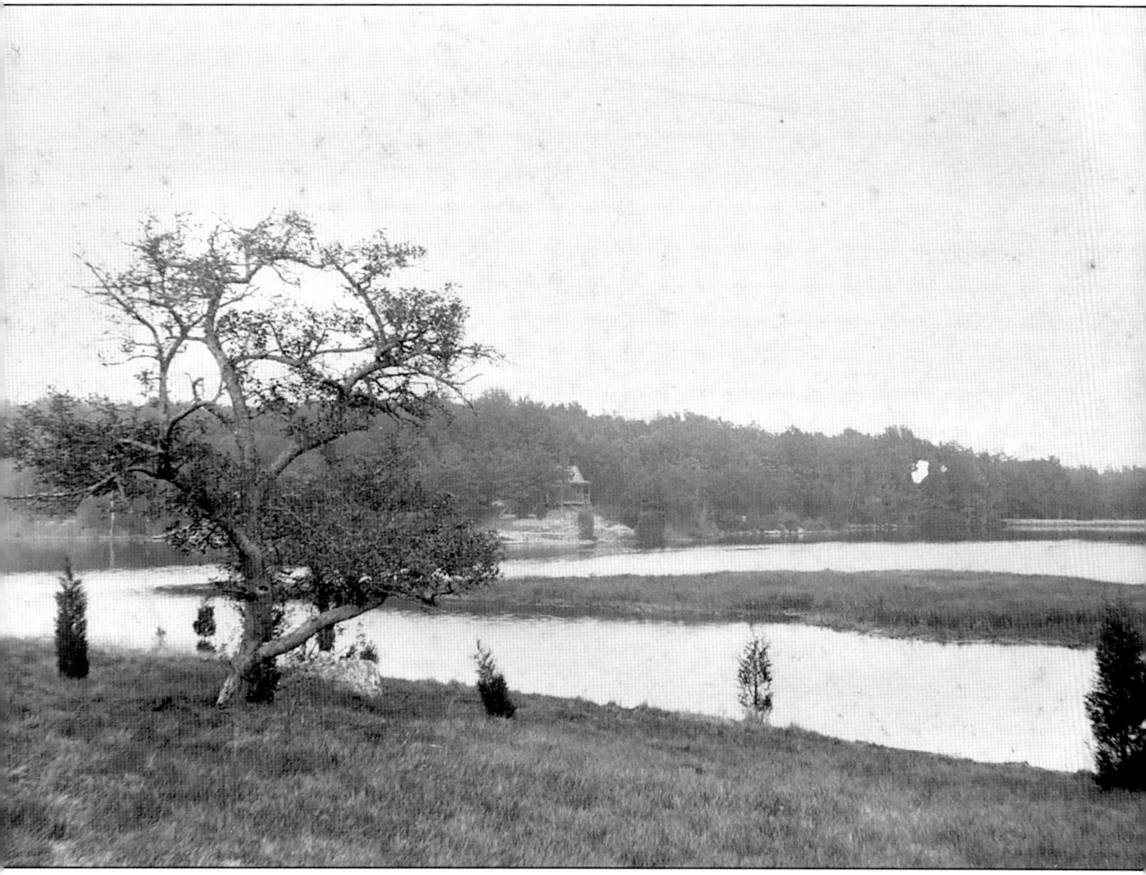

The Charles River has always been an important natural resource for the town. This view shows the Dover Street Bridge from Main Street. The town's area covers 15.3 square miles, or 9,796 square acres. Its perimeter is 23.51 miles long, of which 10.87 miles is the Charles River. The town is an active member of the Charles River Watershed Association, which works hard to improve the water quality of the river.

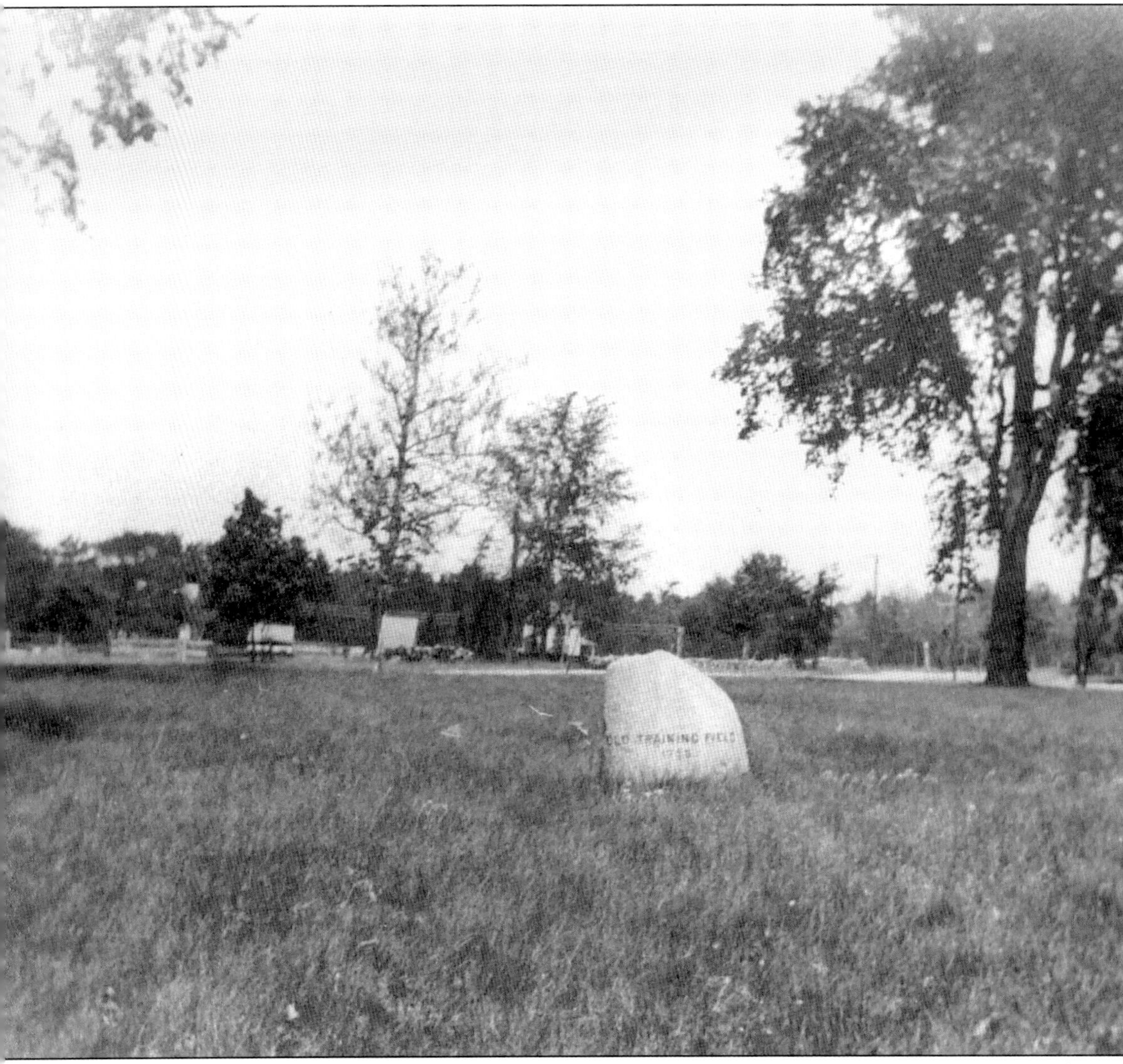

This 1908 view shows the Old Training Field before the Soldiers' Monument was erected behind the stone marker. It was on this field in June 1775 that 17 men of Springfield Parish mustered. They joined with Capt. Daniel Whiting and the Dedham Company, which was positioned in the middle of the battle line on the east slope of Breed's Hill as part of Col. Jonathan Brewer's regiment.

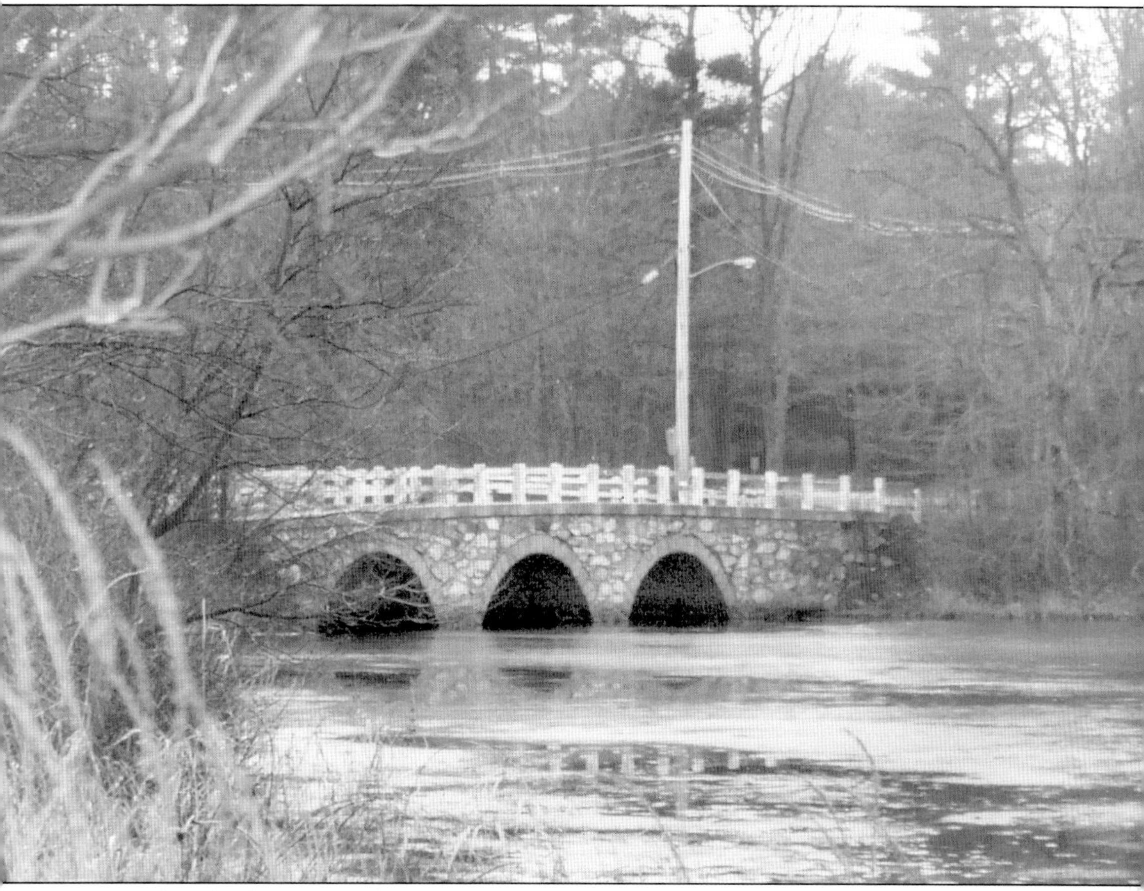

Because the Charles River makes up so much of the town's boundary line, bridges have always been an important part of the community. The three-arch, stone bridge on Centre Street occupies a spot that has hosted a bridge between the towns of Needham and Dover since before 1728. This bridge crosses the river above the dam that served as a power source for the manufacturing industry during the 19th century.

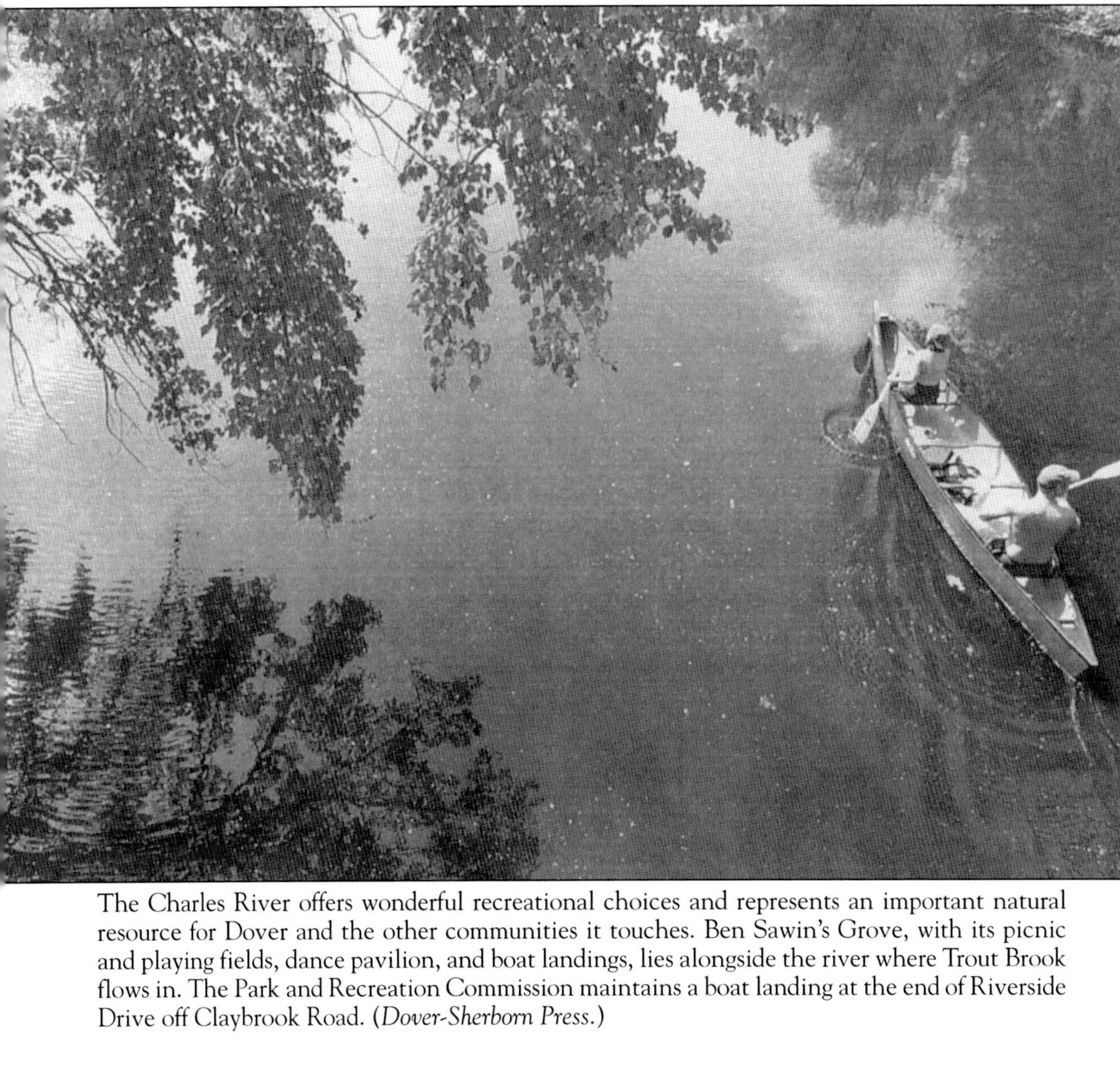

The Charles River offers wonderful recreational choices and represents an important natural resource for Dover and the other communities it touches. Ben Sawin's Grove, with its picnic and playing fields, dance pavilion, and boat landings, lies alongside the river where Trout Brook flows in. The Park and Recreation Commission maintains a boat landing at the end of Riverside Drive off Claybrook Road. (*Dover-Sherborn Press.*)

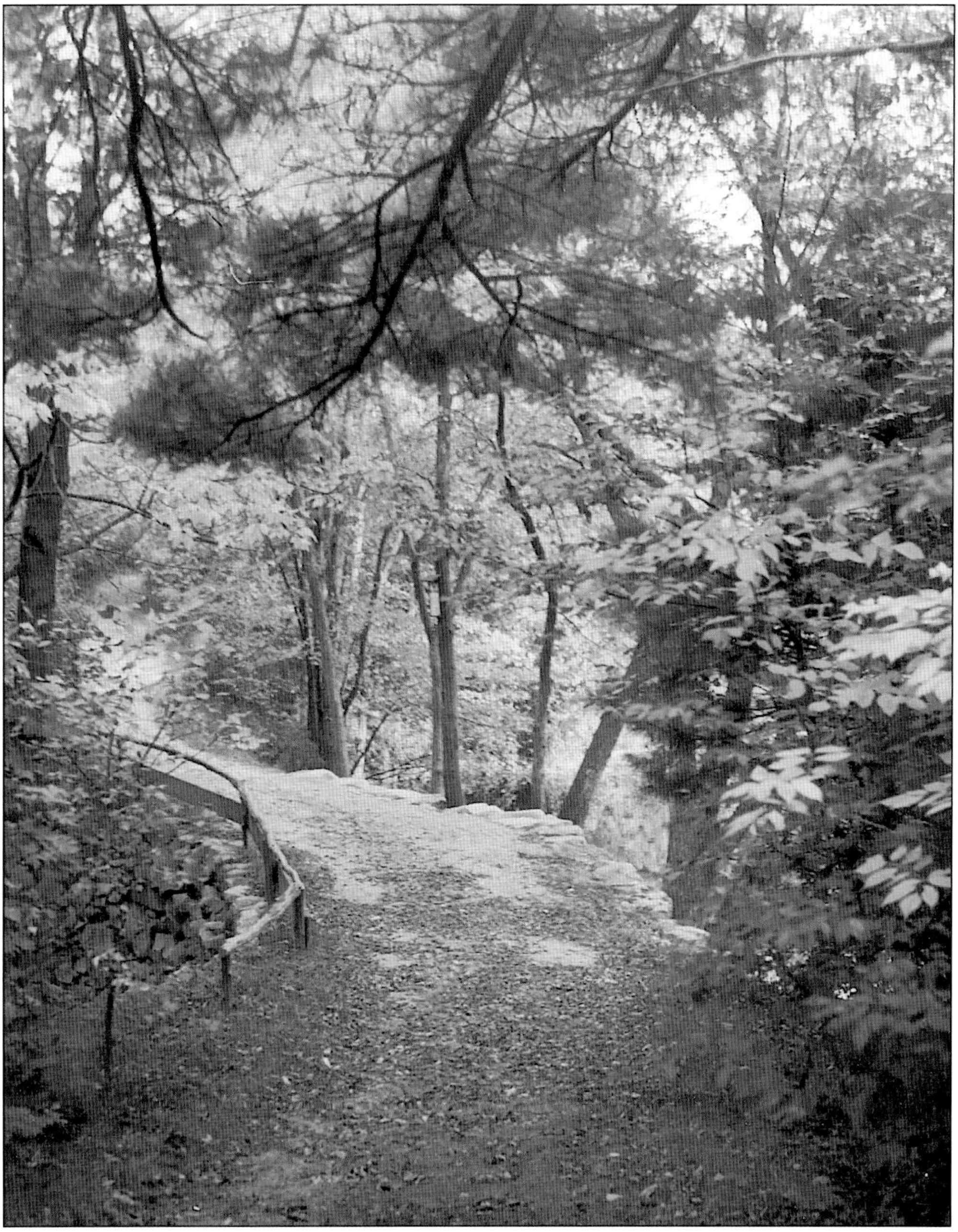

This trail in the Dover woods exemplifies the town's appeal for both townspeople and visitors. Fortunately, the Dover Conservation Commission has stated that it is "committed to the preservation of open space . . . and the rural character of the Town. . . . Critical to this purpose is the interest and involvement of residents not only in conservation planning but also in planning for the inevitable development of Dover in light of the pressures of modern society."

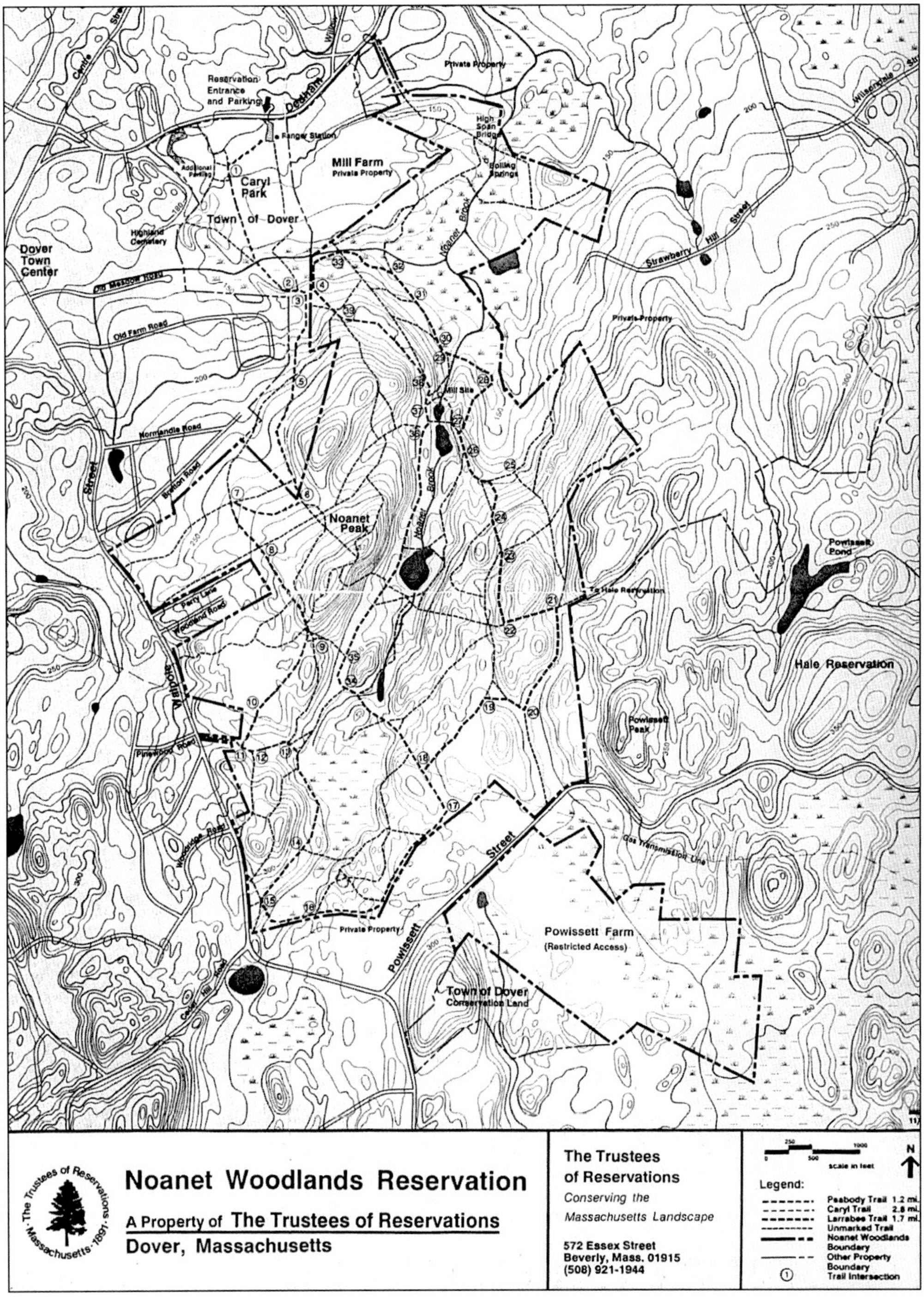

This map of the Noanet Woodlands Reservation illustrates the force of the conservation movement in the town. The reservation is operated by the Trustees of Reservations. Along with the Dover Conservation Land Trust and the Dover Conservation Commission, the community is making an increasingly strong commitment to protecting the land.

Two

CITIZENS OF DOVER

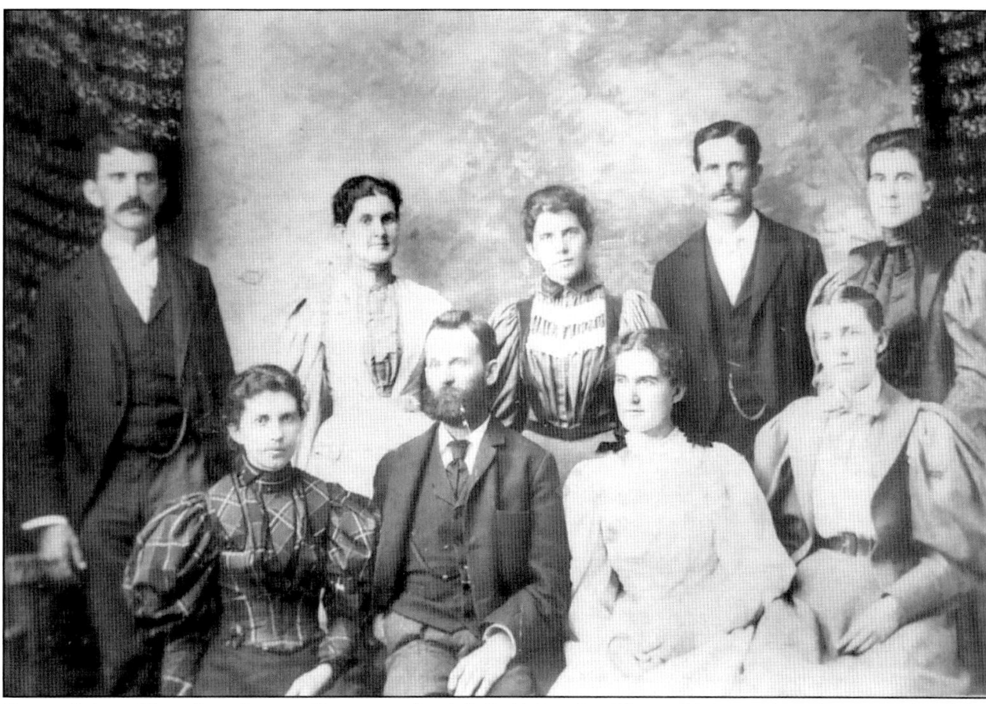

One of the oldest families in Dover is the McGill family. This 1890s studio photograph of the McGill children reminds us how big families were in another era. Farms required a constancy of labor unlike most other occupations. The children grew up at Greystone Farm, now St. Stephen Priory. Seen here, from left to right, are the following: (front row) Annie, James, Jeannie, and Catherine; (back row) Jack, Martha, Margaret, Tom, and Agnes. (Shirley McGill.)

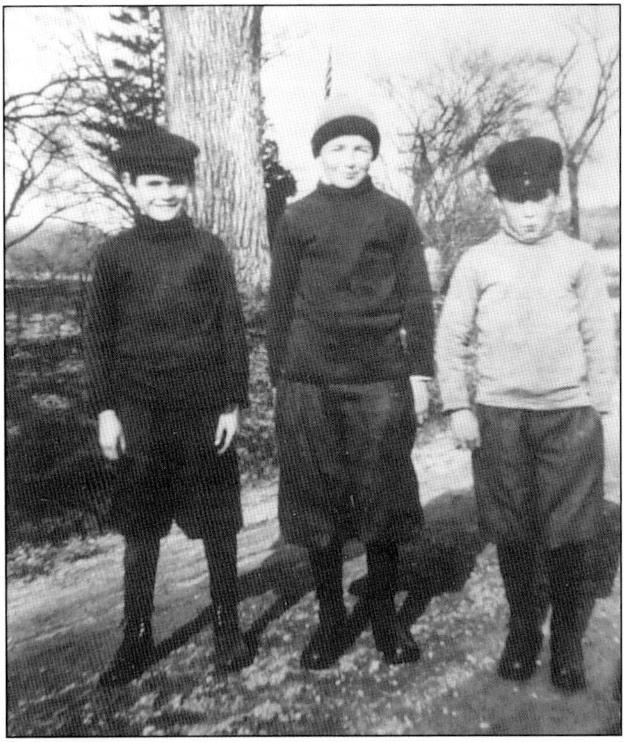

Leo, Francis, and Raymond Comiskey stop in the 1910s to have their picture taken at the family farm on the corner of Main and Haven Streets. Valley Farm Dairy trucks were a familiar sight in Dover and neighboring Needham, Natick, and Wellesley for more than 50 years. (Robert Comiskey.)

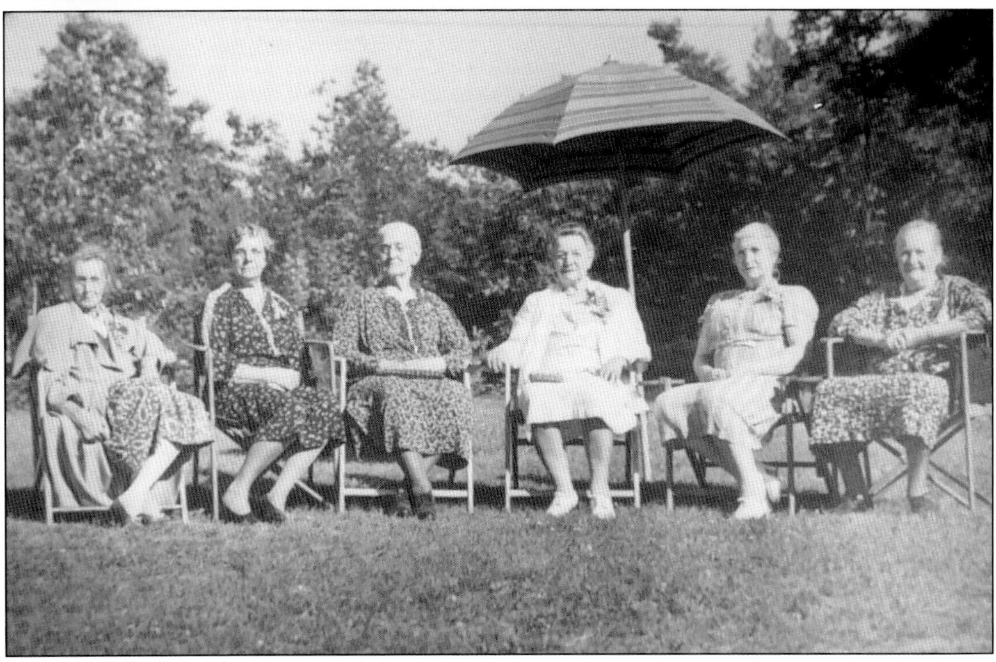

Members of the Dover American Legion Auxiliary gather on the front lawn of the MacKenzie residence on Centre Street in the 1930s. Susan MacKenzie (first on left) and Elizabeth Bond (fifth from left) are the grandmothers of the current property owner. Moments like this were much more common during this era, when time was allocated much differently. (Janet MacKenzie.)

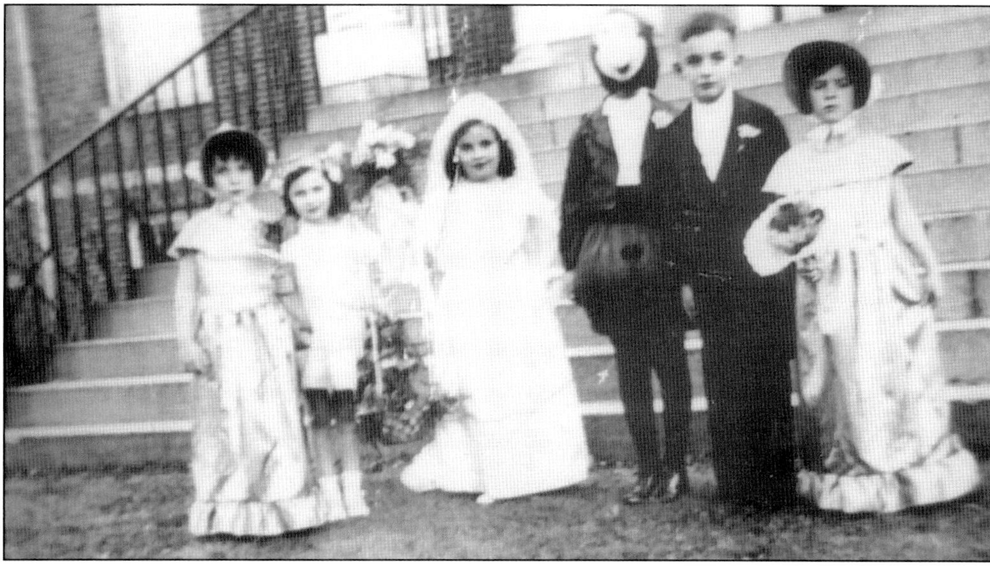

Cartoon characters are always popular. The child wearing the Mickey Mouse mask was married on December 19, 1935. The wedding party received guests at the steps of the Dover Town House. Shown, from left to right, are Barbara Wakelin, Janet MacKenzie, Margaret Thibedeau, Carlton Sherman, John Comiskey, and Dorothy Rasch. (Janet MacKenzie.)

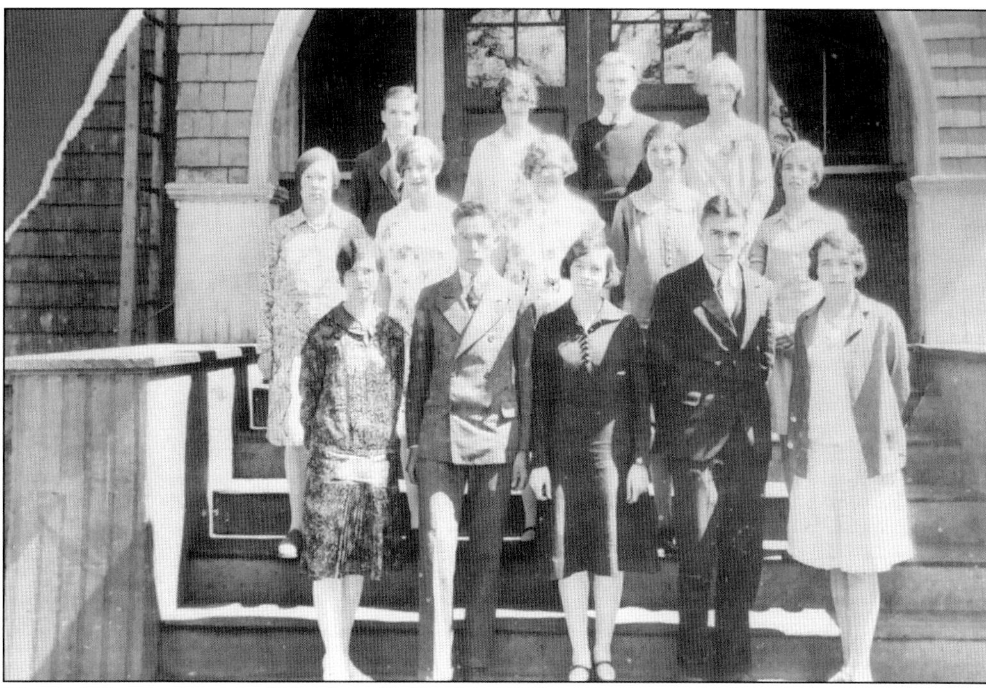

The 1936 Dover Tones yearbook staff of Dover High School assembles on the front steps of the Sanger building. Shown, from left to right, are the following: (front row) Doris Dove (Maker), Kilburn Treadwell, Clair Hinbaugh, Paul Schaffner, and Isabel McCullough; (middle row) Alice Wakelin, Gladys Williams (Treadwell), Ruth Bond, Amy Jacques, and M. Chase; (back row) J. Pascall, Miss Flynn, Carl Walden, and Ruth Hanchett. (Janet Mackenzie.)

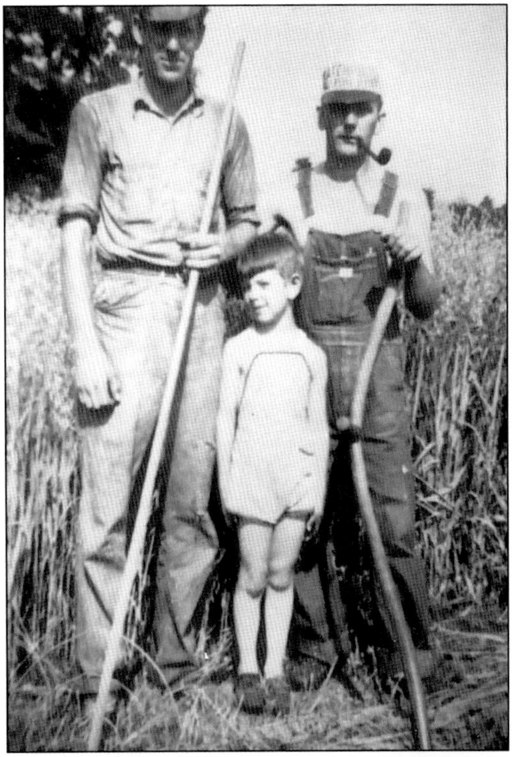

By 1900, Dover's economic base was no longer solely agricultural; however, certain farm chores never ended. The town had many horses and cows, which required feed. Haying, milking, and tending vegetable gardens all required human energy. In this 1937 photograph, Jerry Tupper, Samuel Lockhart, and Chet Heinlein Jr. pose in the field where they were working. (Marion Gerrity.)

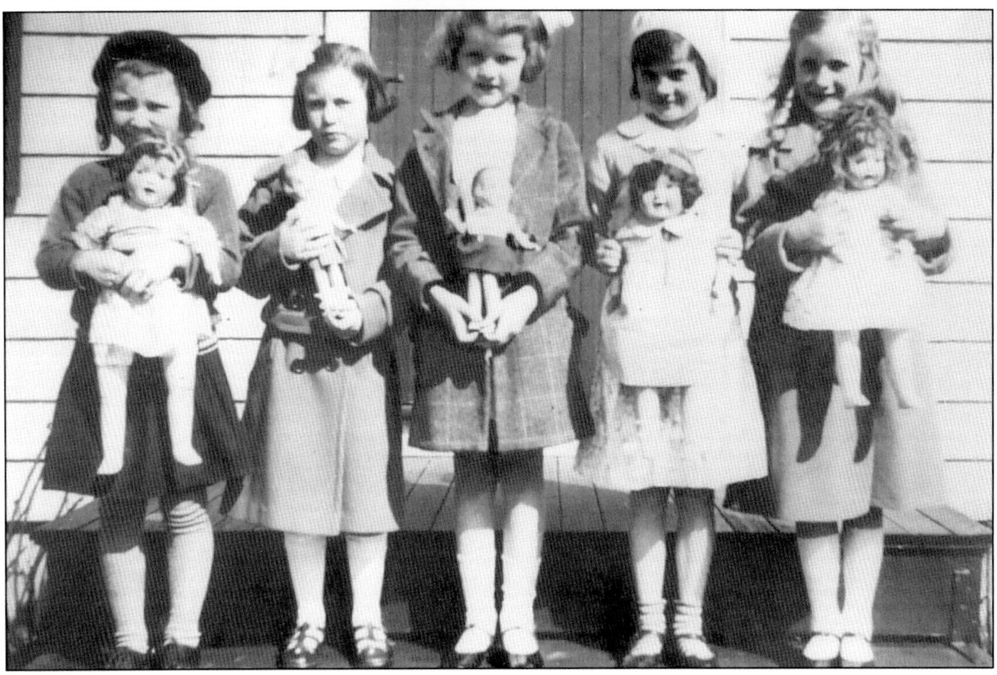

Birthday parties, as well as dolls, always seem to be in favor. Little girls enjoy dressing up for a party. Assembled at Ruth Kettelty's party sometime in the 1930s are, from left to right, Priscilla March, Betty Maker, Annette Burbank, Marion Heinlein, and Ruth Kettlety. (Marion Gerrity.)

In New England, weather and food mark the seasons. Apples and cider-making have been an autumn tradition. In this 1940 photograph, Charles and Betsy Jackson work a cider press in their driveway. There are no preservatives here; this is the real stuff. (Molly Jackson.)

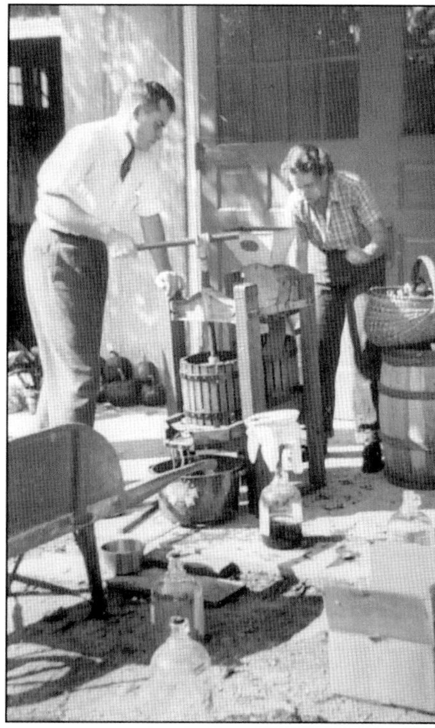

Groom Fred Hicks exercises Cassilis Naiad at Frostfield on October 15, 1937. Horses may be a wonderful recreational sport, but they require a great deal of work. Mucking out stables, walking, and exercising are all part of the daily routine. Horses also demand a great deal of responsibility, which many Dover youngsters learned early in their lives. Tax records for 1998 indicate that there were 135 horses in town. (Cornelia Clark Roberts.)

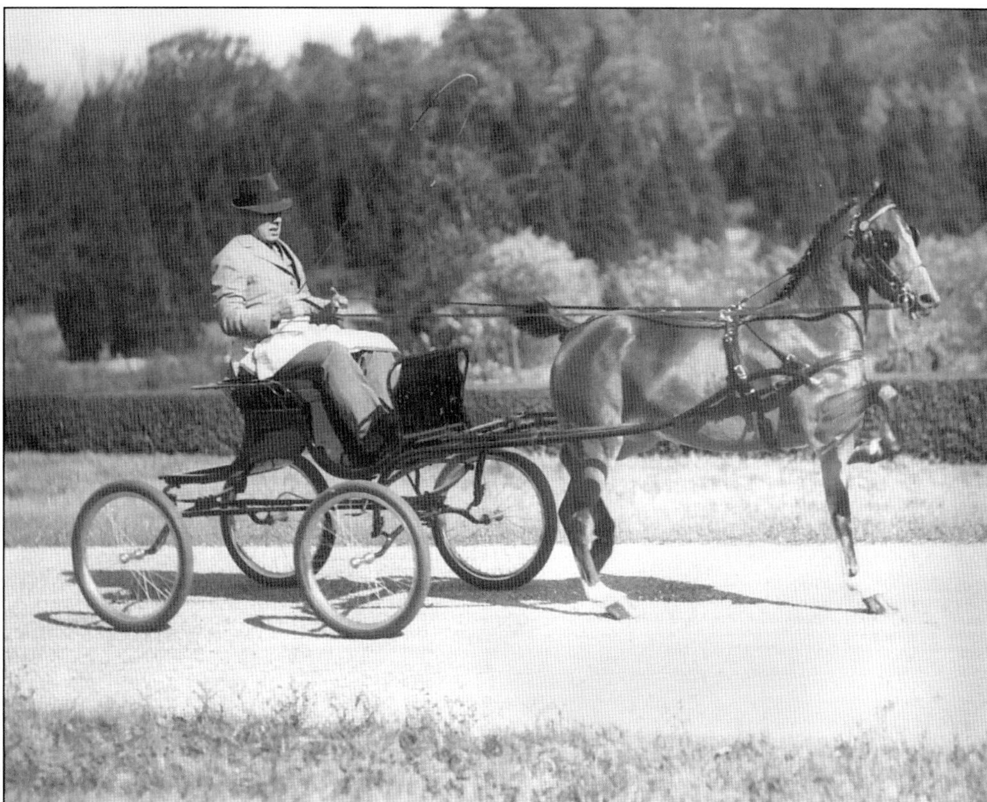

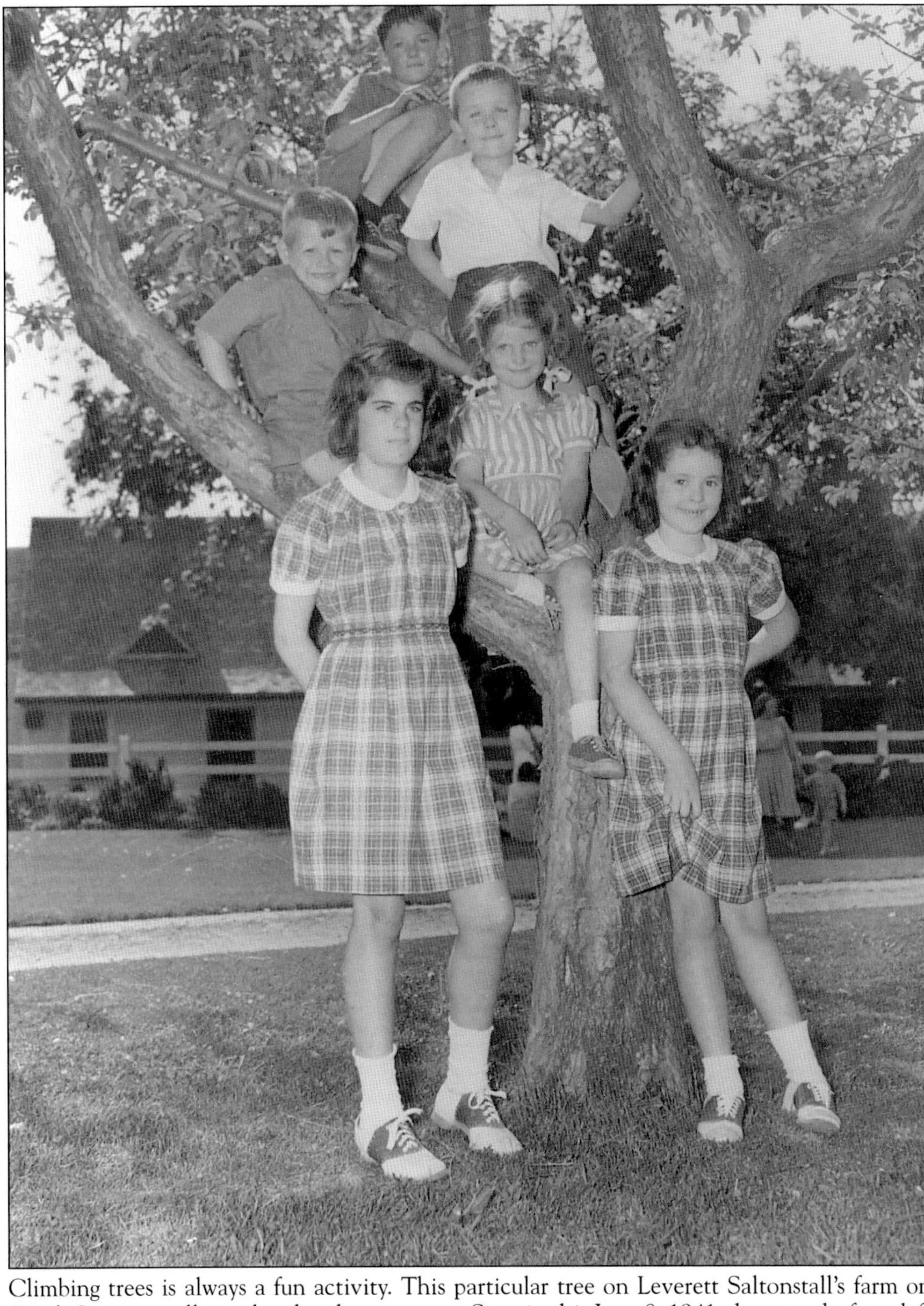

Climbing trees is always a fun activity. This particular tree on Leverett Saltonstall's farm on Smith Street is well populated with youngsters. Seen in this June 8, 1941 photograph, from left to right, are the following: (bottom row) Francis and Carol Pratt; (middle row) Lindsey Rice and Marian Francis; (top row) Walter Cabot and Daniel Codman.

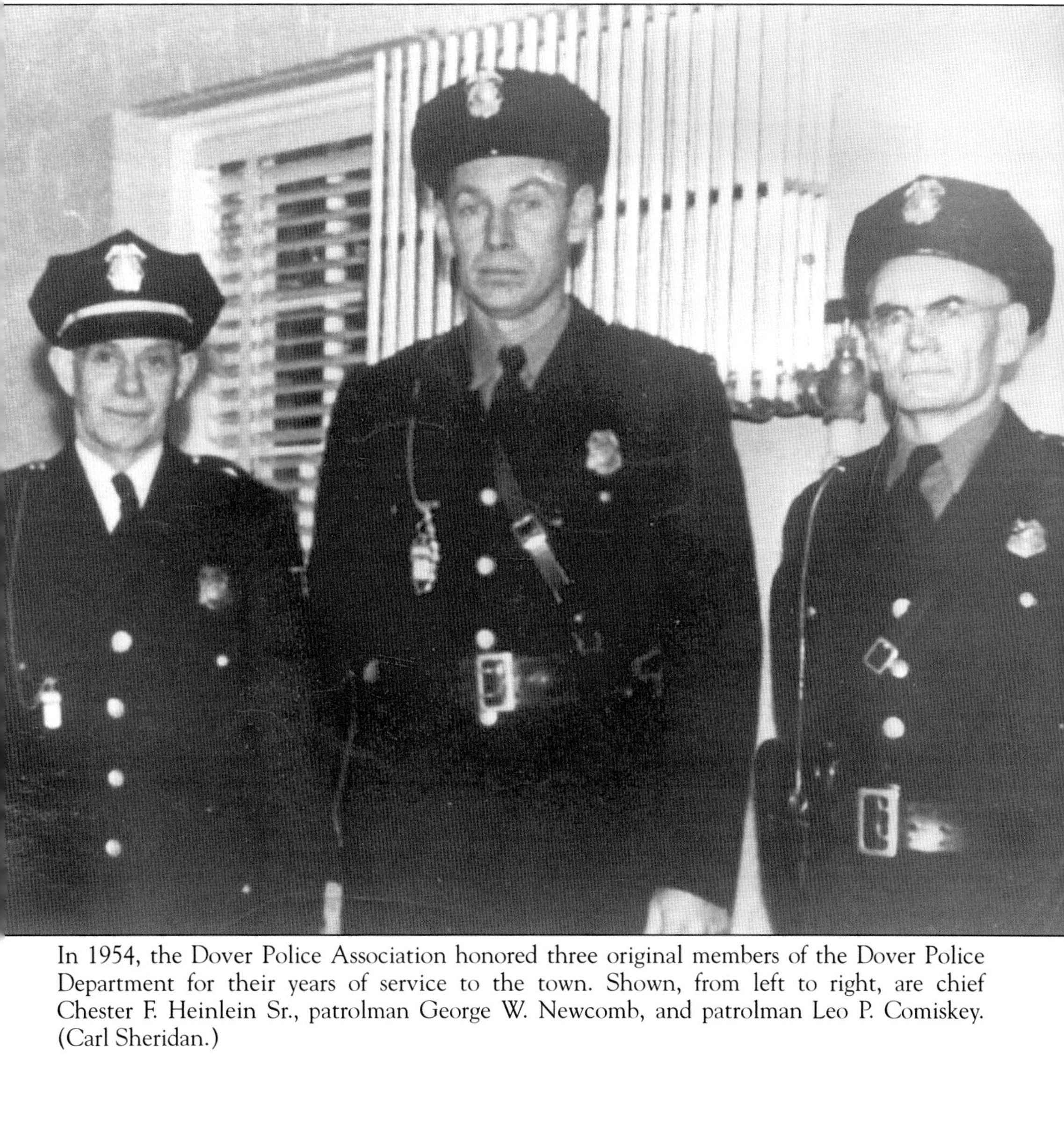

In 1954, the Dover Police Association honored three original members of the Dover Police Department for their years of service to the town. Shown, from left to right, are chief Chester F. Heinlein Sr., patrolman George W. Newcomb, and patrolman Leo P. Comiskey. (Carl Sheridan.)

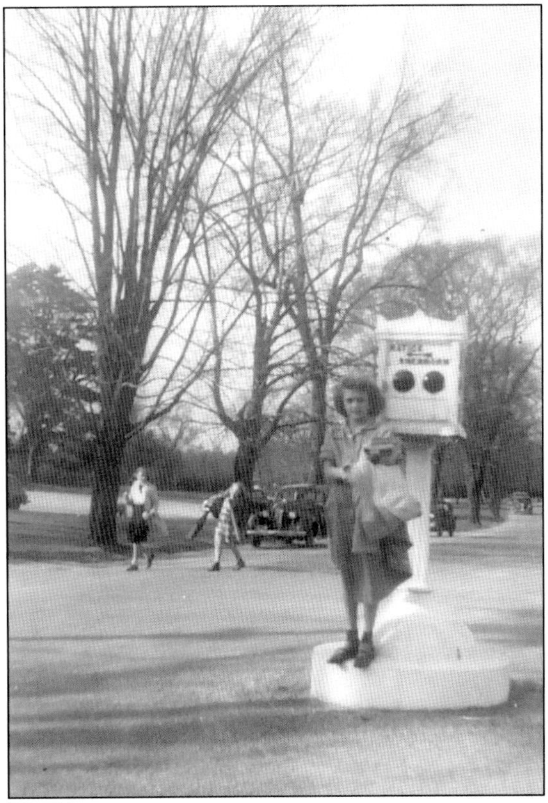

Over the past century, the increasing reliance on the automobile has made traffic a greater part of our lives. The traffic in Dover Center was much different in the spring of 1947. Here, Jean Warwick stands in the middle of Centre Street at Walpole Street and Springdale Avenue. Today, townspeople often discuss how to alleviate the increased traffic. (Nancy Scholz Beckwith.)

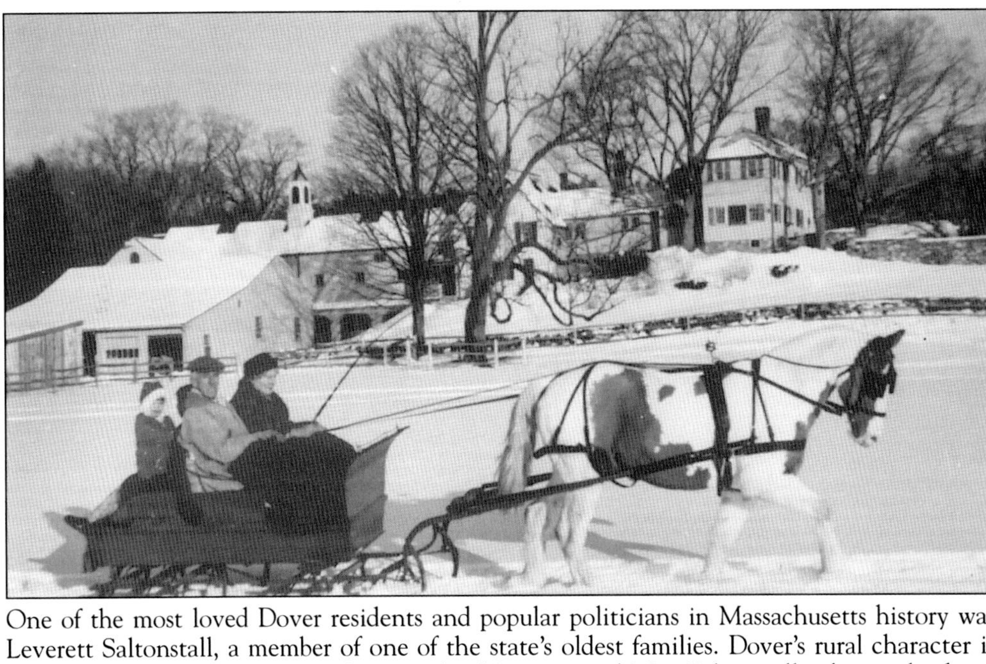

One of the most loved Dover residents and popular politicians in Massachusetts history was Leverett Saltonstall, a member of one of the state's oldest families. Dover's rural character is shown in this Christmas 1960 photograph of Senator and Mrs. Saltonstall riding a sleigh on their farm. (Saltonstall family scrapbook.)

Although Doverites are close to Boston, they need to travel no further than the town limits to enjoy big-city entertainment. The community-based Dover Foundation fills that need with plays, complete with the excitement of the big top. Henry Stone shows his skill as he rides a unicycle in the 1948 Dover Follies. (Dover Foundation archives.)

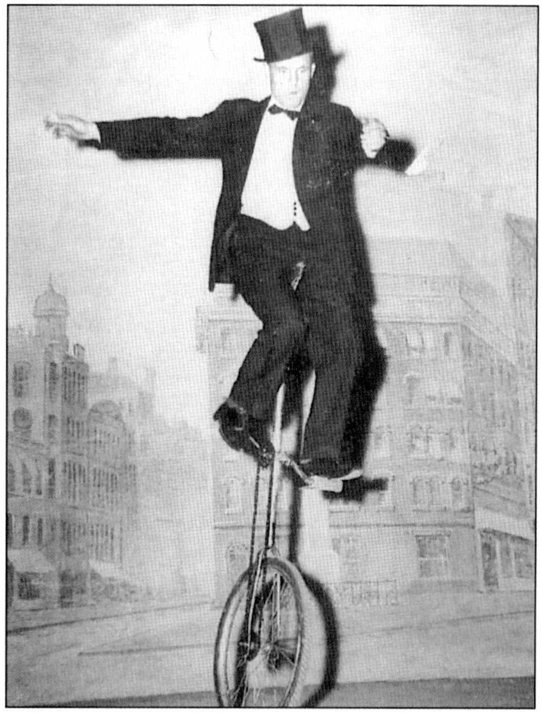

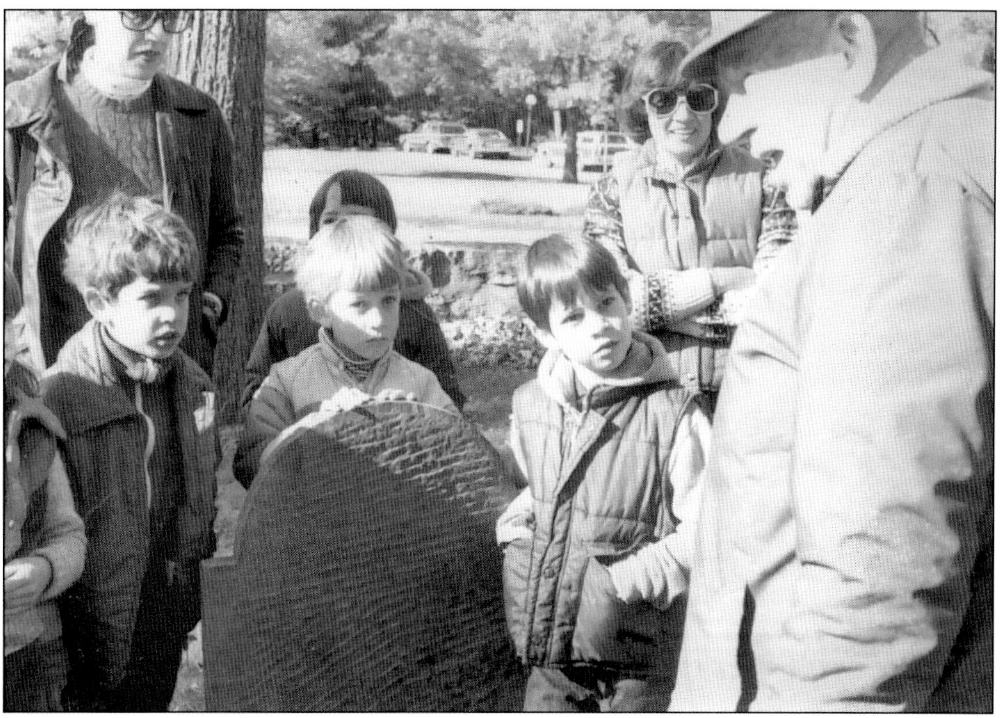

One Dover citizen who loved to talk about his town was Harry A. Bertschy, the cemetery commissioner in the 1980s. Here, he gives a historical talk to some kids in the Highland Cemetery. In 1980, Bertschy wrote and published a brief history of the cemetery. There are about 400 early gravestones in the cemetery that are being carefully protected.

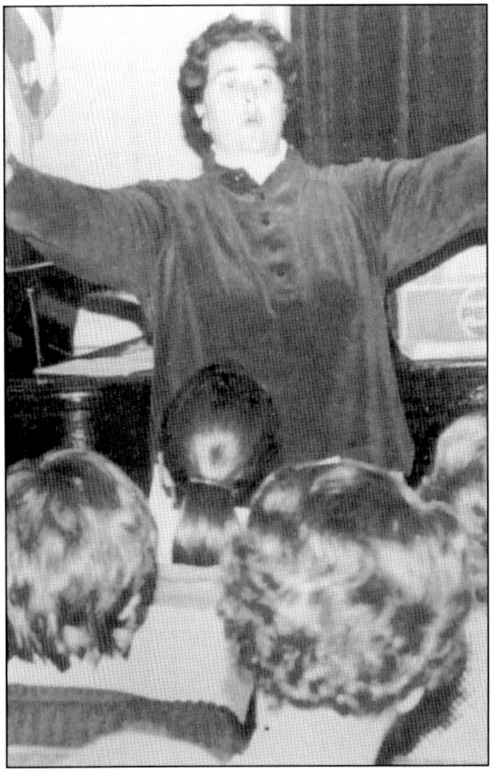

Another 1970s cultural mainstay was Georgiana Berry, director of music at the high school. Georgie lent her many talents to both the schools and the community. Here, she directs the Dover Foundation chorus for one of its many productions. (Dover Foundation archives.)

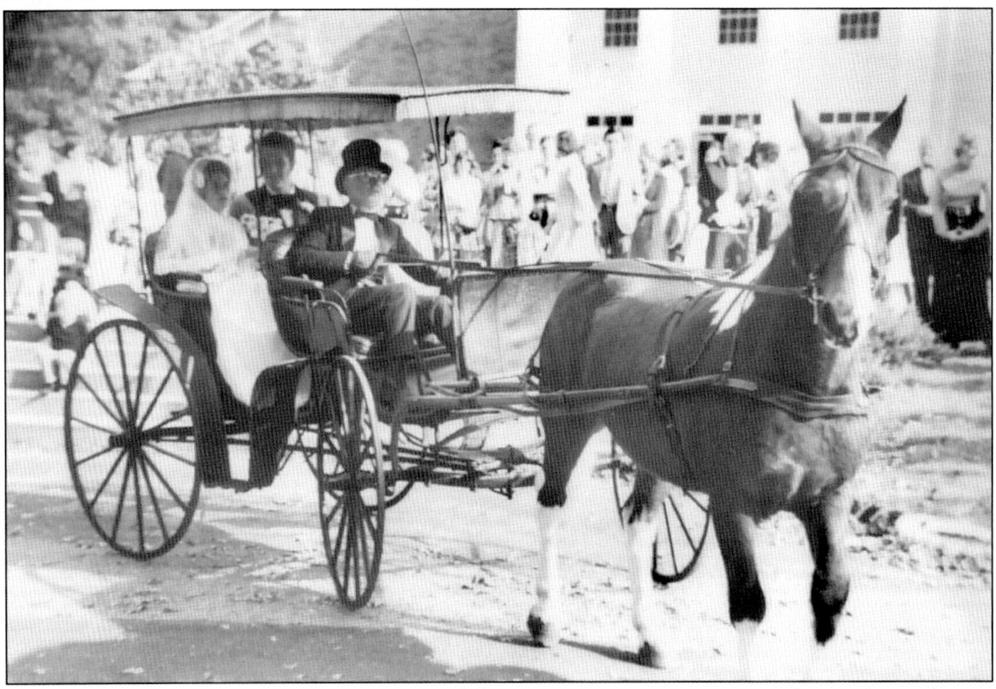

Young people seek ways to make their celebrations more interesting; a horse-drawn buggy always seems romantic. Harry Snow drives newly married Elizabeth Gerrity and Joseph Devine Jr. away from the Dover Church in a flashy rig on October 7, 1973. (Marion Gerrity.)

Antoinette Weathers stands ready at Highland Cemetery for the Memorial Day parade. She is a member of the Chickering family that has long been in Dover. A veteran of WWII and a member of the George B. Preston American Legion Post No. 209, she was the first female commander of the post.

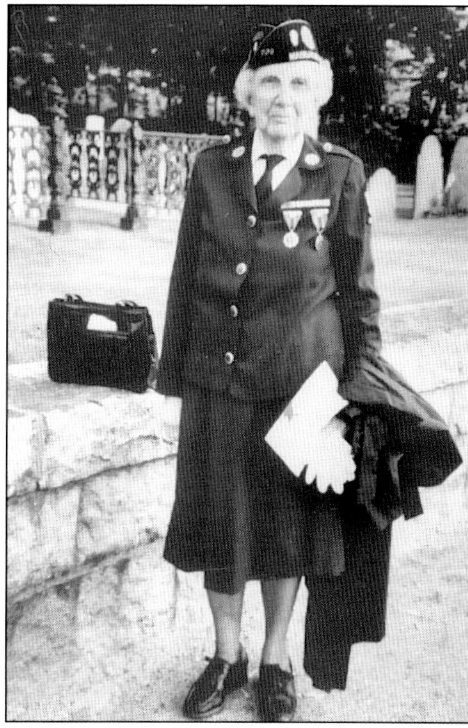

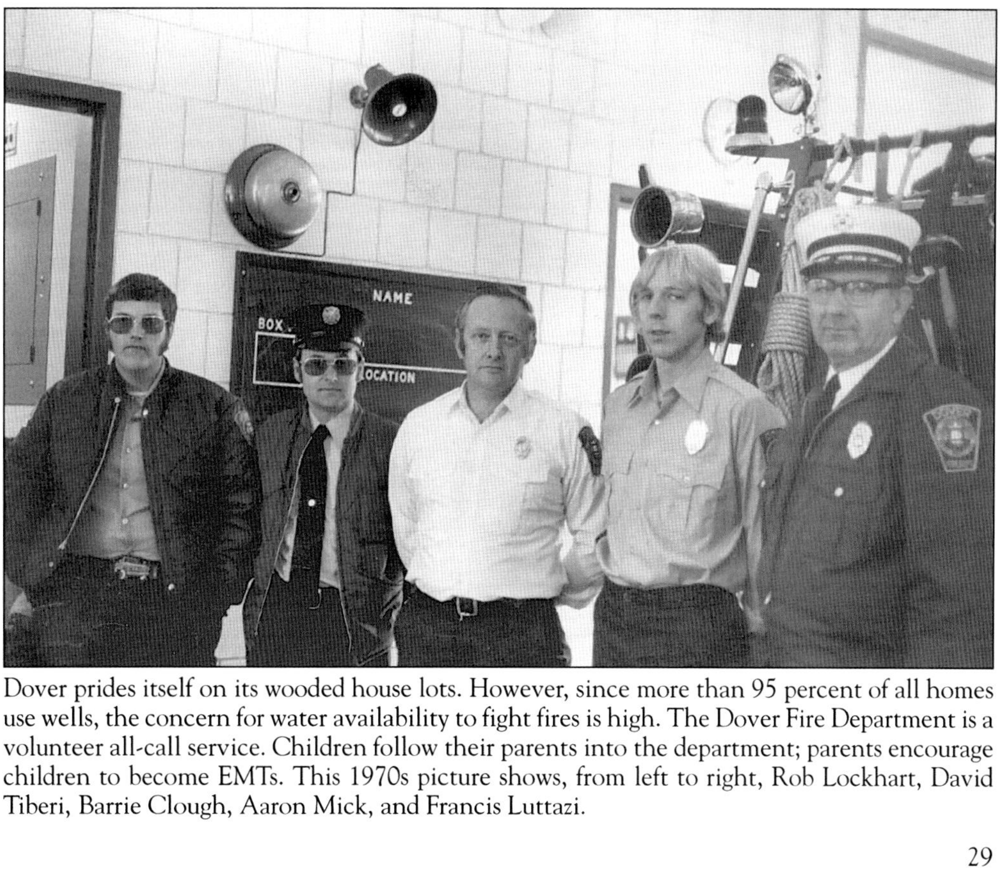

Dover prides itself on its wooded house lots. However, since more than 95 percent of all homes use wells, the concern for water availability to fight fires is high. The Dover Fire Department is a volunteer all-call service. Children follow their parents into the department; parents encourage children to become EMTs. This 1970s picture shows, from left to right, Rob Lockhart, David Tiberi, Barrie Clough, Aaron Mick, and Francis Luttazi.

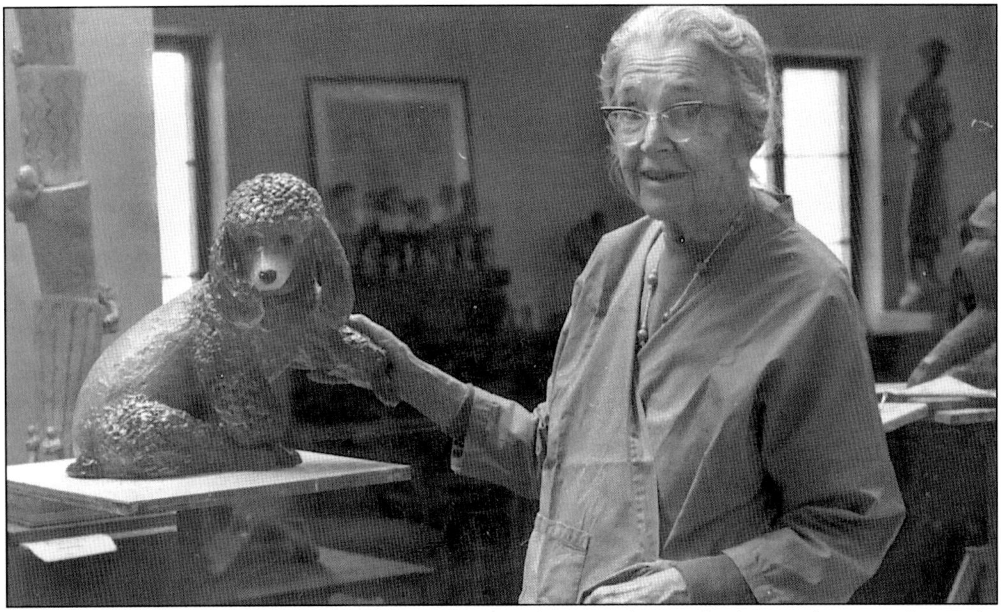

On May 16, 1961, Tufts University dedicated the Amelia Peabody Pavilion at the Tufts University School of Veterinary Medicine in Grafton, Massachusetts. The university conferred an honorary Doctorate of Fine Arts degree on Dover resident Amelia Peabody. At the ceremony, they announced, "the craftsmanship, beauty, and sensitivity of your sculpture have made your work beloved throughout the nation. You have dedicated your art and life to the welfare of God's creatures, man and animals alike." (Barbara Bedell.)

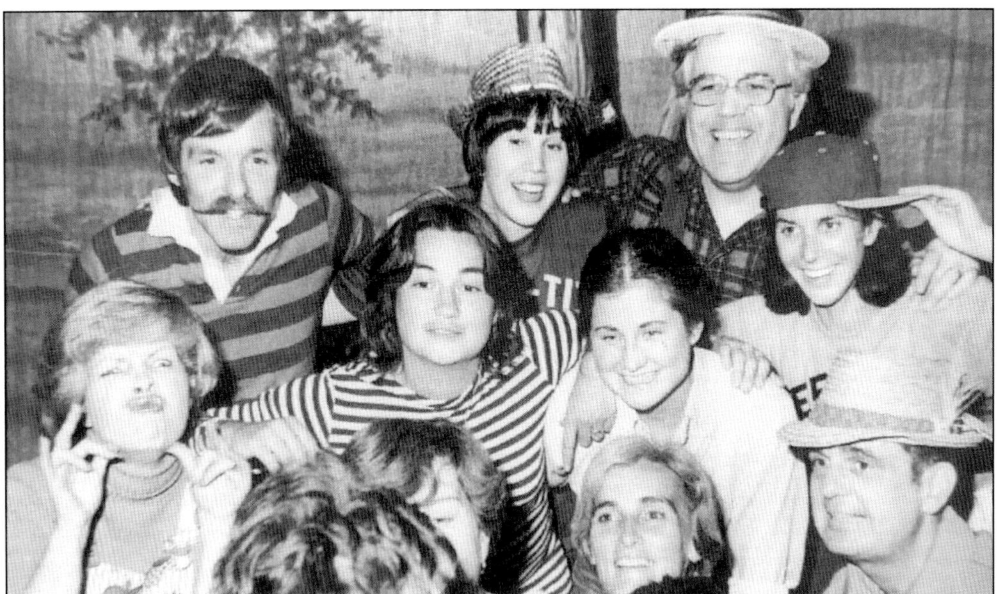

The Dover Foundation is one of the town's most popular organizations. The 1977 cast of *Pajama Game*, from left to right, is as follows: (front row) Ann Courtney, Pat Berger, and Scott Ricketson; (middle row) Darlene Crump, Gail Bambrick, Maggie Coggeshall, and Pooh Lockwood; (back row) Dick Stewart, Judy Conrad, and Carl Krause. (Dover Foundation Archives.)

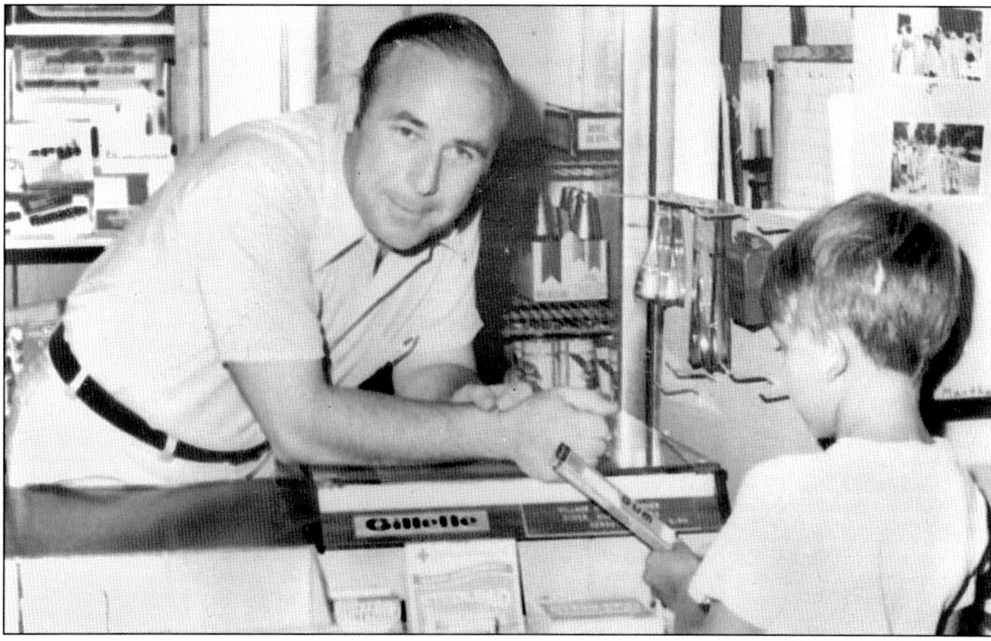

In this 1970s photograph, Ken Ball waits on an unidentified youngster at Village Drug of Dover. For many years, he was the first friendly face to greet newcomers to the town. He was also a great friend to many kids in town as an active member of the Dover Park and Recreation Commission. (Don Ball.)

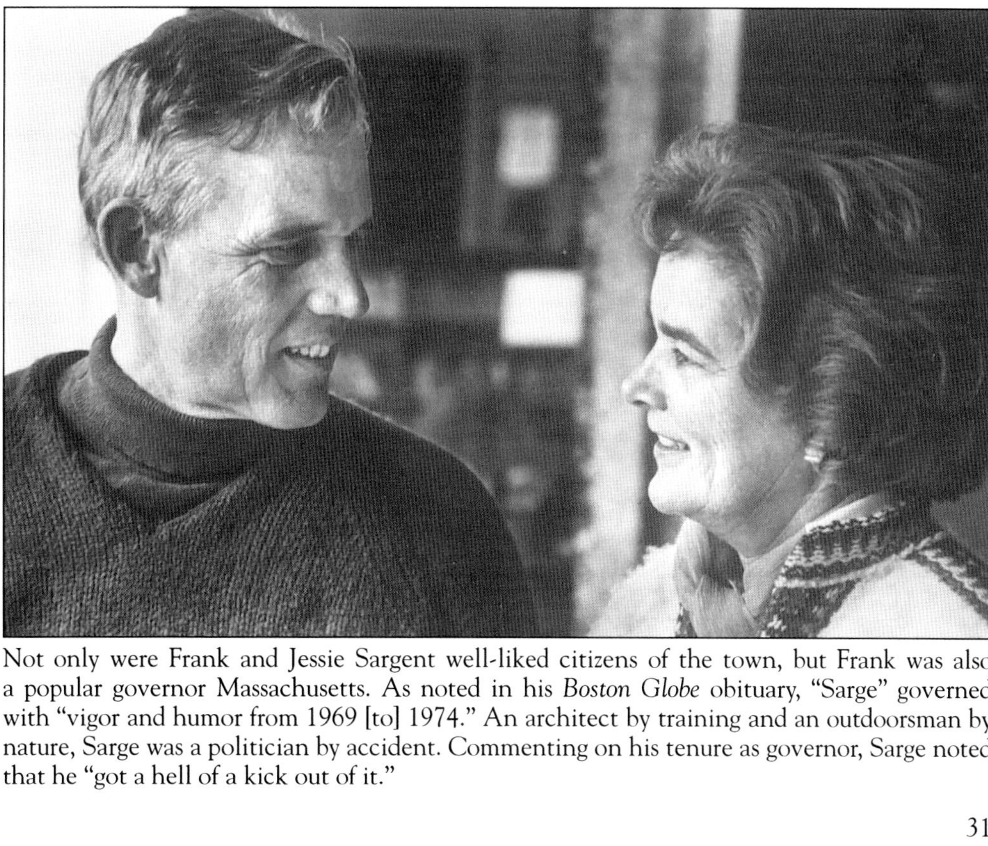

Not only were Frank and Jessie Sargent well-liked citizens of the town, but Frank was also a popular governor Massachusetts. As noted in his *Boston Globe* obituary, "Sarge" governed with "vigor and humor from 1969 [to] 1974." An architect by training and an outdoorsman by nature, Sarge was a politician by accident. Commenting on his tenure as governor, Sarge noted that he "got a hell of a kick out of it."

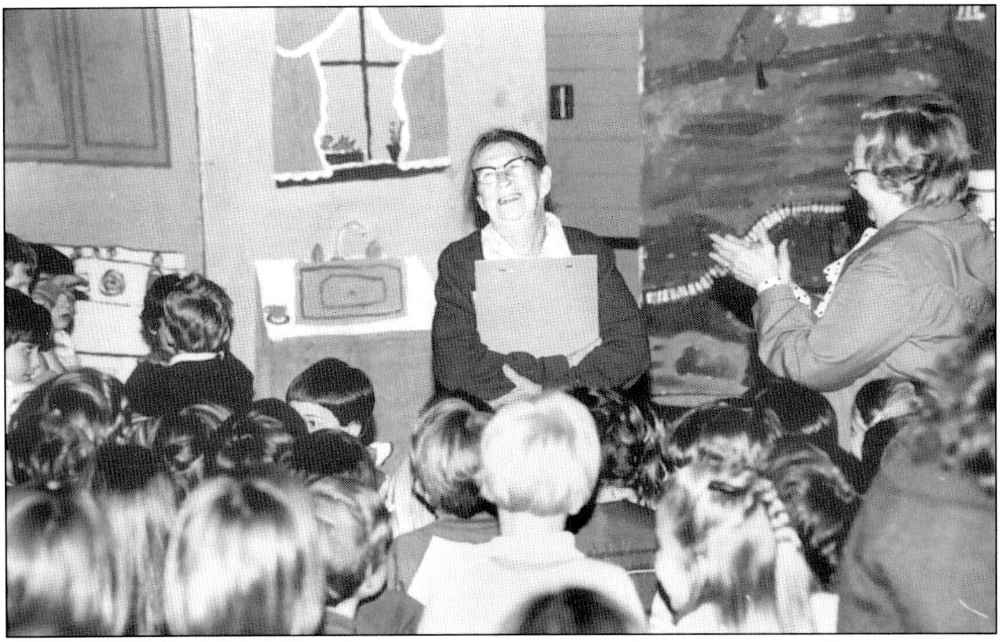

The Charles River School has been an important part of the community. For many years, Frances Neale, who was the head cook at the school, served as a confidant, mother, and good friend to the pupils. Here, she laughs with appreciation at her retirement party in May 1982. (Harry Neale.)

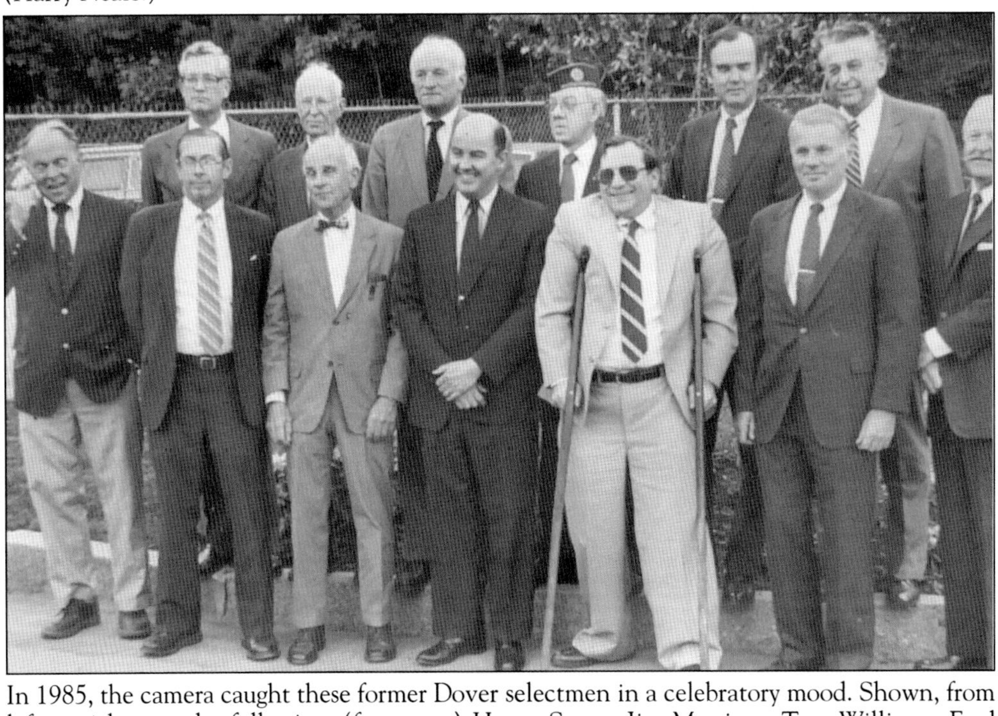

In 1985, the camera caught these former Dover selectmen in a celebratory mood. Shown, from left to right, are the following: (front row) Henry Stone, Jim Martinez, Tom Williams, Fred Maier, Nick Sarris, John Gray, and Charlie Rheault; (back row) Norm Nicholson, Ted Chase, Dave MacIntosh, Chet Heinlein Jr., Charlie Cabot, and Walter Attridge.

Two of Dover's most popular citizens, former town librarian Emily Bertschy and author Dick Vara of *Dover Days Gone By*, strike a pose during the 1986 sesquicentennial celebration. On March 31, 1836, the General Court of the Commonwealth of Massachusetts incorporated "the District of Dover into a Town by the name of Dover." On May 2, 1836, the inhabitants of the district voted to approve that act. (Marion Gerrity.)

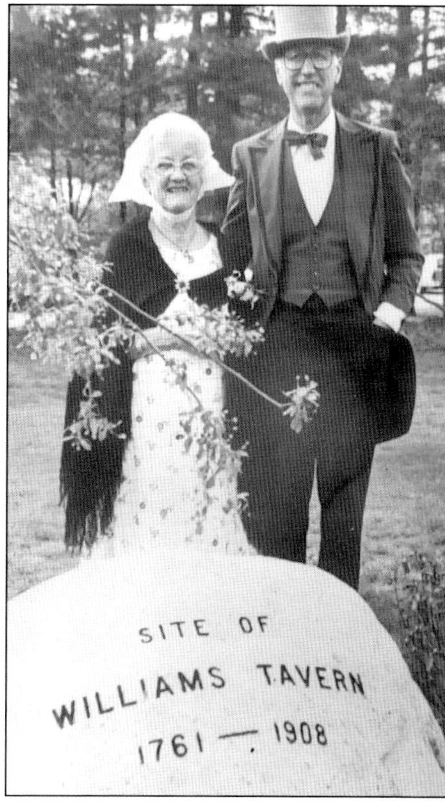

Kapers for Kids, a volunteer organization supported by donations, sponsors the annual Back to School Concert, the Halloween Costume Party, the Breakfast and Photo with Santa, and the Easter Egg Hunt. The members of this 1988 Easter Egg Hunt crew seem to be enjoying themselves. Louise Ball is wearing the Easter Bunny costume. (Sandy Ball.)

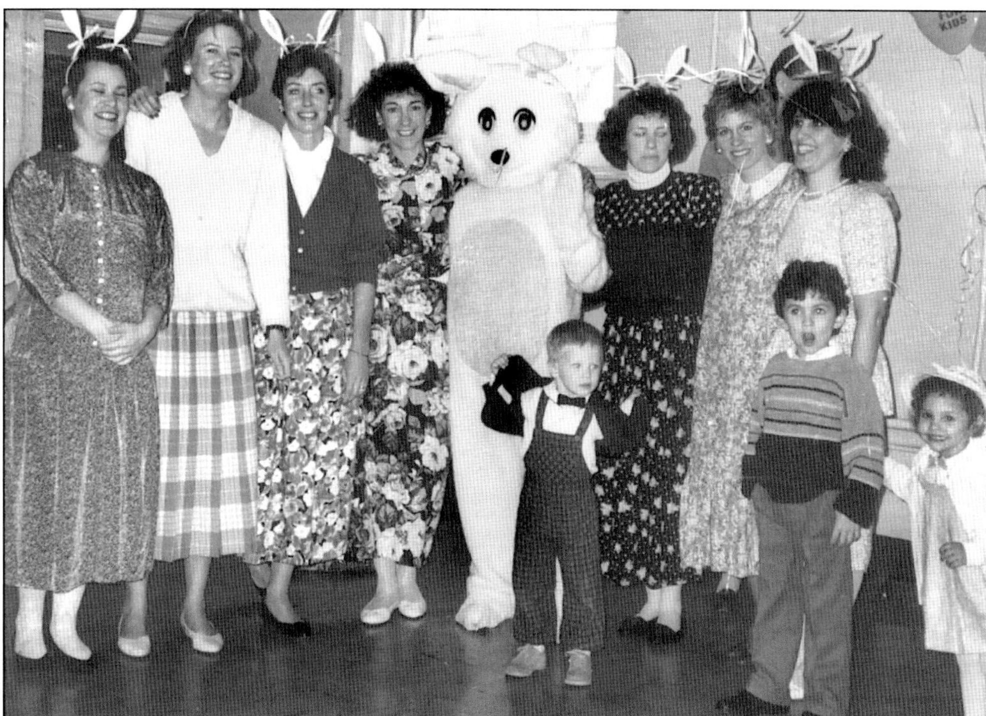

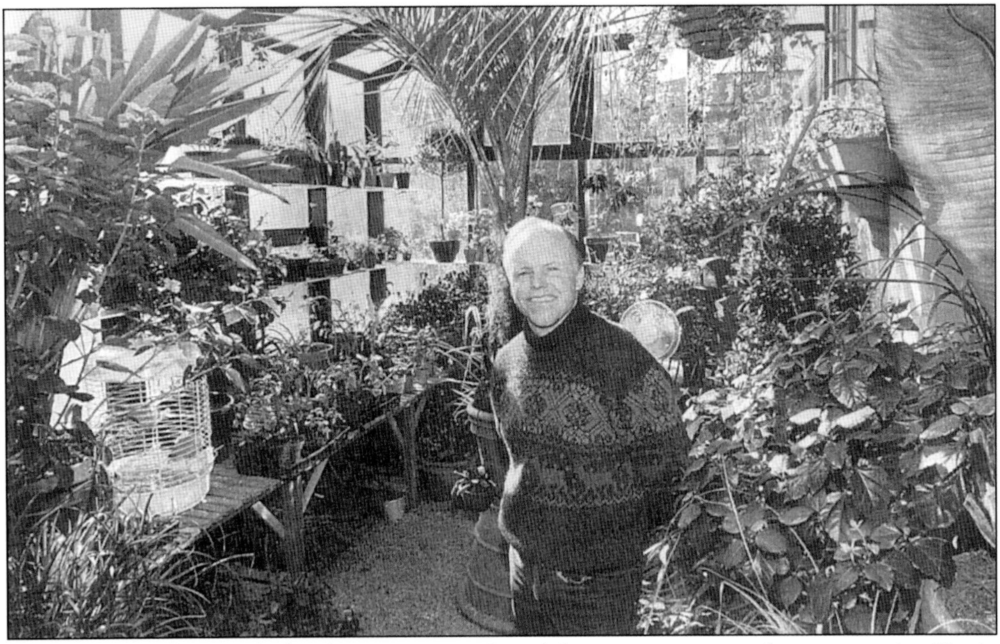

The town overflows with floral activities; garden club projects support the community. Kevin Doyle, shown in his Wilsondale Street greenhouse, is a nationally known master gardener. In the spring, summer, fall, and winter, Kevin makes the seasons come alive for all around him through courses or his own floral settings. (*Dover-Sherborn Press.*)

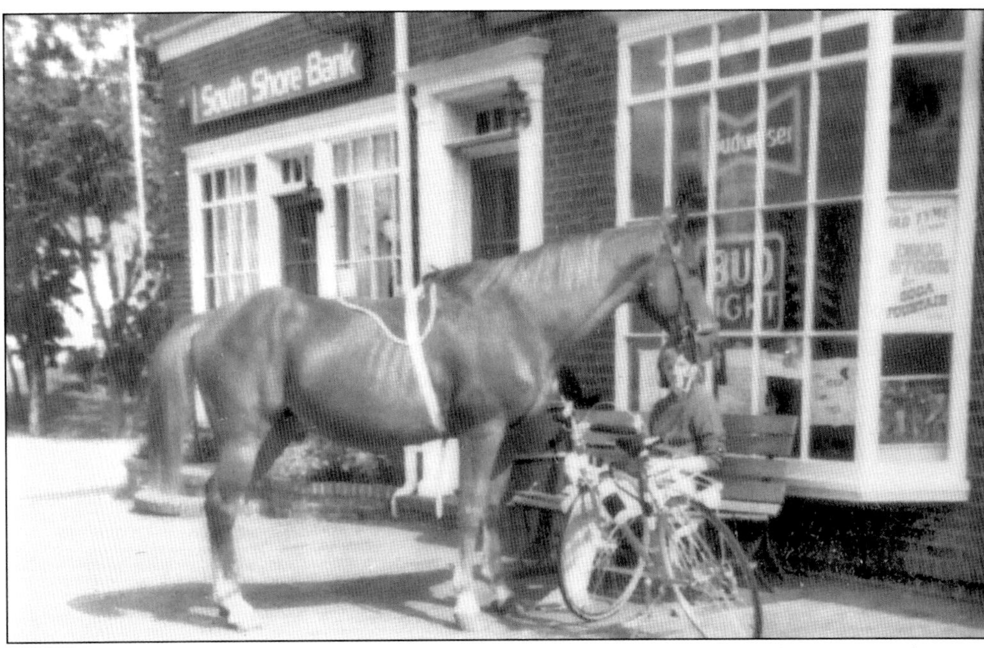

The environmental movement has made us much more conscious of what we are doing to our surroundings. Horses and bicycles have been with us this entire century, but now seem to be vehicles of choice in this environmental age. What better place to stop for a rest than the friendly benches in front of the Dover Store? The rider is unidentified. (Don Ball.)

Three

NORFOLK HUNT CLUB

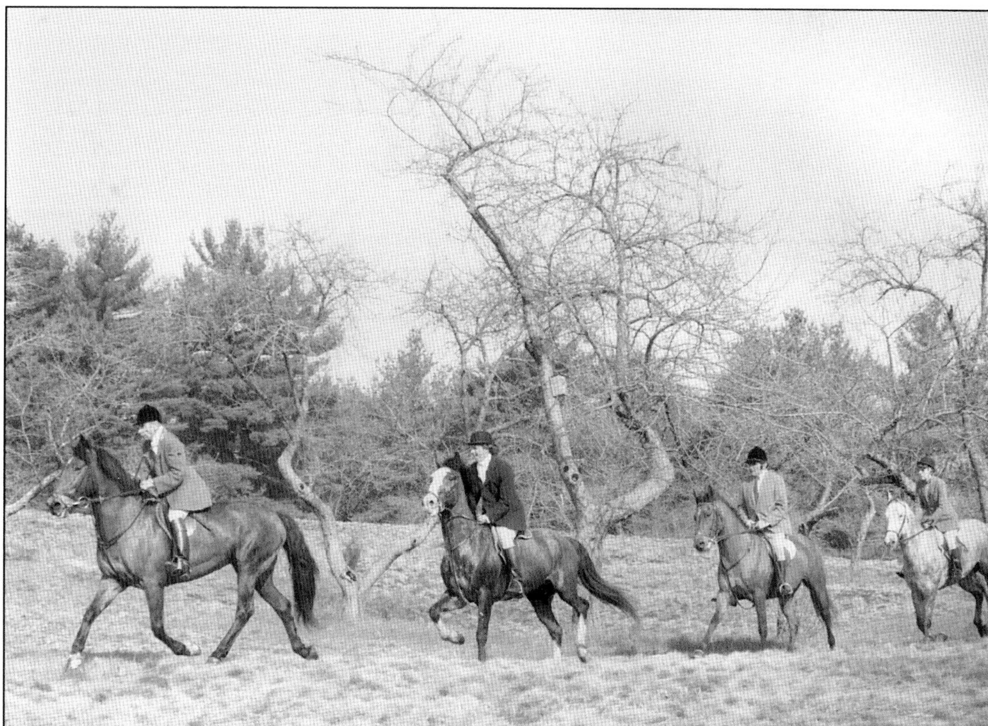

The *Dedham Transcript* of September 12, 1896 announced that a "new hunt club, similar to Myopia, has been organized at Dedham . . . to be known as the Norfolk Hunt, and the field of operations will be . . . mostly about the towns of Medfield, Dover, and Dedham. . . . The membership . . . is largely made-up of members of the Dedham Polo Club." The Norfolk Hunt Club moved to the Medfield-Dover line in 1900. In 1901, the club was incorporated and purchased the Wardener Farm on Centre Street.

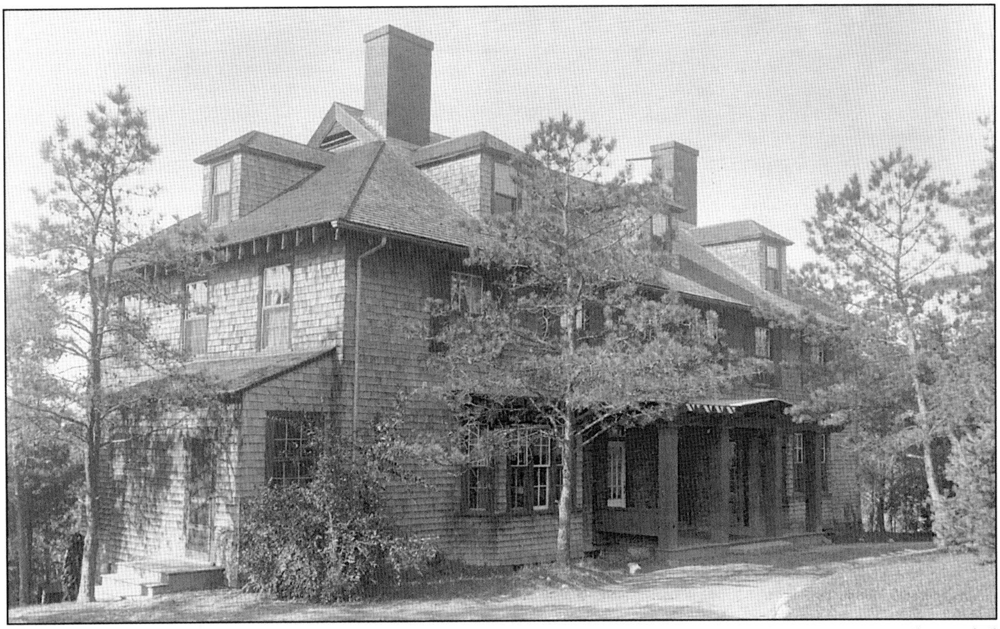

The Norfolk Hunt Club built its clubhouse on Centre Street in 1902. As many members did not live in Dover, the clubhouse served as a hotel during a hunt. Although it was easily reached by rail from Boston, many hunt members decided to purchase land and build houses in Dover. The clubhouse has been renovated and is now a private residence.

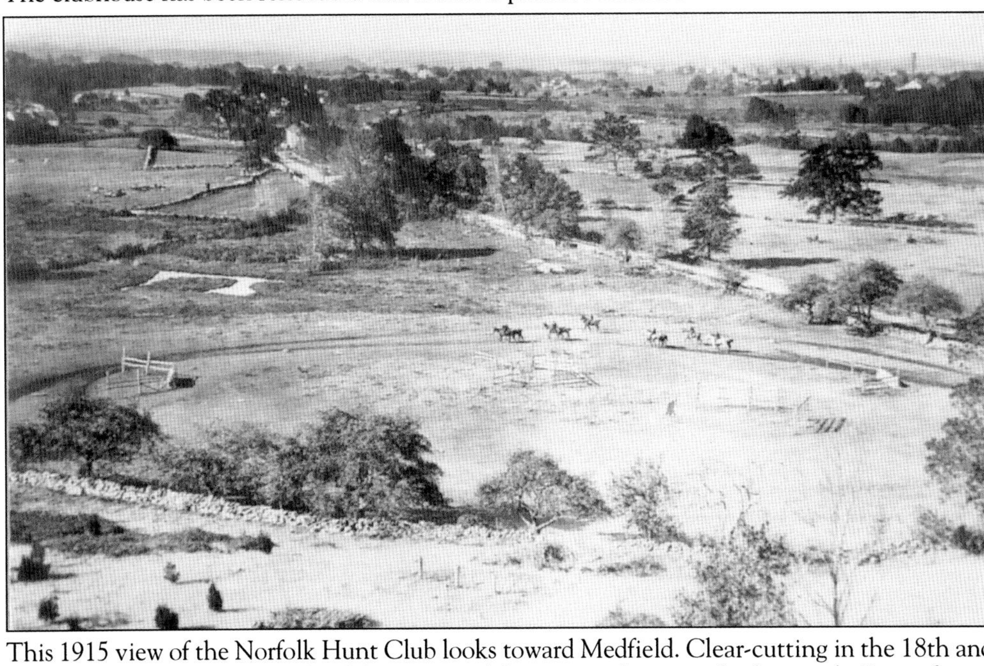

This 1915 view of the Norfolk Hunt Club looks toward Medfield. Clear-cutting in the 18th and 19th centuries opened more land for increased farming and pasture for livestock. Stone fences and natural obstacles provided tests of skill for the riders. The Norfolk Hunt Club obtained permission to drag hunt with the proviso of repairing all damages. The emphasis has always been on conservation of the land and cooperation with the owners who are trying to preserve the open space for all to enjoy. (Norfolk Hunt Club.)

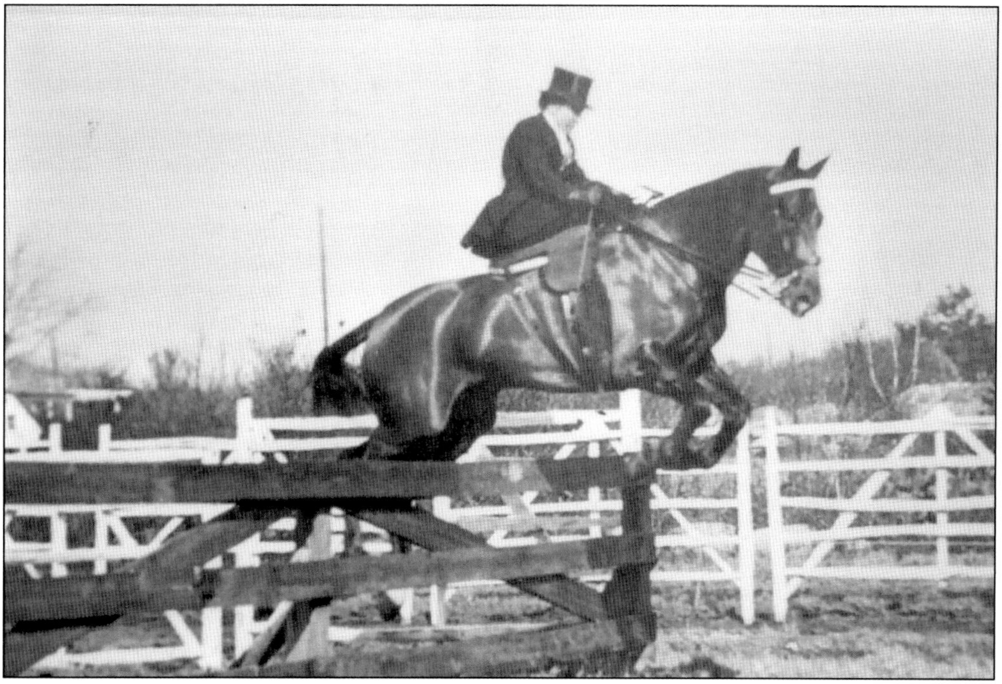

Amelia Peabody, a noted sculptress and a great charitable benefactress in Boston, jumps a fence in the 1920s. Peabody was the only child of the founder of Kidder Peabody. She grew up on Commonwealth Avenue in Boston. As a young girl, she was attracted by the Norfolk Hunt Club and eventually moved to Dover, buying the Mill and Powissett Farms, which include Noanet Woodlands. She left almost 1,000 acres to the Trustees of Reservations. (Norfolk Hunt Club.)

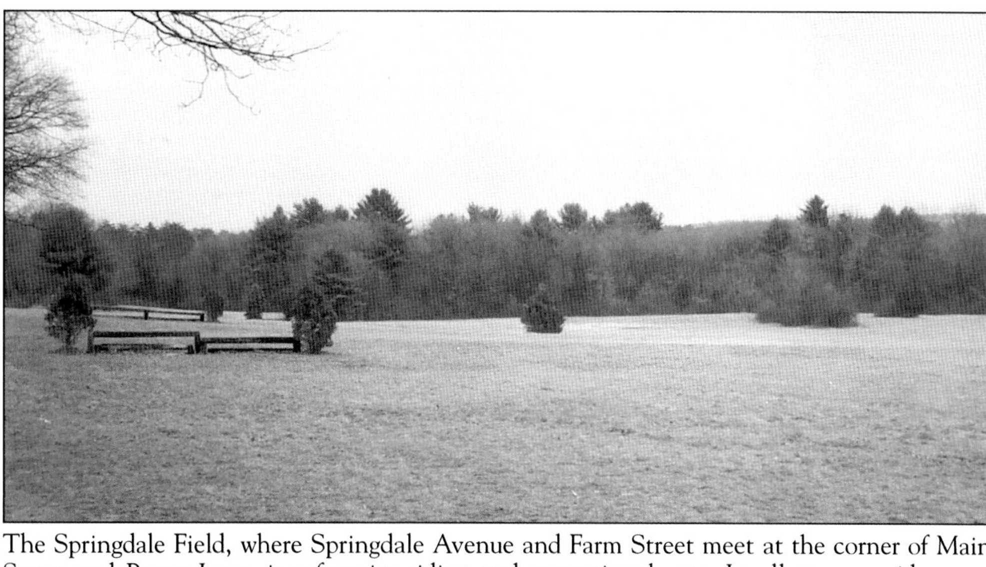

The Springdale Field, where Springdale Avenue and Farm Street meet at the corner of Main Street and Pegan Lane, is a favorite riding and recreational area. In all seasons, riders can be seen working their mounts while others work their dogs. Maintained by the Dover Land Conservation Trust, this field will remain open in perpetuity.

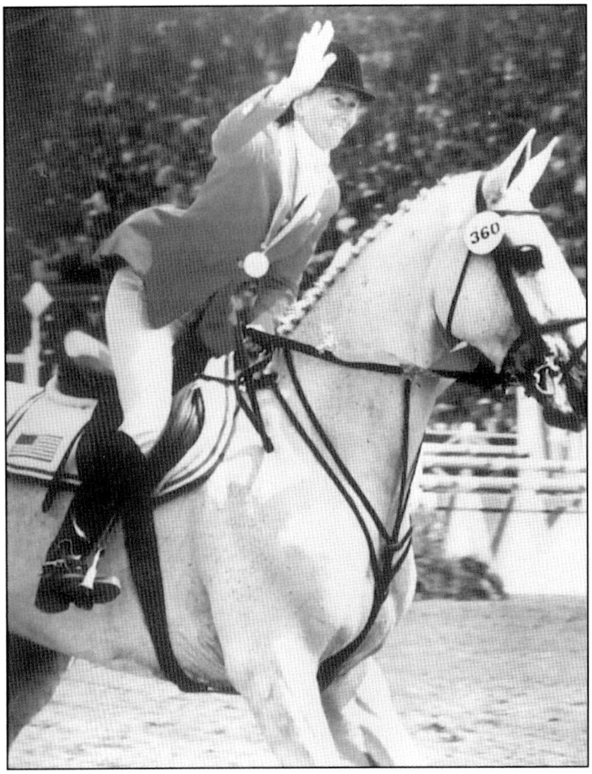

Karen Wennberg Stives of Stonehenge Farm on Pine Street rides her horse, Ben Arthur, at the 1984 Los Angeles Olympics. Participating as a member of the United States Equestrian Team, she won a Team Gold medal and an Individual Silver medal. Karen was a member of the Norfolk Pony Club as a youngster. Riding in Dover continues to be a popular activity. (Karen Stives.)

Mary Ryerson Frost, left, and her daughter, Jane McKay Frost, jump cleanly in this 1934 photograph. Generations of Dover families have enjoyed riding and have loved horses. Besides family riding, many have gone on to become accomplished riders and trainers. (Cornelia Clark Roberts.)

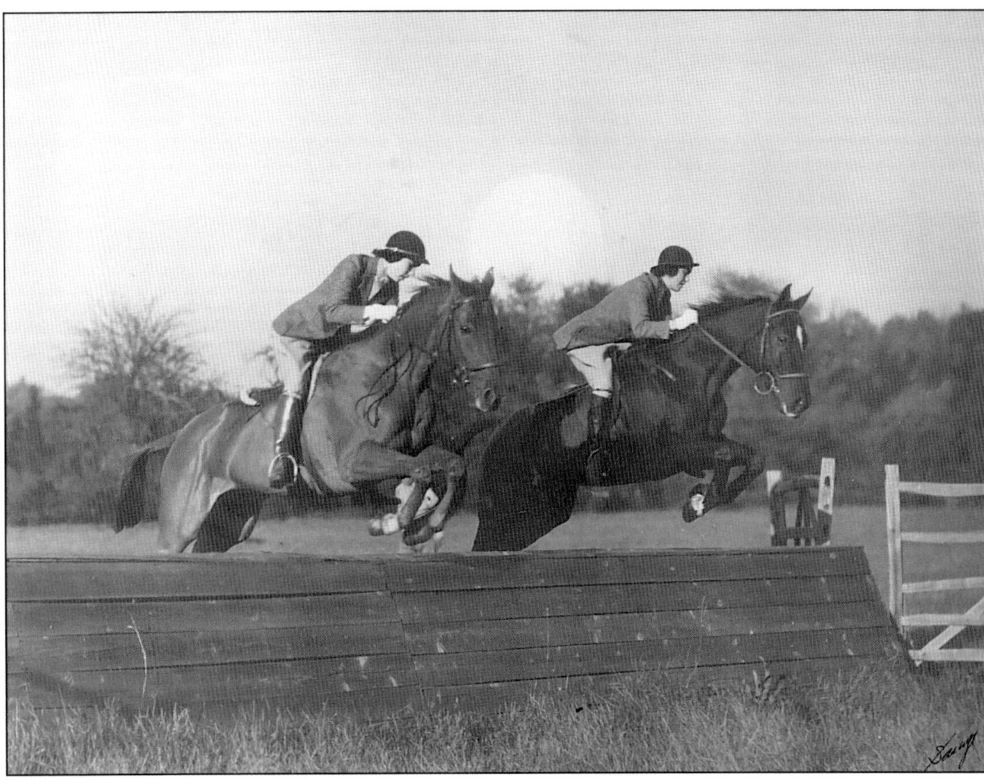

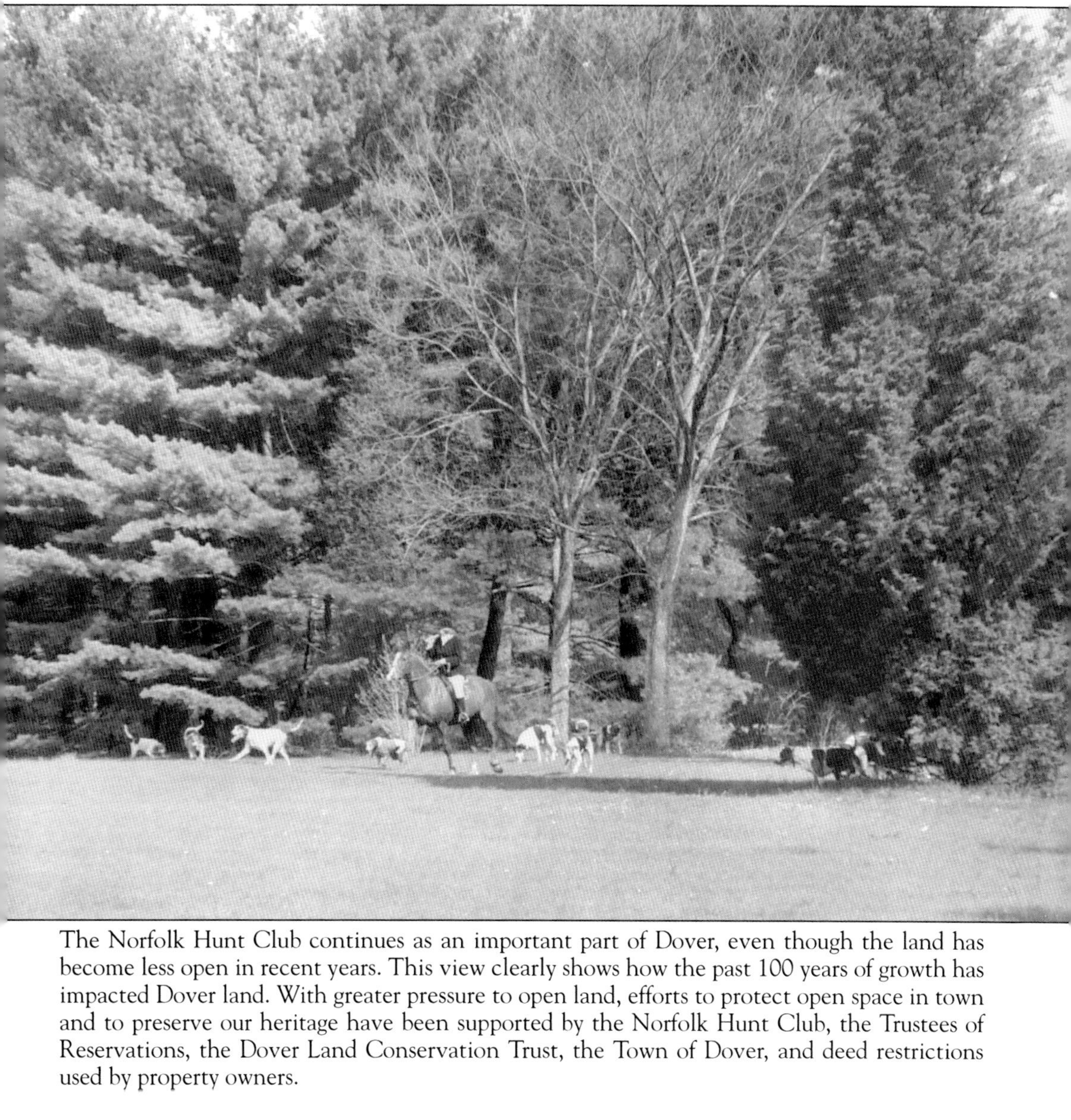

The Norfolk Hunt Club continues as an important part of Dover, even though the land has become less open in recent years. This view clearly shows how the past 100 years of growth has impacted Dover land. With greater pressure to open land, efforts to protect open space in town and to preserve our heritage have been supported by the Norfolk Hunt Club, the Trustees of Reservations, the Dover Land Conservation Trust, the Town of Dover, and deed restrictions used by property owners.

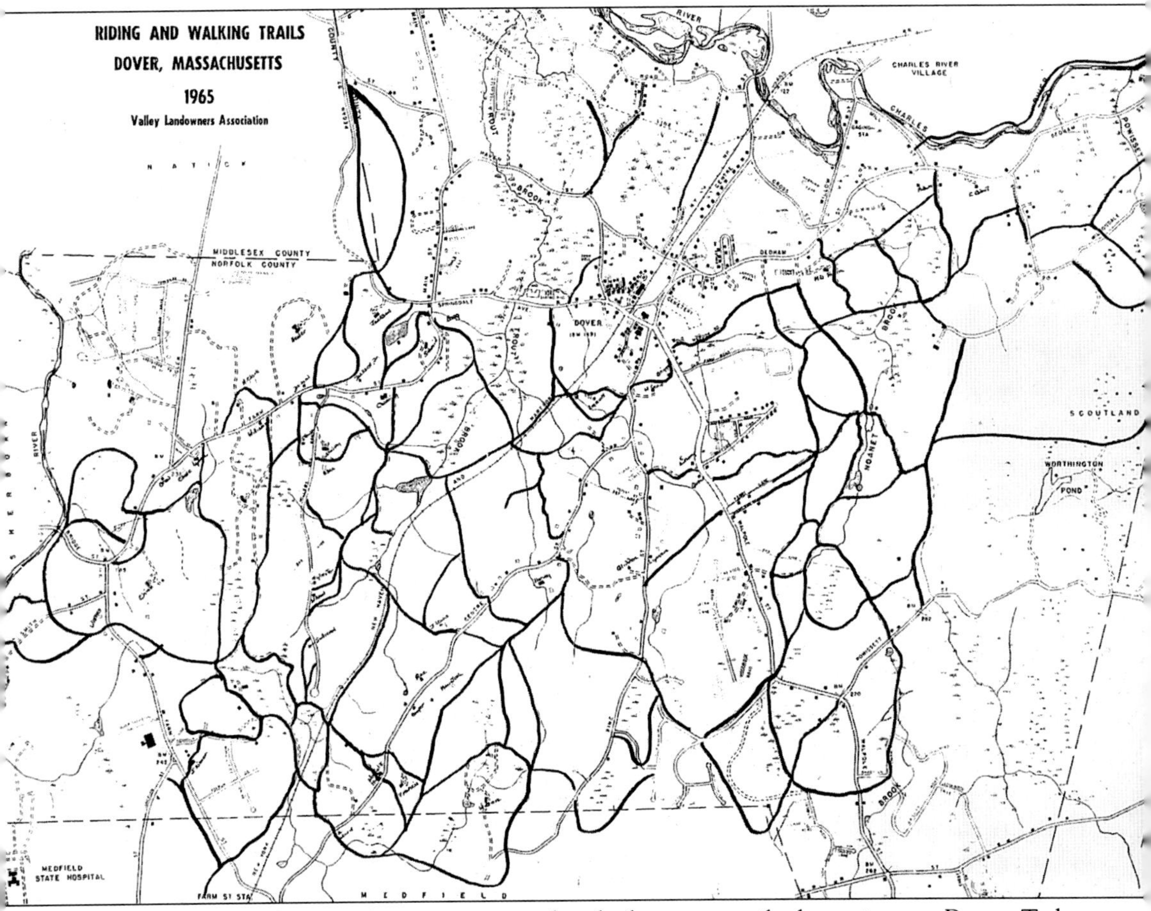

This Valley Landowners Association map details the many trails that crisscross Dover. Today, the Dover Conservation Commission works with developers to restore interrupted connections and to keep the remaining trails open where possible.

Four

ECONOMIC AND GOVERNMENT MATTERS

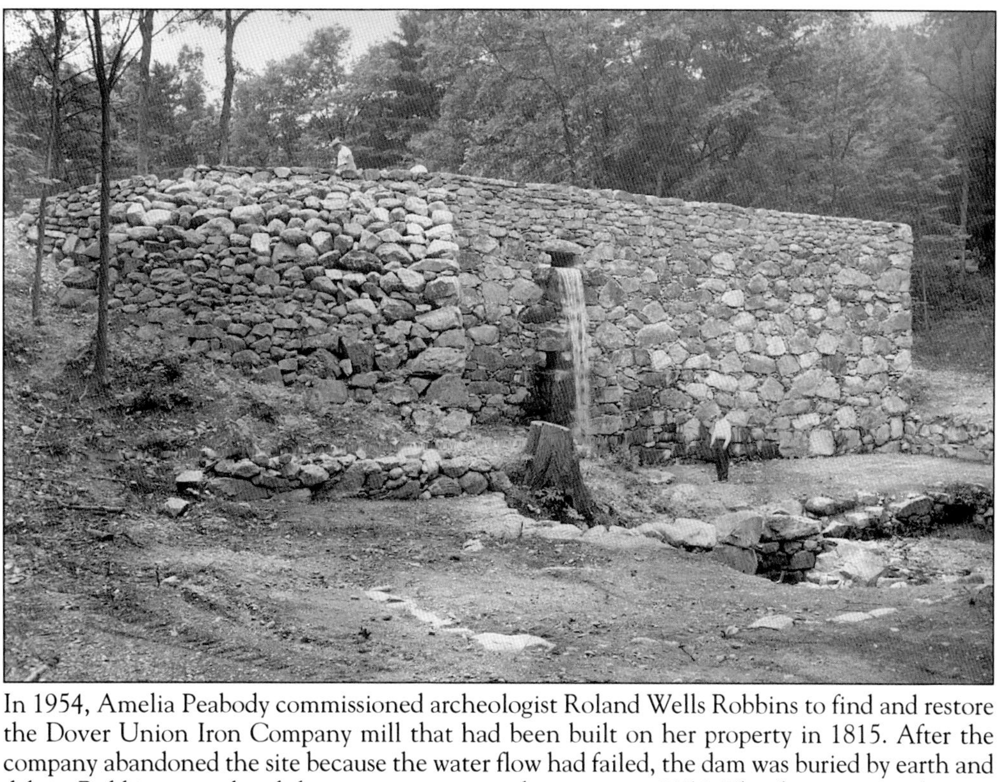

In 1954, Amelia Peabody commissioned archeologist Roland Wells Robbins to find and restore the Dover Union Iron Company mill that had been built on her property in 1815. After the company abandoned the site because the water flow had failed, the dam was buried by earth and debris. Robbins completed the reconstruction in late summer 1954. The dam is a popular part of the Noanet Woodlands Reservation.

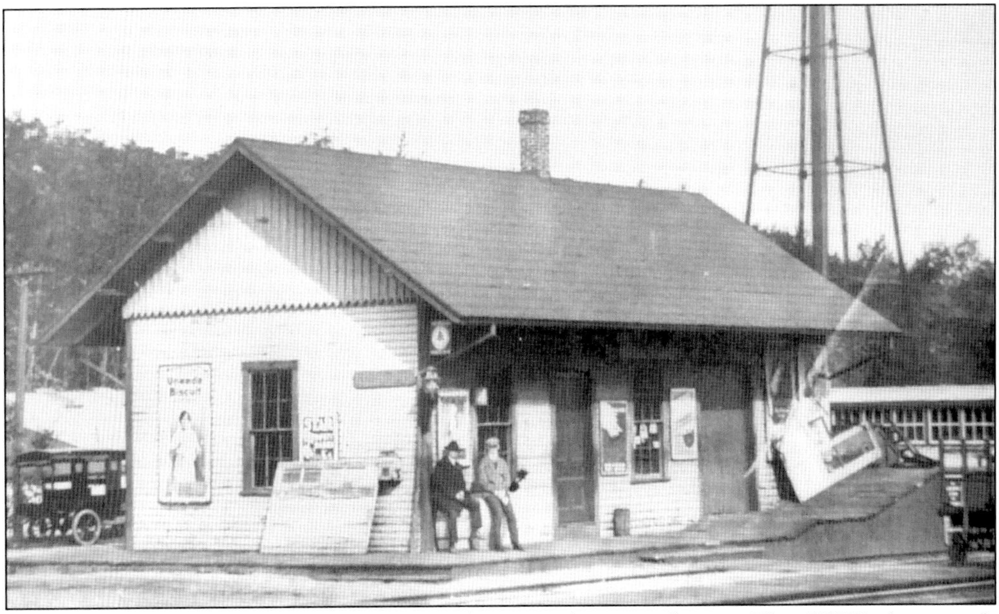

The railroad came to Dover in the 1850s, changing the town forever. This WWI photograph shows a school barge parked to the left behind the station. To the right, the old water tower looms above the Hodgson portable house factory. A railroad siding that branched from the main line to the station facilitated the loading of freight cars, allowing the company to ship goods all over the world. (George Michel.)

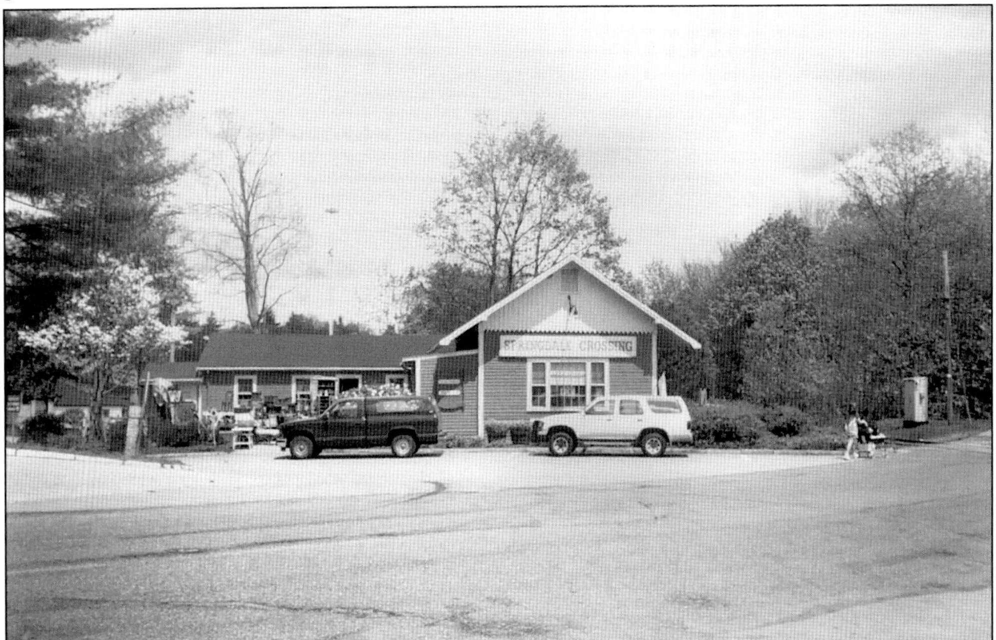

The Dover Country Store, popular in the 1950s, 1960s, and 1970s as a repository of people's good junk for a price, has become Springdale Crossing, housing an antique store and a real estate office. The railroad tracks to the right still carry freight to Medfield, but passenger service does not exist. The nearest commuter station is at Needham Junction.

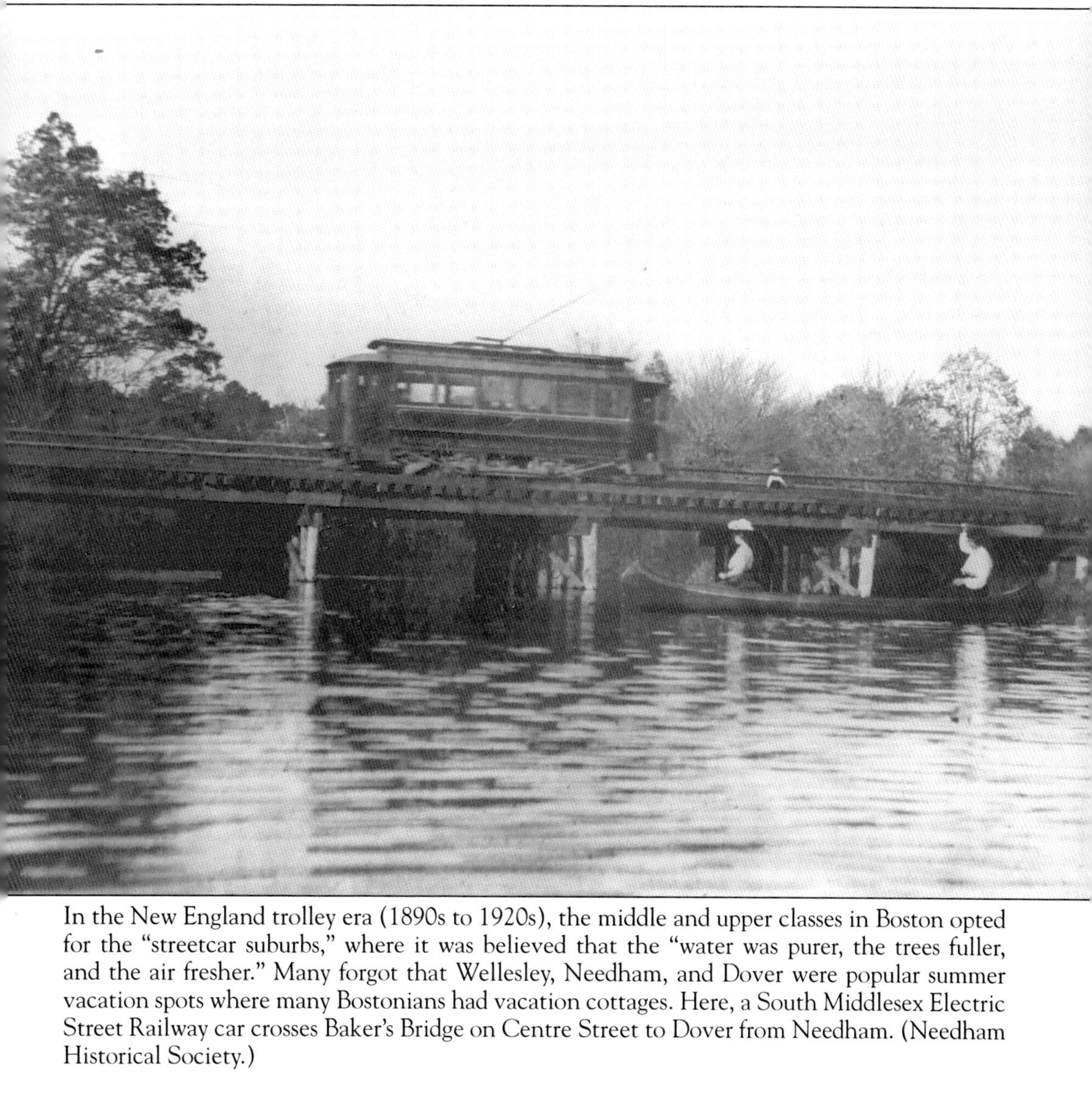

In the New England trolley era (1890s to 1920s), the middle and upper classes in Boston opted for the "streetcar suburbs," where it was believed that the "water was purer, the trees fuller, and the air fresher." Many forgot that Wellesley, Needham, and Dover were popular summer vacation spots where many Bostonians had vacation cottages. Here, a South Middlesex Electric Street Railway car crosses Baker's Bridge on Centre Street to Dover from Needham. (Needham Historical Society.)

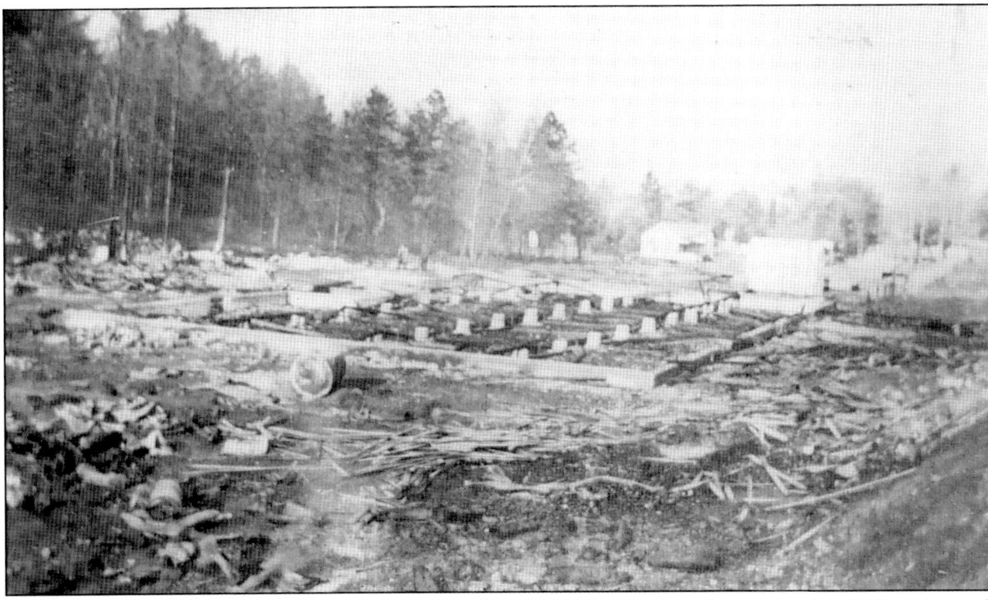

Shortly after moving into new quarters, fire leveled E.F. Hodgson's factory in 1911. He took advantage of the catastrophe to rebuild near the railroad station and the new town center. In doing so, Hodgson gained direct access to a railroad siding and an easy means to ship his completed product.

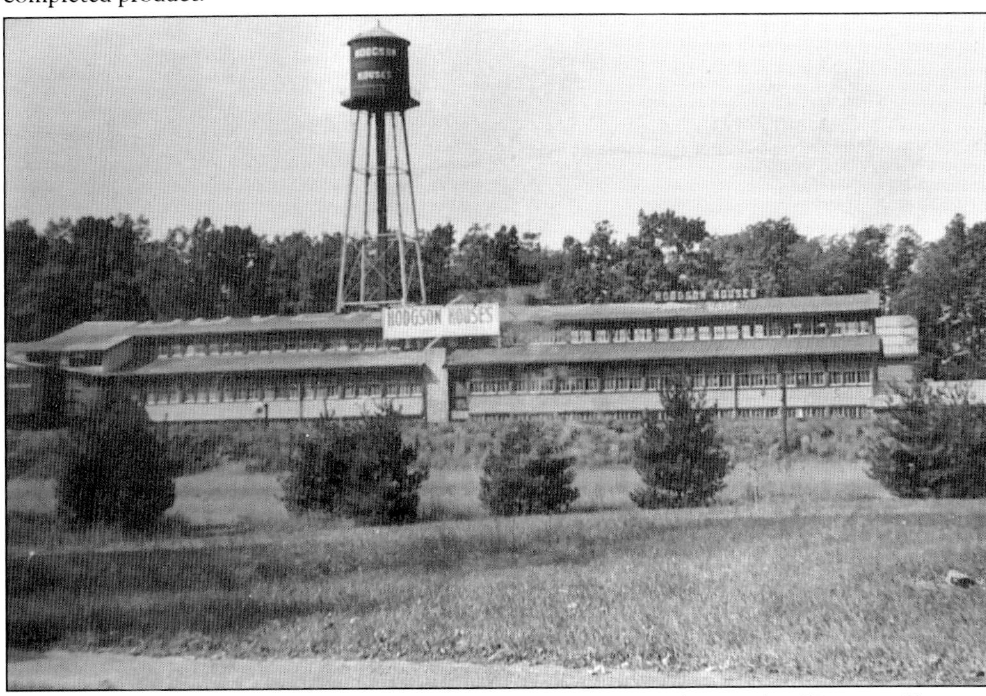

E.F. Hodgson's portable house factory dominated the center of town for 50 years. From its small beginnings on his father's Farm Street property in 1896, Hodgson's business expanded throughout the first half of the century and served an international market. The business was sold in 1961. Most of the factory was dismantled, with the Dover Highway Department taking over the site.

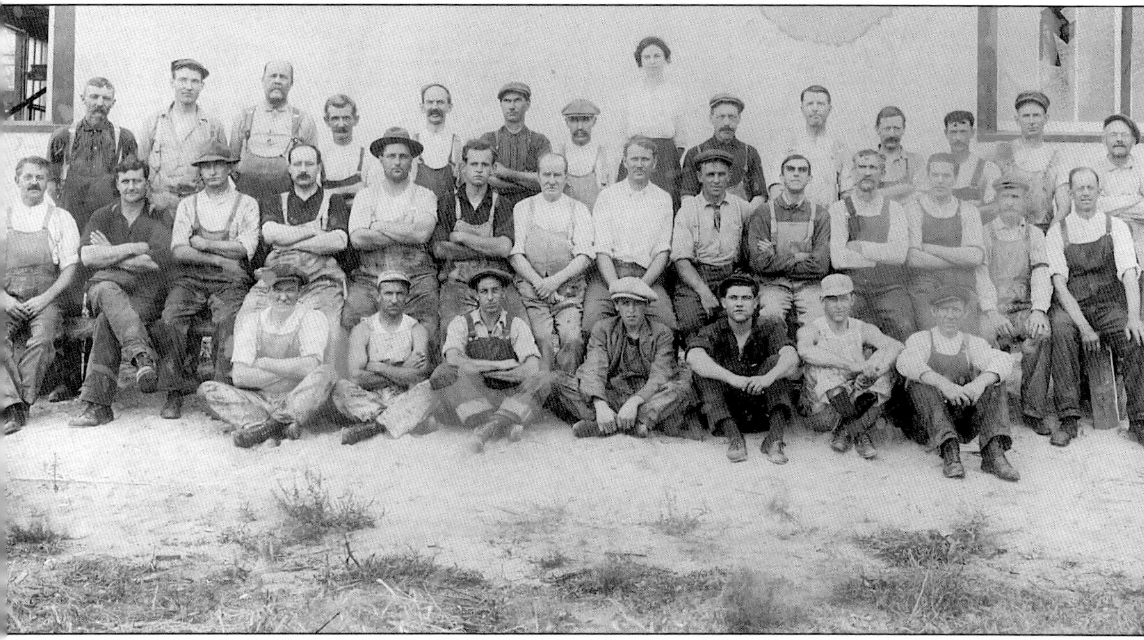

Workers at the E.F. Hodgson Company assemble in front of the main building, c. 1914–1915. In the middle row center sits Ernest Hodgson, owner, with James H. Chickering, superintendent, on his left. Mary Wall, clerk, stands in the back row, center right. Many of the workers lived in Dover, but others came from Medfield and other neighboring towns.

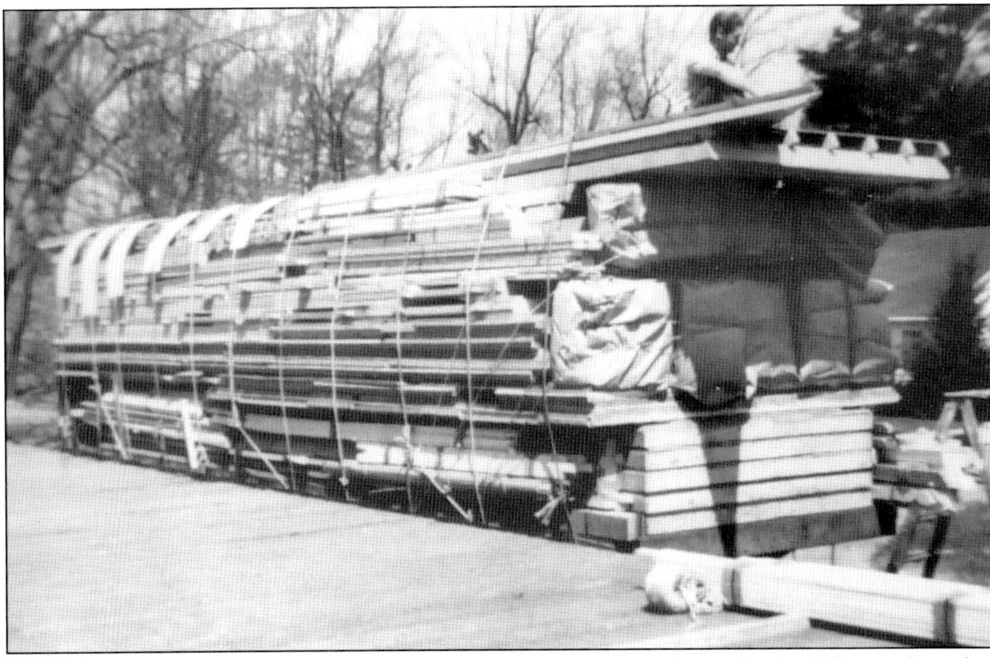

This 1950s photograph shows what an E.F. Hodgson Company house looked like, packaged to go. And go they did—all over the world. In 1916, the Belgian Royal Family ordered a Hodgson portable building to be used as an orphanage. Vacation homes abound all up and down the New England coast. By 1926, Sears, Roebuck & Company began competing by selling prefabricated homes by catalog. (Janet MacKenzie.)

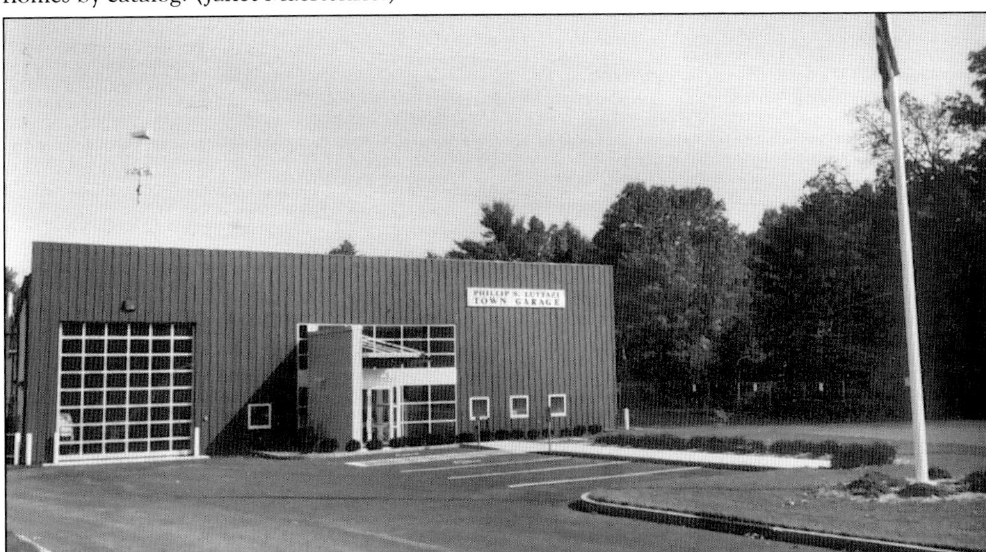

The 1996 Dover town meeting failed to approve a new town garage. On March 31 and April 1, 1997, a spring snowstorm caused a portion of the town garage to collapse, and the remaining structure was condemned. Consequently, a new town garage was completed in October 1998 and named for Phillip S. Luttazi. Luttazi was a Harvard graduate, a WWII veteran, and the superintendent of roads for 34 years. He replaced his father, Settimio E. Luttazi, the former superintendent who died in 1950.

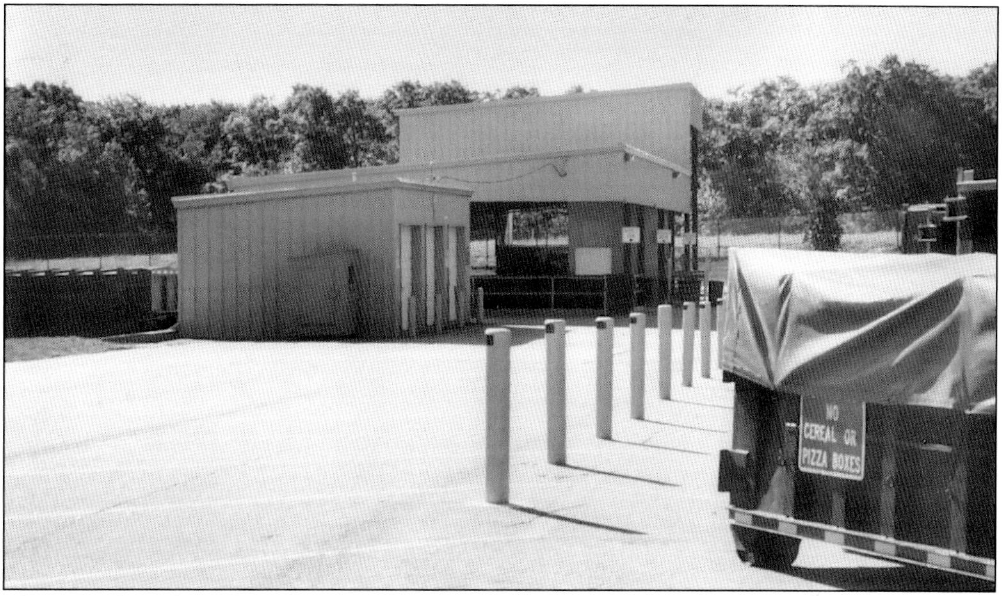

The town has always been environmentally conscious. The Powissett Street sanitary landfill, near the Westwood line, became a serious problem in the late 1960s. In the 1970s, the site became a transfer station with non-recyclable solid waste trucked to an energy facility in Millbury, Massachusetts. Residents have since become accustomed to the separation of materials as required by law.

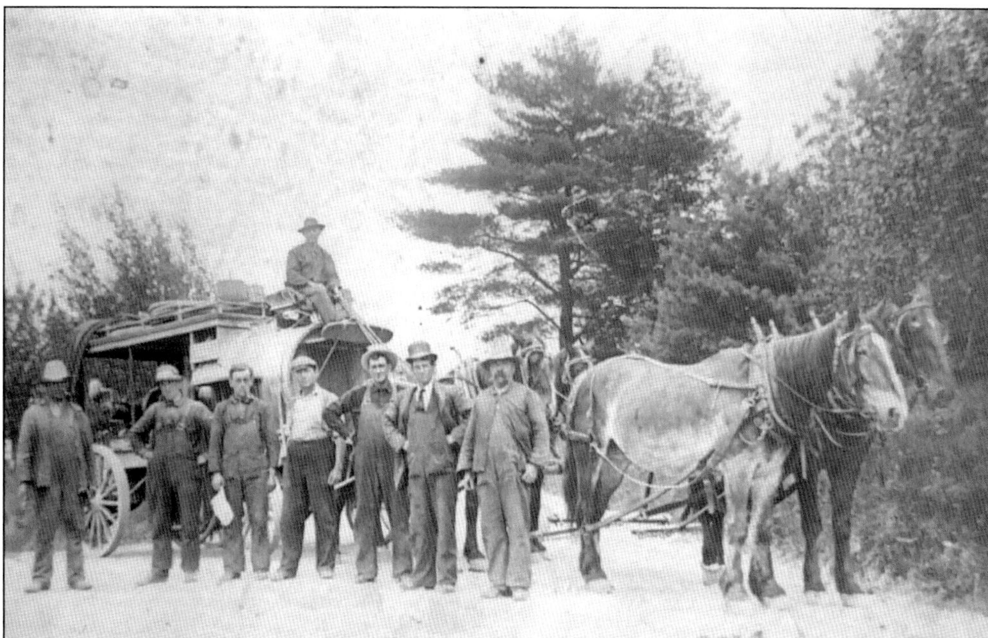

Sometimes, residents wake up in the early hours of a spring morning and hear the Norfolk County mosquito control truck spraying the sides of the roads. This horse-drawn gypsy moth spraying wagon worked the roads from 1906 to 1917. Harold MacKenzie is third from the left, Roderick MacKenzie is first on the right, and B. Snee is in the driver's seat. (Janet MacKenzie.)

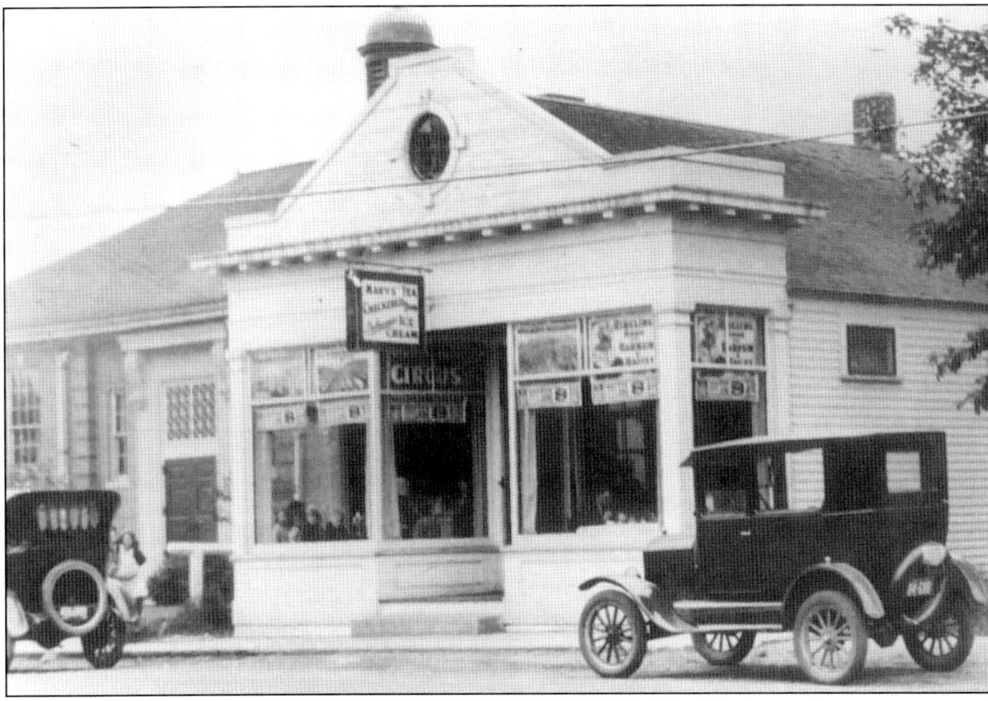

In 1925, the reliable Ford Tin Lizzie was designed with country roads in mind; it was equipped with heavy duty spokes, high road clearance, running boards, and mudguards. These cars—seen parked in front of Mary Hanchett's Checkered Tea Room on Springdale Avenue next to Caryl School—changed Dover and America forever. (Emmons scrapbook.)

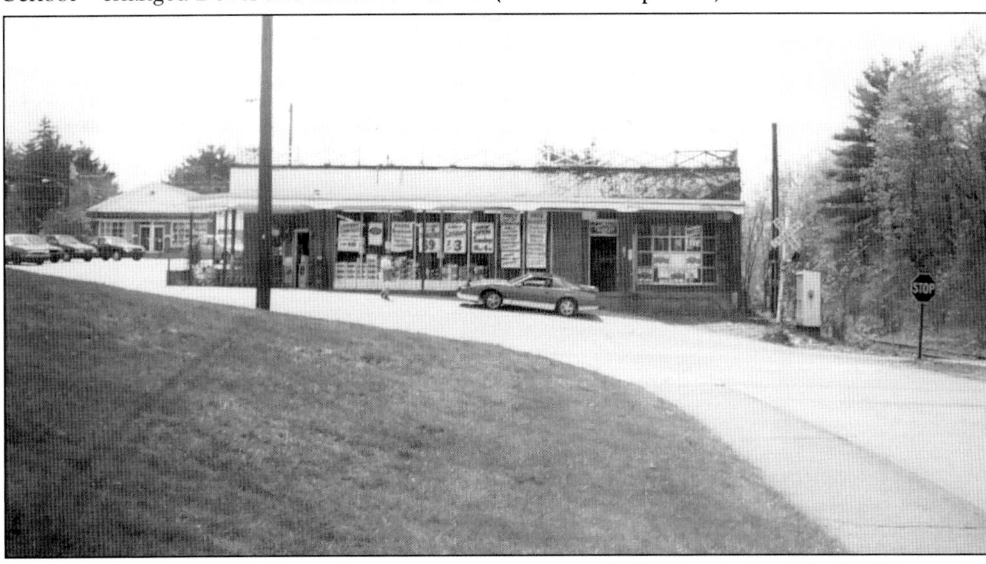

Complete with a package store, this present incarnation of J.W. Higgins's original 1880s market on Springdale Avenue would have caused him some concern. Old Jedediah Higgins was president of the Dover Temperance Society for nine years and clerk of the Massachusetts Total Abstinence Society. Treadwell's service station and the post office used to occupy the parking lot to the left, until the station moved to Whiting Road and the post office moved into the Breagy and Roach building on Centre Street.

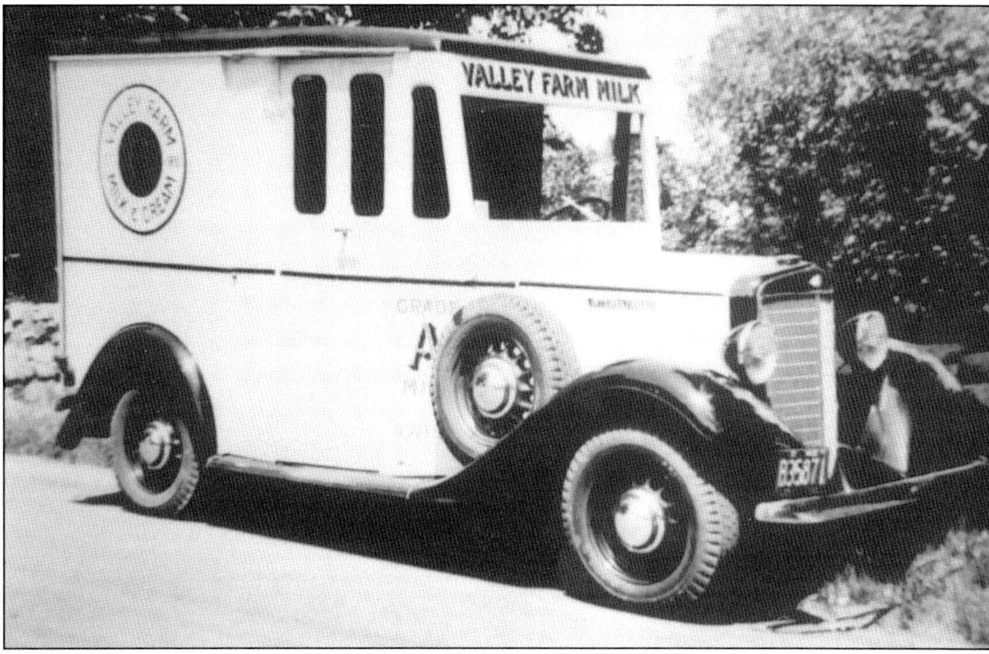

Michael Comiskey established Valley Farm Dairy in 1891 on Dedham Street at the present location of Mill Farm. Shortly after 1900, Comiskey moved the farm to a larger tract of land at the corner of Haven and Main Streets. The initial route went to Dana Hall in Wellesley and spread to Natick, Needham, Medfield, Westwood, and Millis. By 1920, the first of four Comiskey sons joined the business. The farm ceased operation in 1960. (Robert Comiskey.)

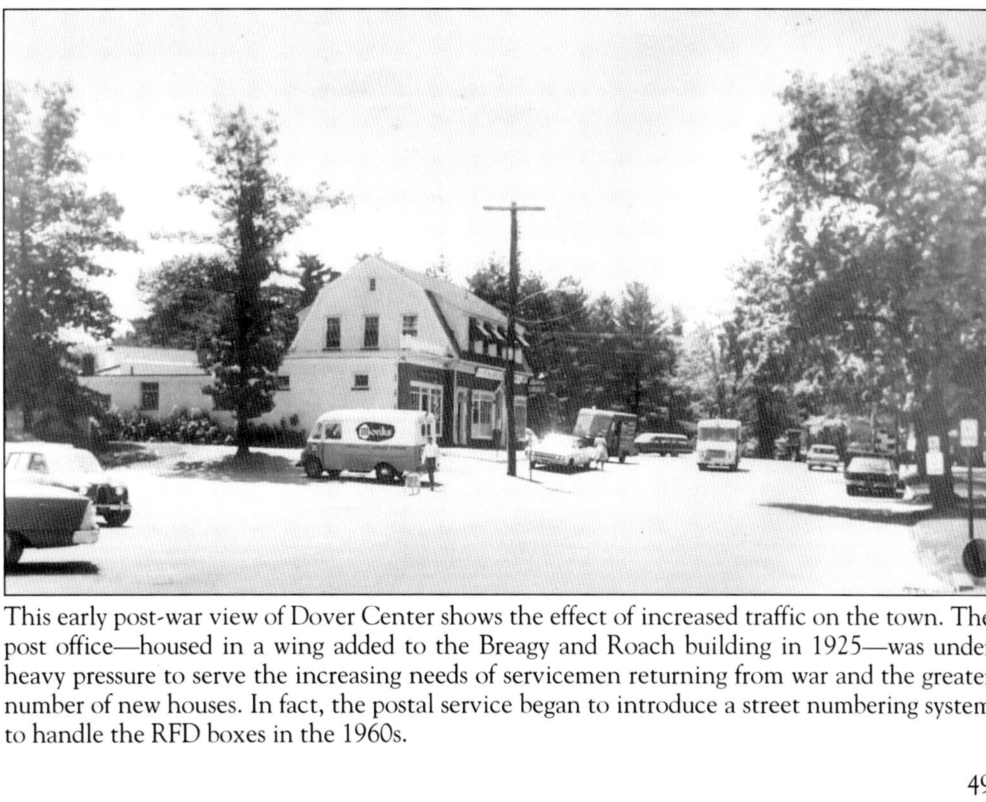

This early post-war view of Dover Center shows the effect of increased traffic on the town. The post office—housed in a wing added to the Breagy and Roach building in 1925—was under heavy pressure to serve the increasing needs of servicemen returning from war and the greater number of new houses. In fact, the postal service began to introduce a street numbering system to handle the RFD boxes in the 1960s.

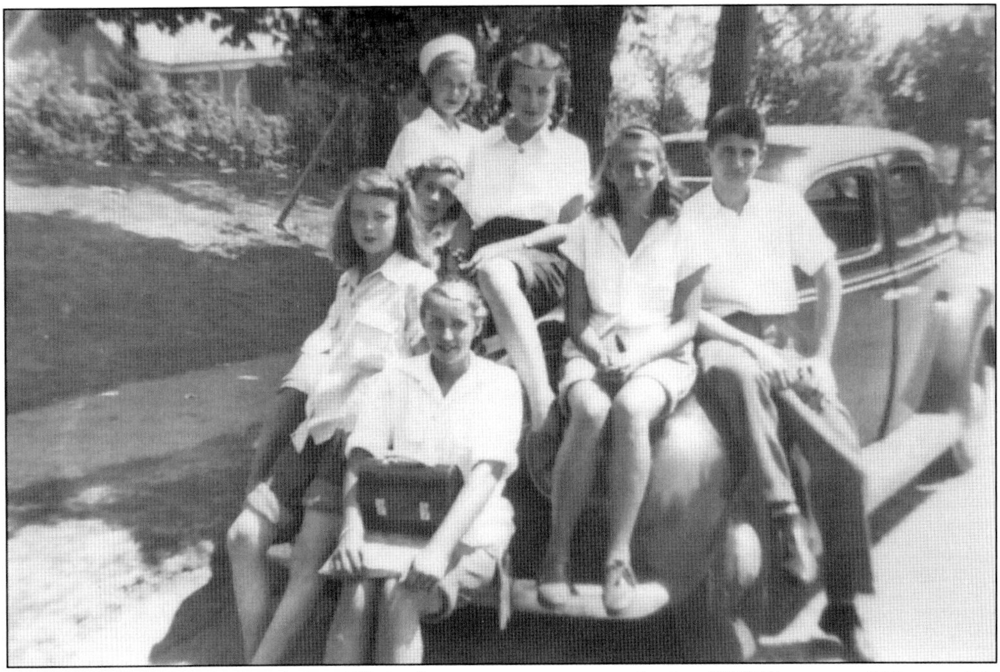

Farming requires constant labor. With the young men away during WWII, crews of Dover girls worked the fields during the summer harvest. This picture shows the 1945 summer Mill Farm work crew and a friend. Clockwise from the front, they are Elva Goucher, Dorothy DeBrynkops, Shirley Bond, Dale Morse, Marjorie Maker, Betty Piper, and Ralph Cote. (Shirley McGill.)

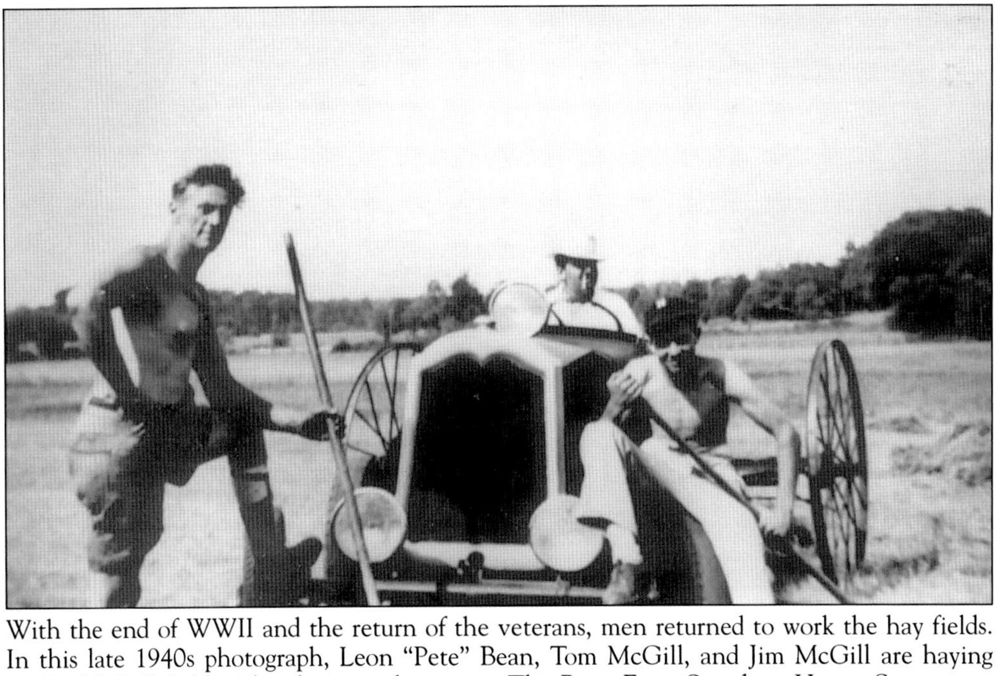

With the end of WWII and the return of the veterans, men returned to work the hay fields. In this late 1940s photograph, Leon "Pete" Bean, Tom McGill, and Jim McGill are haying in the McGill field with a homemade tractor. The Bean Farm Stand on Haven Street near McGill Corners was a familiar summer stopping place. Truck farming in this area has changed to organic farming. (Shirley McGill.)

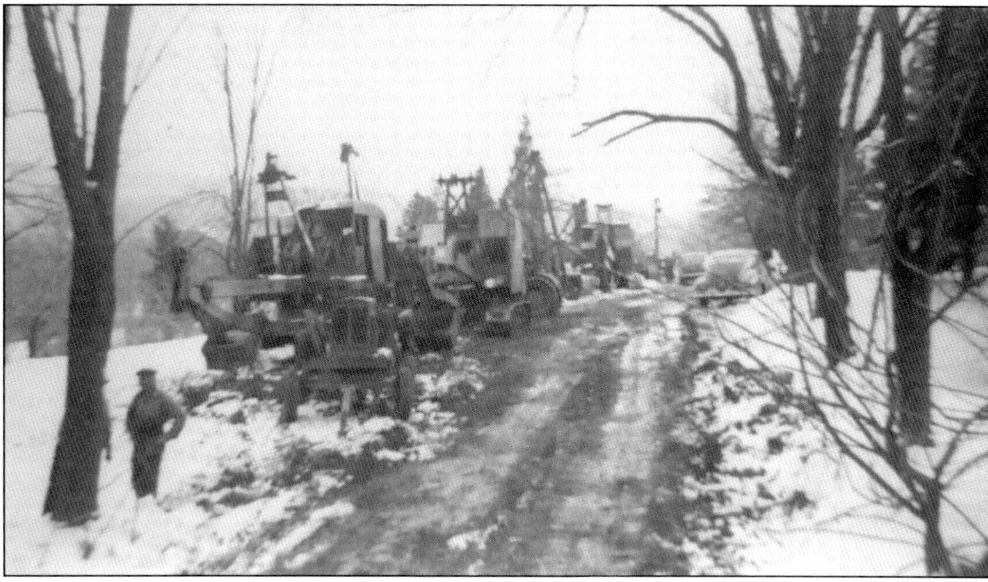

In 1955, the gas line arrived in Dover. This view shows heavy equipment beside the road near Channing Field. The town saw its first all electric houses before WWI and its first solar house in 1948. Energy is still a major concern and newer houses incorporate current heating and air-conditioning technology. (Janet MacKenzie.)

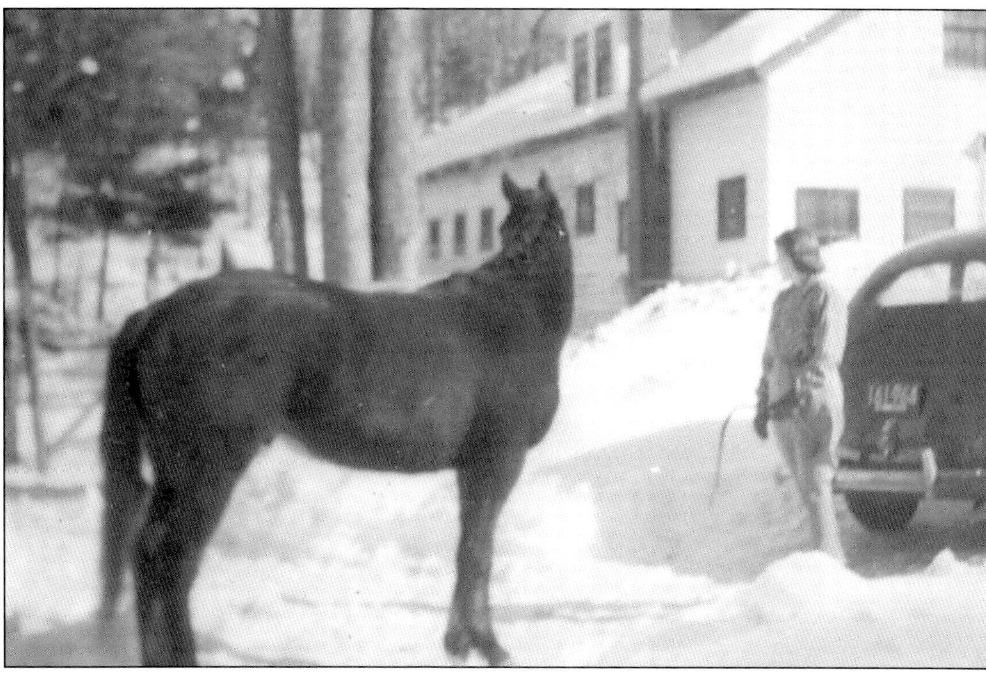

James Power, superintendent of the Dedham Country and Polo Club stables, bought property on Dedham Street to establish his own business, but died in 1927 before he could realize his dream. His wife, Annie, and their four children made the stable a reality. For decades, the Power family taught the joy of riding and the love of horses. Daughter Anna, shown here, ran the Power's Stables from 1951 to 1973, when the business was sold and became Wildwood Stable. The stables are now the Mt. Ida College Equestrian Center. (Helen P. Fenton.)

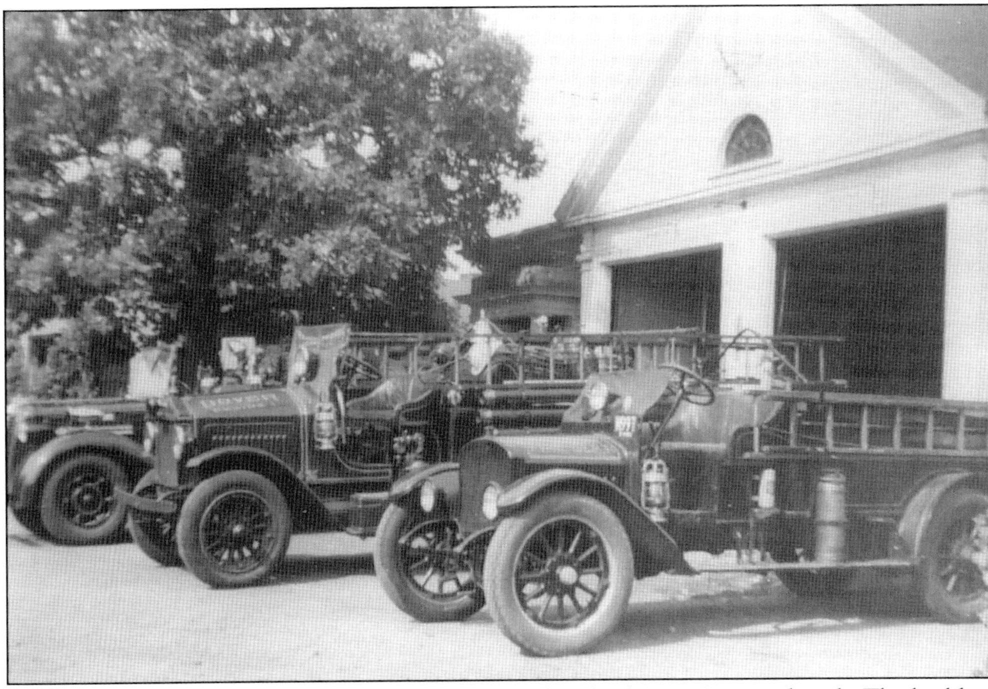

In the 1920s, the Dover Fire Department was housed in the former Baptist church. The building had been moved from Springdale Avenue to Whiting Road. Today, a call department consisting of Dover citizens—who are paid when called to a fire, ambulance call, or training session—is on duty 7 days a week, 24 hours a day. (Robert Comiskey.)

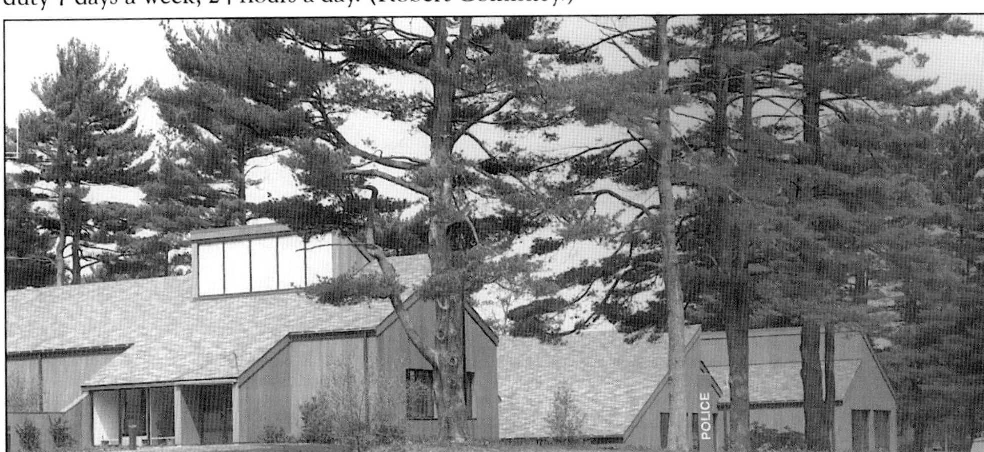

Population changes have put increased stress on both police and fire units in the town. The town meeting voted to erect a new joint protective services building, which was built in 1975 on the Bryant-Hynes property at the corner of Walpole and Centre Streets. The neighboring Frost House was moved to the regional school site.

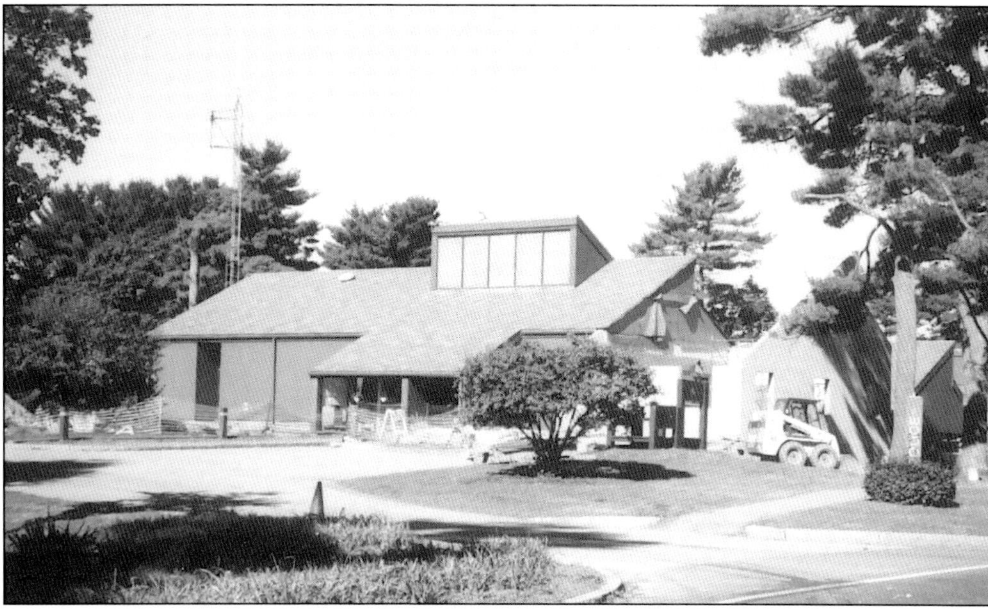

In 1998, Police Chief Joseph Q. Griffin reported that "crime statistics in Dover . . . mirrored the downward trend of most Greater Boston communities. . . . Service delivery rather than crime is, thankfully, the principal function of the department." Similar service demands were placed on the fire department by the increase in housing construction. The 1999 town meeting voted a building expansion plan, which was completed in 2000.

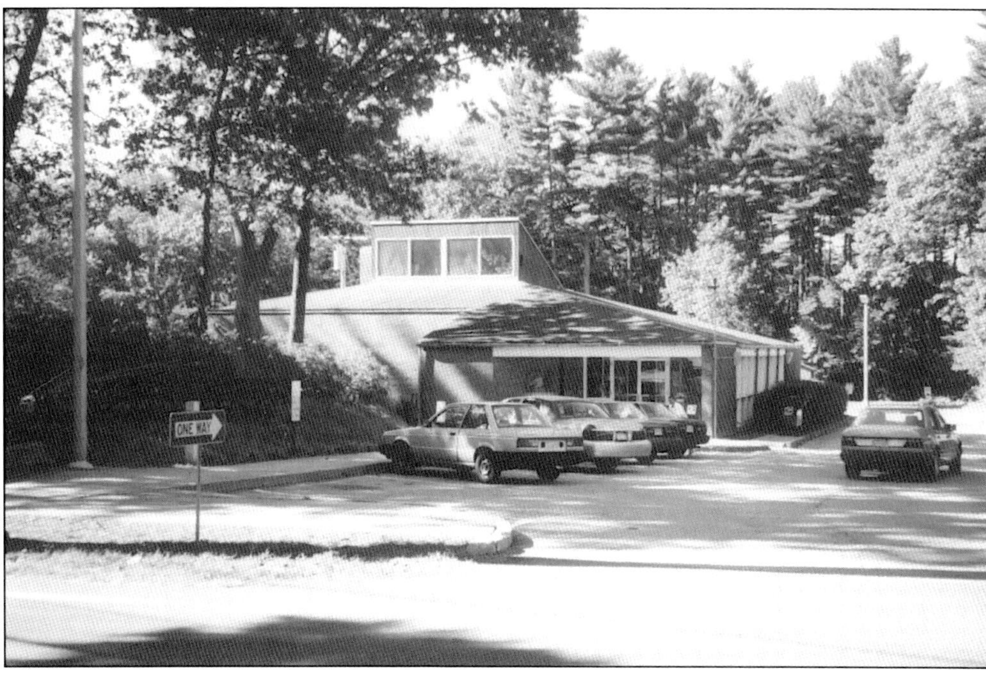

In the 1960s, the town's population outgrew the small post office wing of the Village Drug Store. In 1976, the U.S. Postal Service opened a new post office on Walpole Street beside the new protective services building. By fiscal year 1999, zip code 02030 was handling 2,624,272 pieces of mail and generating almost $500,000.

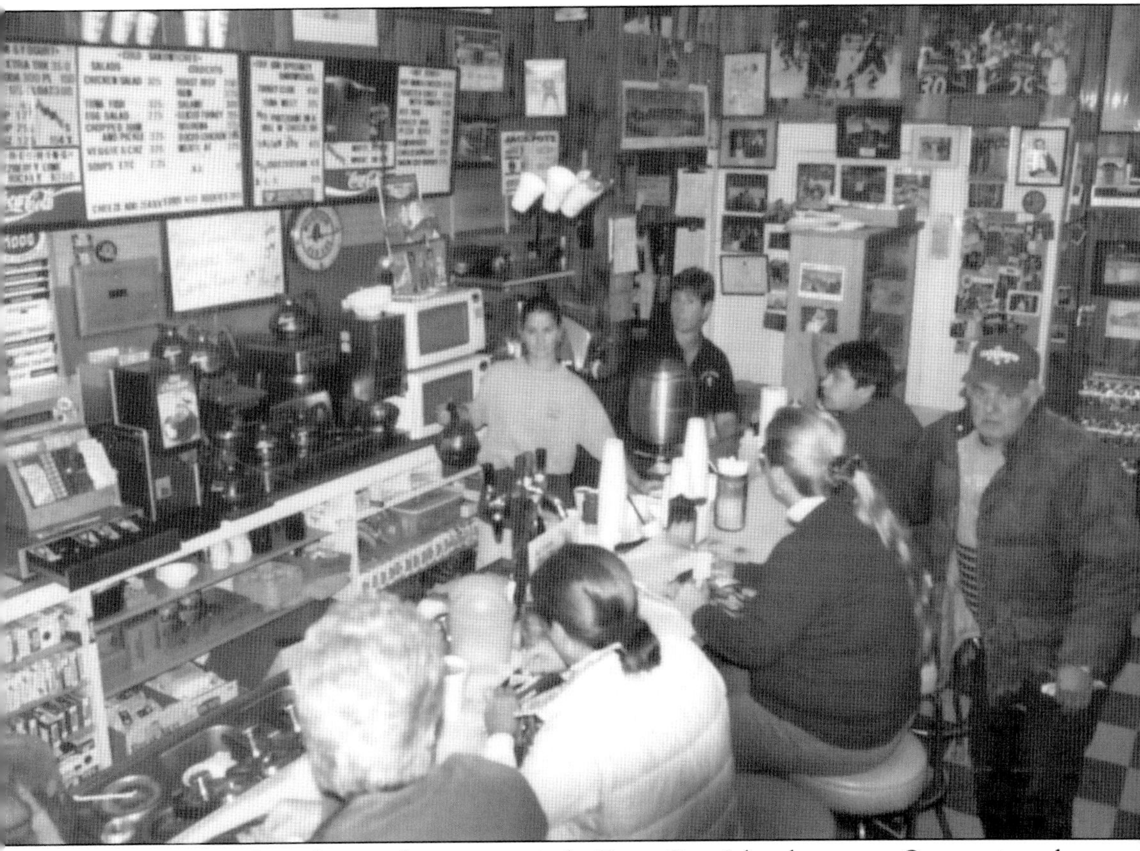

The most popular gathering place in town is the Dover Store's lunch counter. On any given day, one can meet selectmen, friends, police officers, teachers, and visitors for a cup of coffee or a soft drink. From town politics to the Red Sox, the Bruins, the Celtics, or the Patriots, anything and everything is fair game for discussion. In the center background, Sandy Ball oversees operations; she runs the store with her father, Don. "Give me a large black, three sugars, and a jelly doughnut."

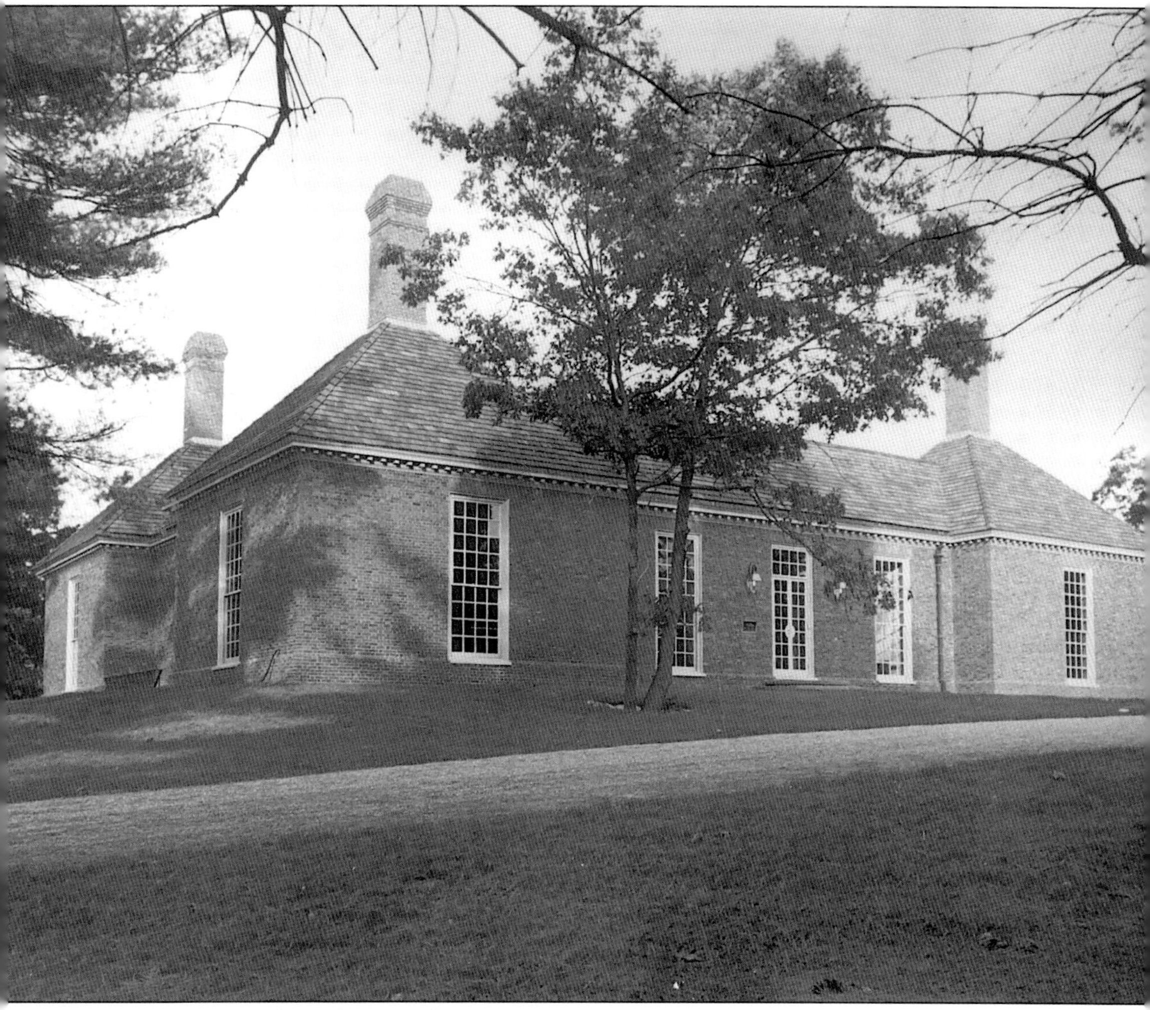

The Dover Town Library had a collection of 200 volumes as early as 1817. In 1804, the town meeting had appropriated $500 for books and furnishings for a room to house 794 volumes in the town hall. In 1922, the new Dover Town House was built with a library wing. The present library building, opened on December 1, 1968, was renovated and rededicated on May 3, 1996. Membership in the Minuteman Library Network and access to the Internet have enlarged the library beyond its physical collection. (Marvin Rosenkrantz.)

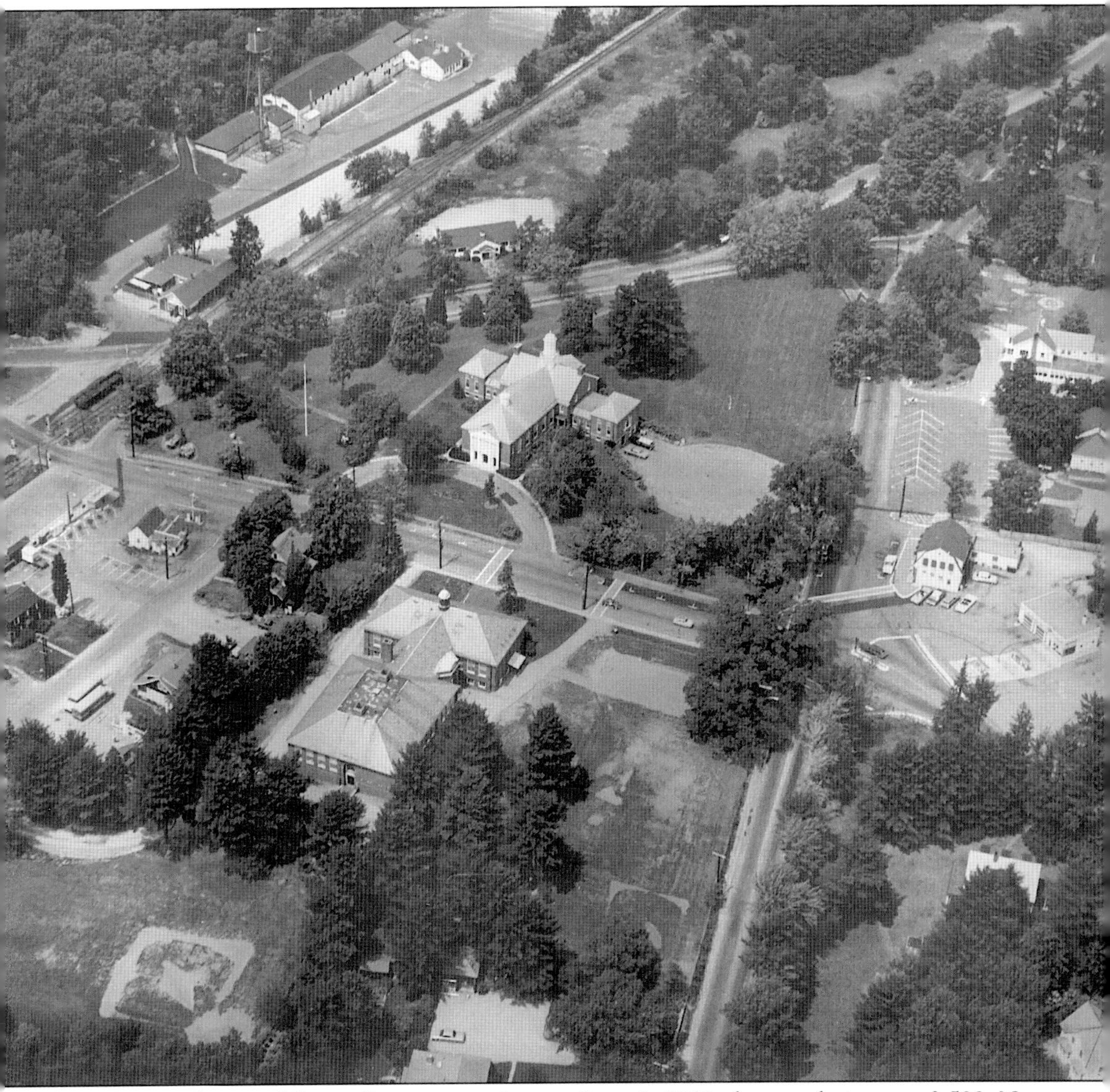

This aerial view of Dover Center was taken on June 5, 1966; the population was 3,592. Note the changes that have taken place. The old town garage and the water tower are gone. The old training field has been cleared and the library sits in the upper right corner. Caryl School, in the center, was rebuilt after the 1970 fire. The Frost House on the corner of Walpole and Centre Streets is gone, as is the traffic island in the center of the intersection. The protective services group now sits in the lower right corner. Treadwell's is gone from the Dover Market–Higgins parking lot. The Mobil station has had a face lift and the Dover Country Properties building fills the side edge of the station. Charles River School's parking lot has grown a new science center. Across the center, trees have been cut down and the landscape has changed. However, at whatever age, the center remains a striking part of the town.

Five

HOUSES OF DOVER

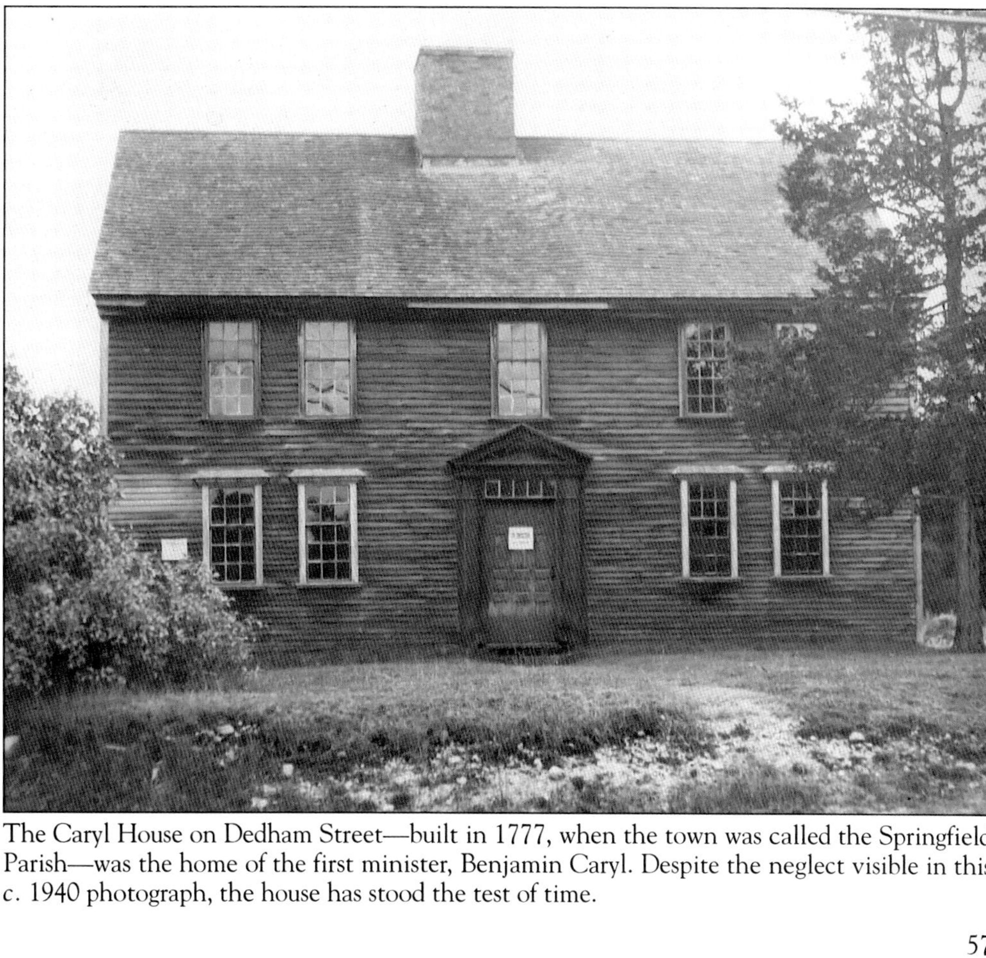

The Caryl House on Dedham Street—built in 1777, when the town was called the Springfield Parish—was the home of the first minister, Benjamin Caryl. Despite the neglect visible in this c. 1940 photograph, the house has stood the test of time.

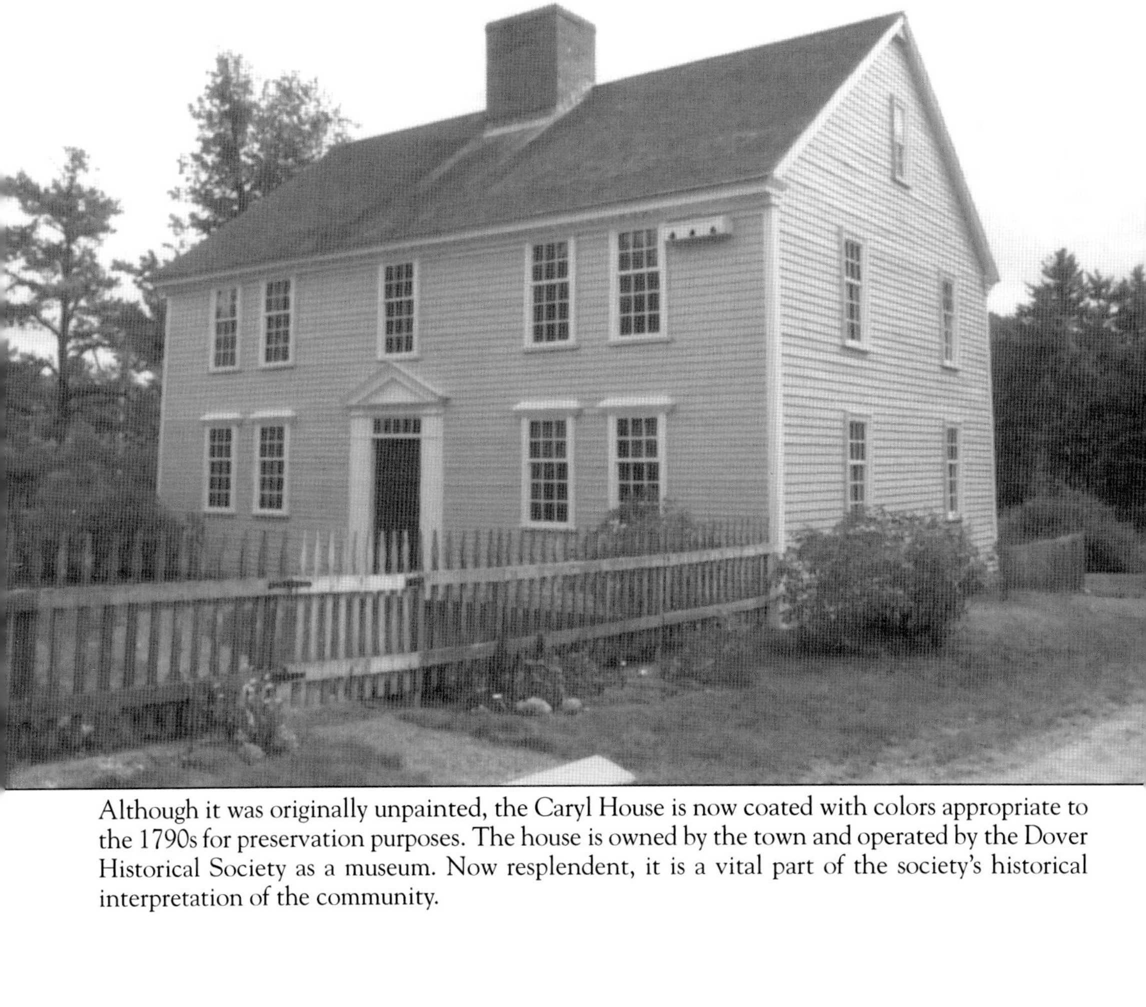

Although it was originally unpainted, the Caryl House is now coated with colors appropriate to the 1790s for preservation purposes. The house is owned by the town and operated by the Dover Historical Society as a museum. Now resplendent, it is a vital part of the society's historical interpretation of the community.

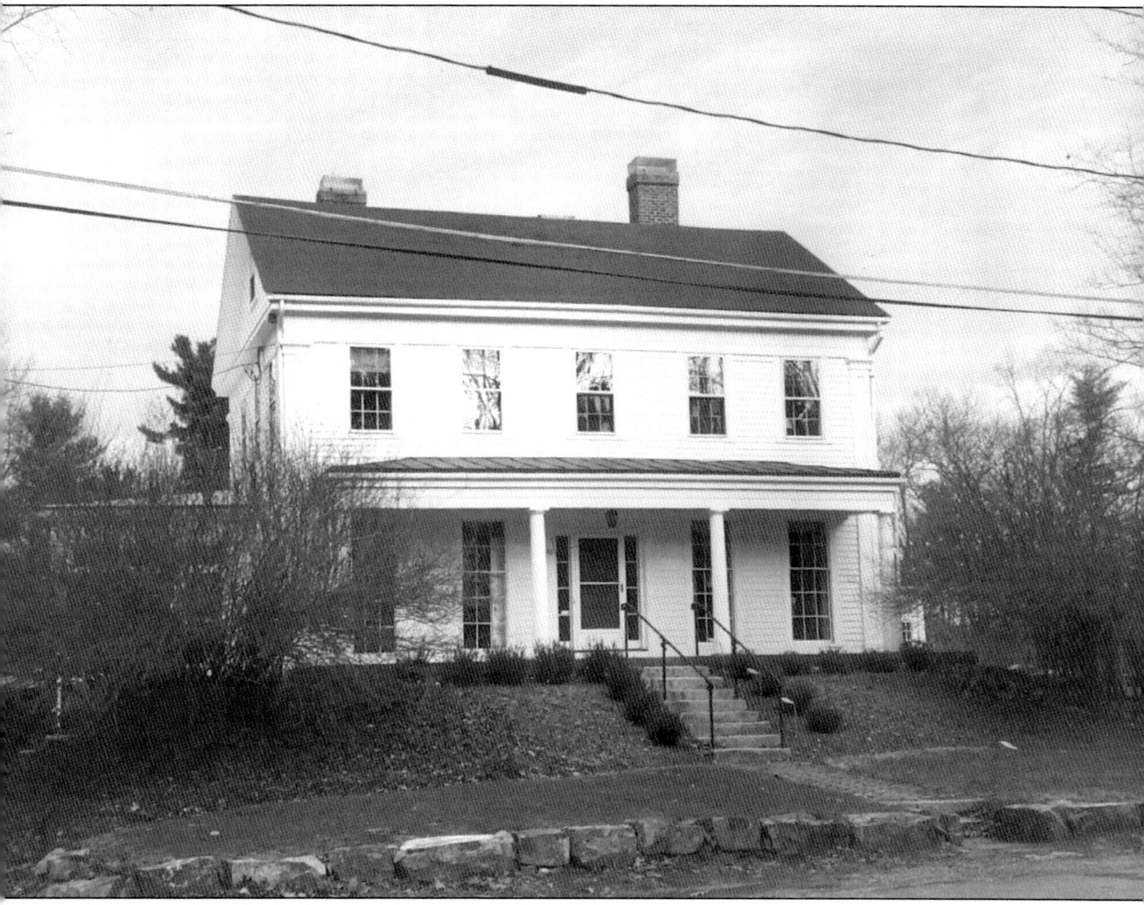

Ephraim Wilson built this farmhouse on Wilsondale Street in the early 1850s for his bride; the style of the house was typical of the era. It certainly has stood the test of time and has remained as originally built, with only minor changes.

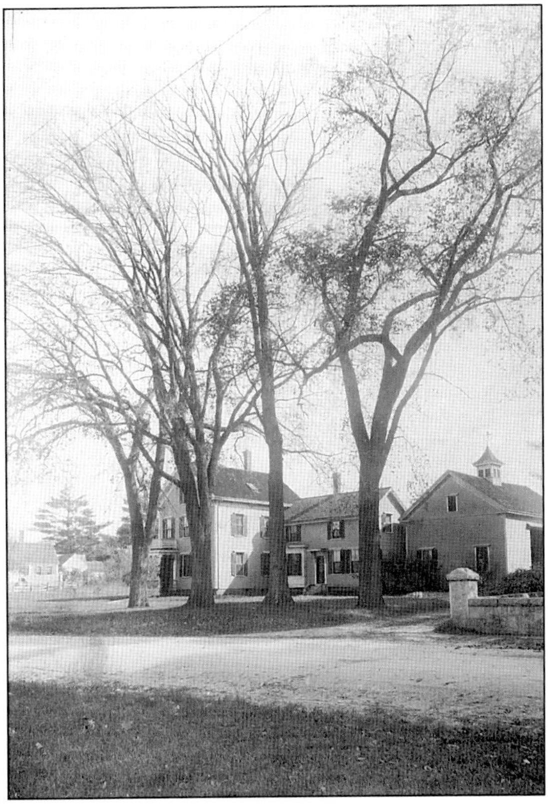

The Bertschy House on Centre Street, across from the library, was built in 1877. The house on the left was connected to the barn to the right. You can just see the front edge of Highland Cemetery on the right. Part of the house was used as an early telephone exchange.

In 1917, the Bertschy House was separated from the barn, which was later converted into a house. From 1926 to 1927, the house was referred to as the Teacher's Lodge for the teachers who boarded there from the Sanger School up the street. The two parts look this way today.

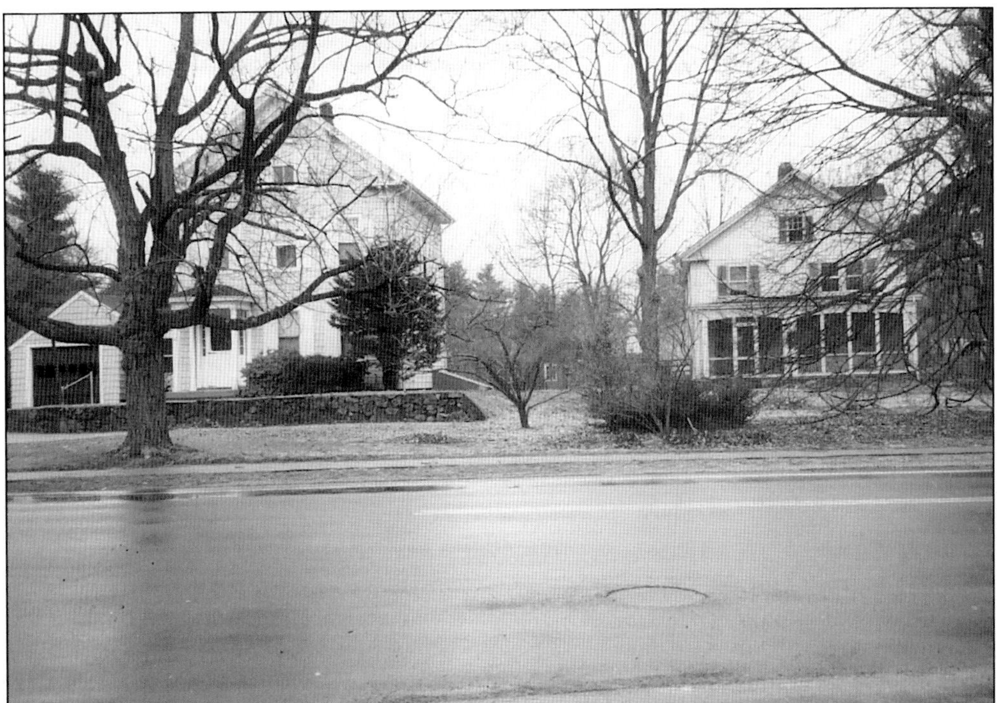

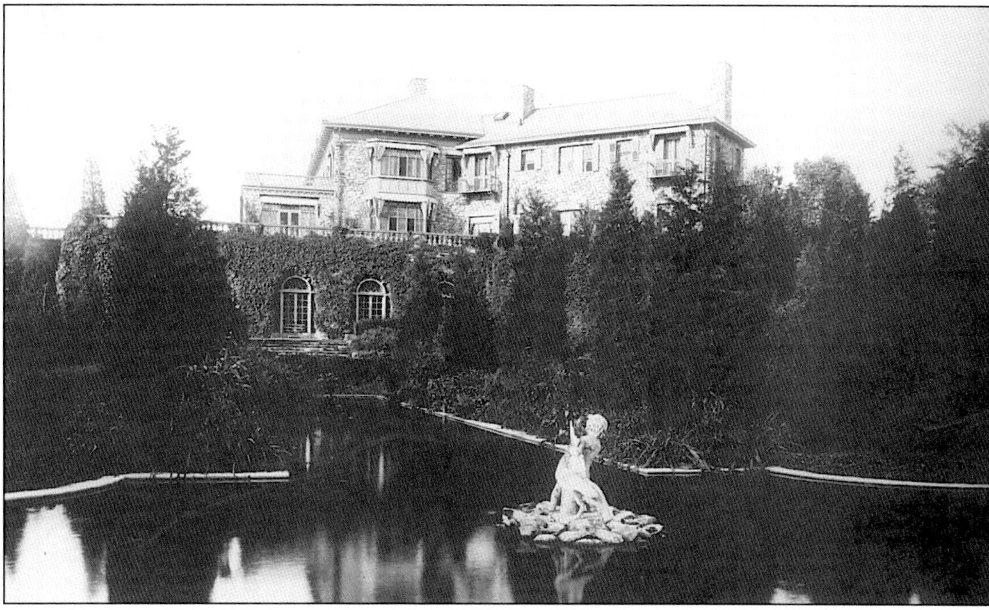

Part of the formal gardens at the current Dominican Priory on Glen Street is shown in this photograph. Mr. and Mrs. Arthur Davis built the estate from 1902 to 1908. Mrs. Davis was the sister of Alice Cheney Baltzell, who built Elm Bank. Olmstead & Vaux of Boston designed the grounds.

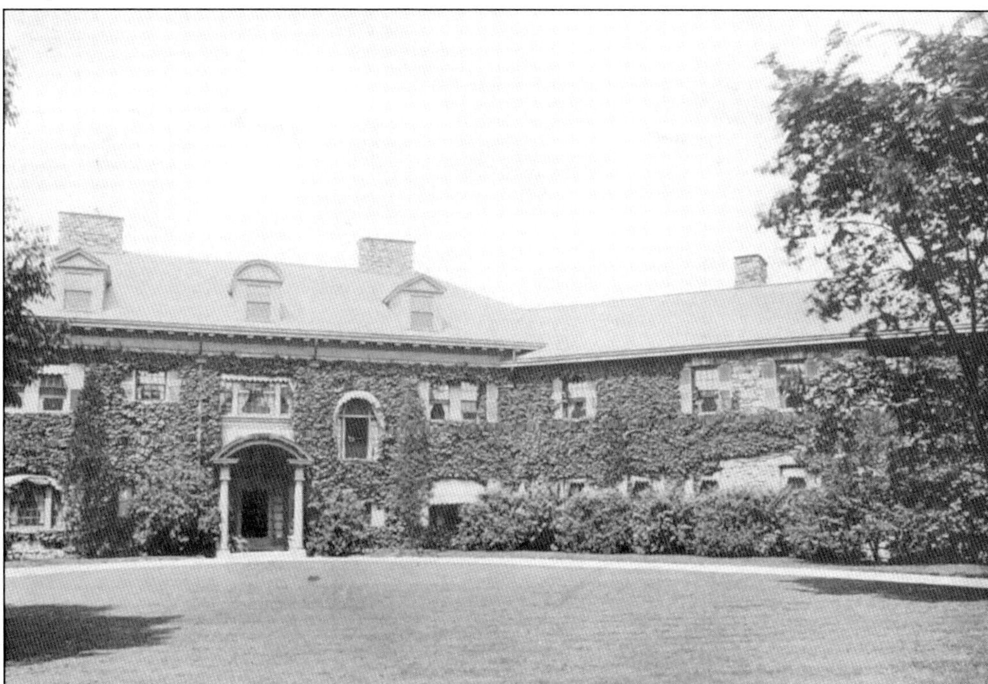

St. Stephen Priory is a center of increased activity. Although the building has been changed, this post-WWII picture shows how much the priory resembles the country estates that dotted the Dover countryside after 1900. The house is approached by a tree-lined drive. The Charles River flows behind the priory.

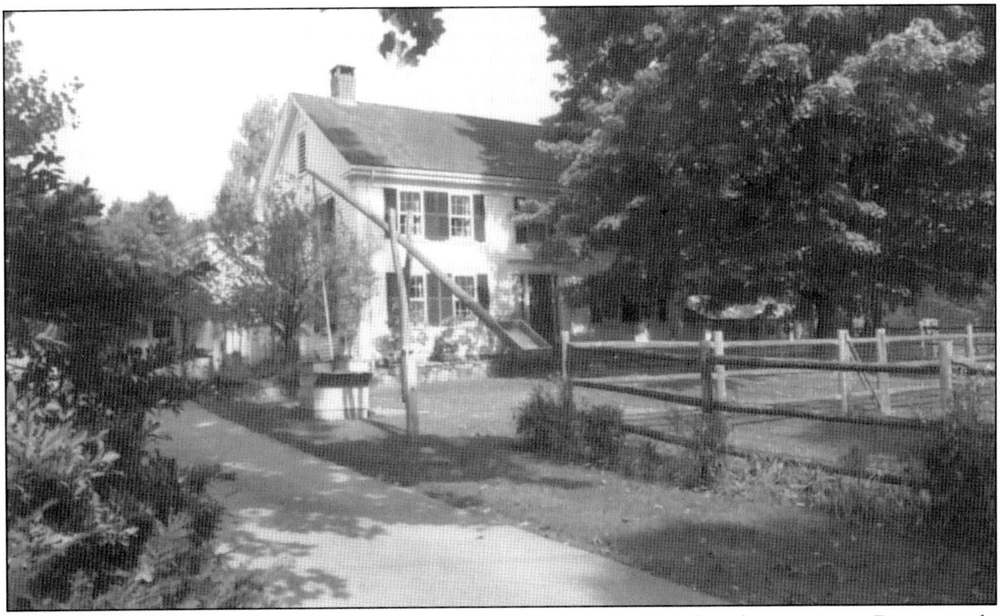

Chickering Farm on Haven Street reflects the history of a family who came to Dover early to farm. James H. Chickering was a community leader, superintendent of the E.F. Hodgson Company, and a town selectman. Chickering School was named after him; his daughter Emily was long the town librarian.

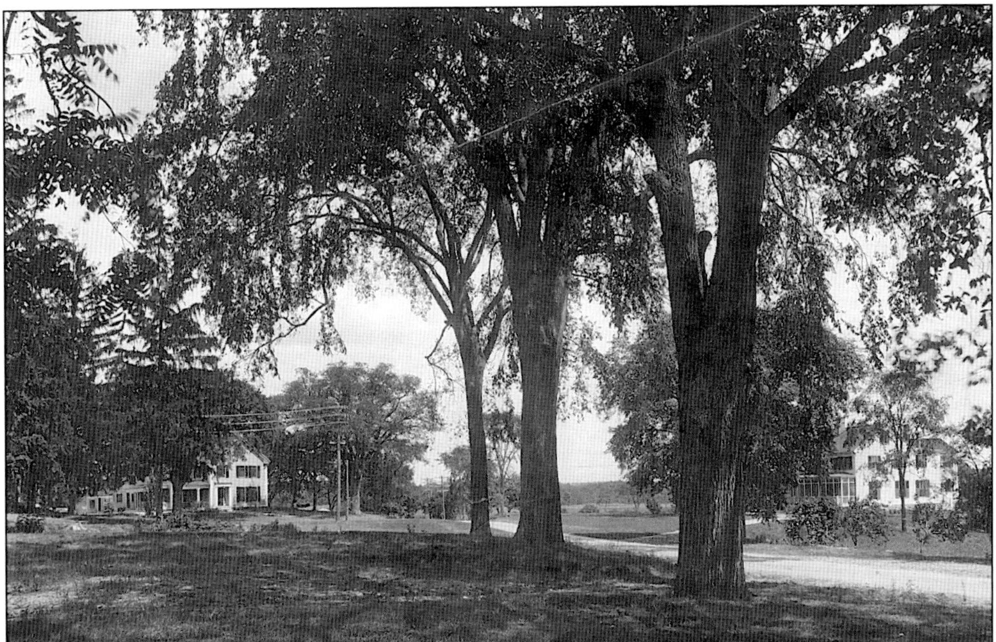

McGill Corner is a familiar Dover sight. To the left is Michael Comiskey's Valley Dairy Farm, which he moved from Mill Farm on Dedham Street in 1900. When it closed in 1960, a group of Dover residents tried unsuccessfully to turn the land into a golf course and country club. In 1967, a 52-acre parcel of the farm was the first purchase of the Dover Conservation Commission.

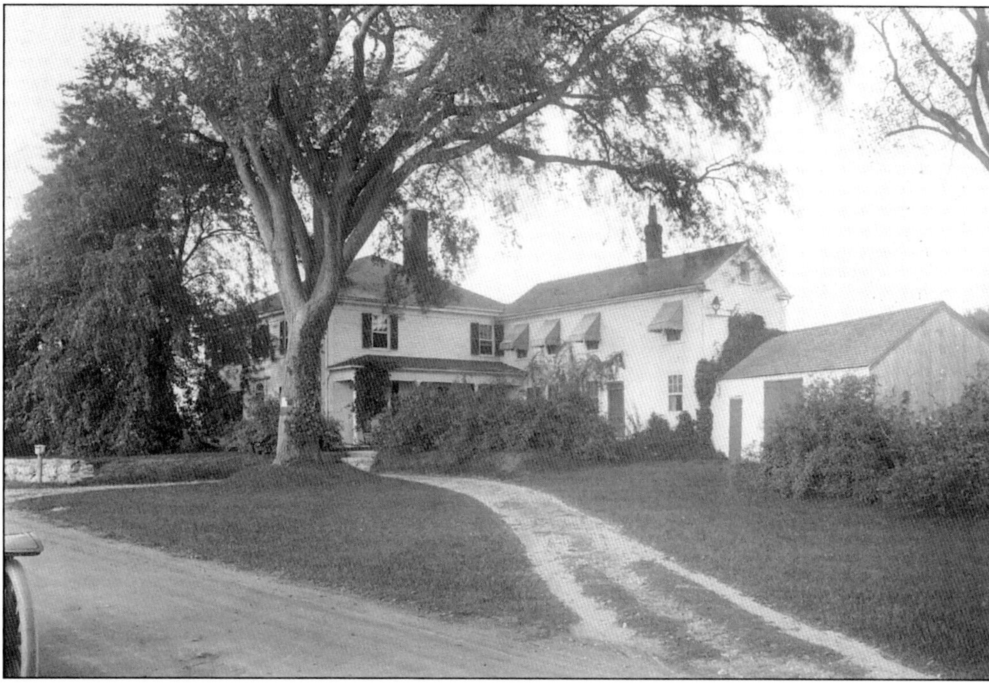

The Pokanoket Club on Farm Street, founded in 1899, was housed in this 1805–1813 Federal-style building, which was originally a dairy farm. The club acquired the farm from James S. Carey on September 17, 1906. The house is currently a private residence.

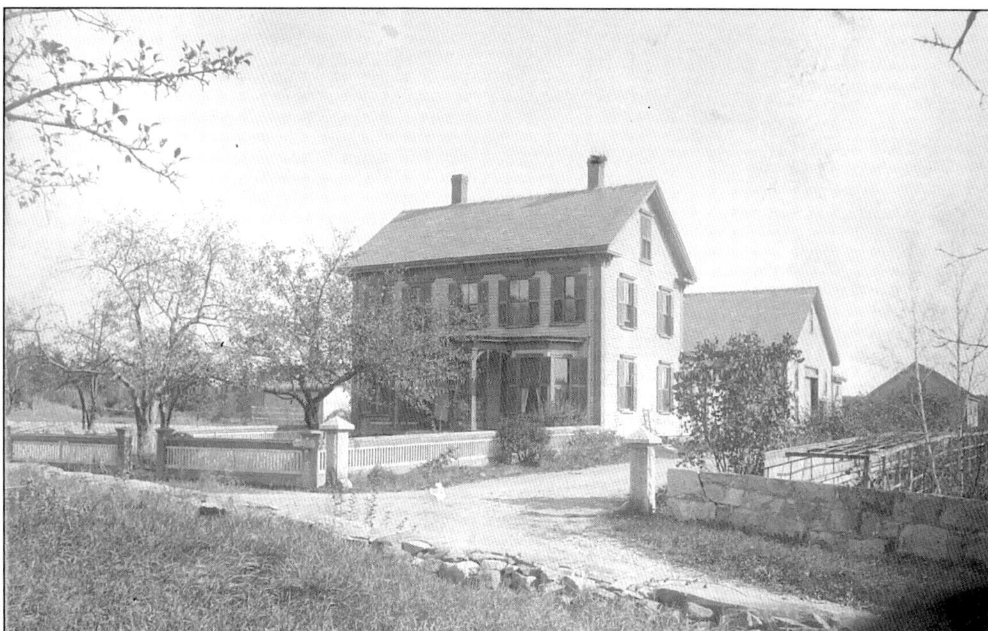

Beautiful Pine Street has been designated a scenic road. This Federal Victorian, built between 1830 and 1850, reminds us of a wondrous age. This neo-classical structure has changed little; however, heavy growth now covers the land. A tennis court has been built in the field to the right.

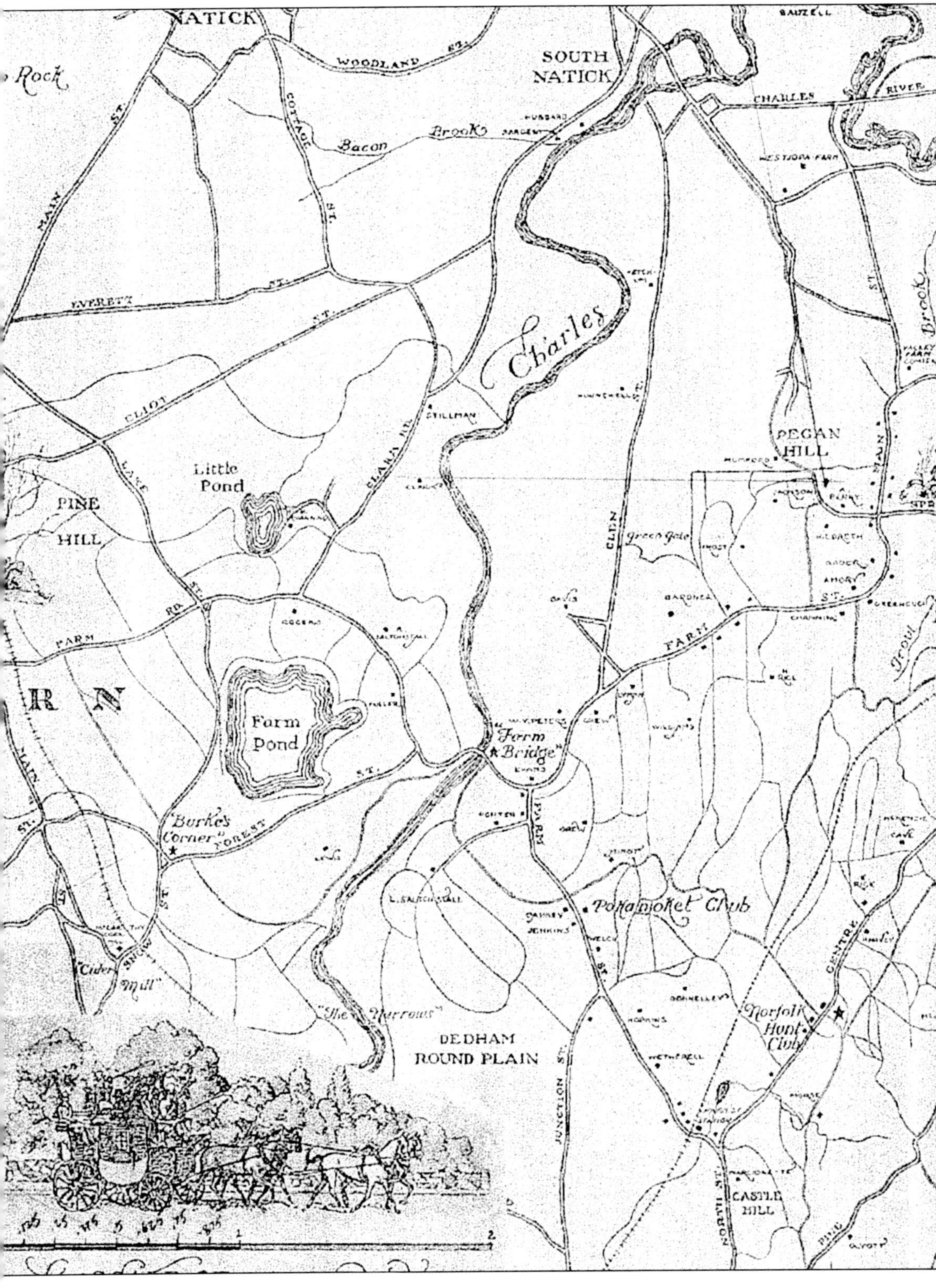
NATICK
SOUTH NATICK
Rock
WOODLAND RD.
COTTAGE ST.
MAIN ST.
Bacon Brook
CHARLES RIVER
EVERETT ST.
ELIOT ST.
Charles
LAKE ST.
Little Pond
PINE HILL
CLARK RD.
STILLMAN
PEGAN HILL
GLEN ST.
Green Gate
FARM RD.
FARM ST.
Farm Pond
Farm Bridge
"Burke's Corner"
FOREST ST.
SNOW ST.
"Cider Mill"
Pokanoket Club
"The Narrows"
DEDHAM ROUND PLAIN
JUNCTION ST.
Norfolk Hunt Club
CENTRE ST.
NORTH ST.
CASTLE HILL
AMORY ST.

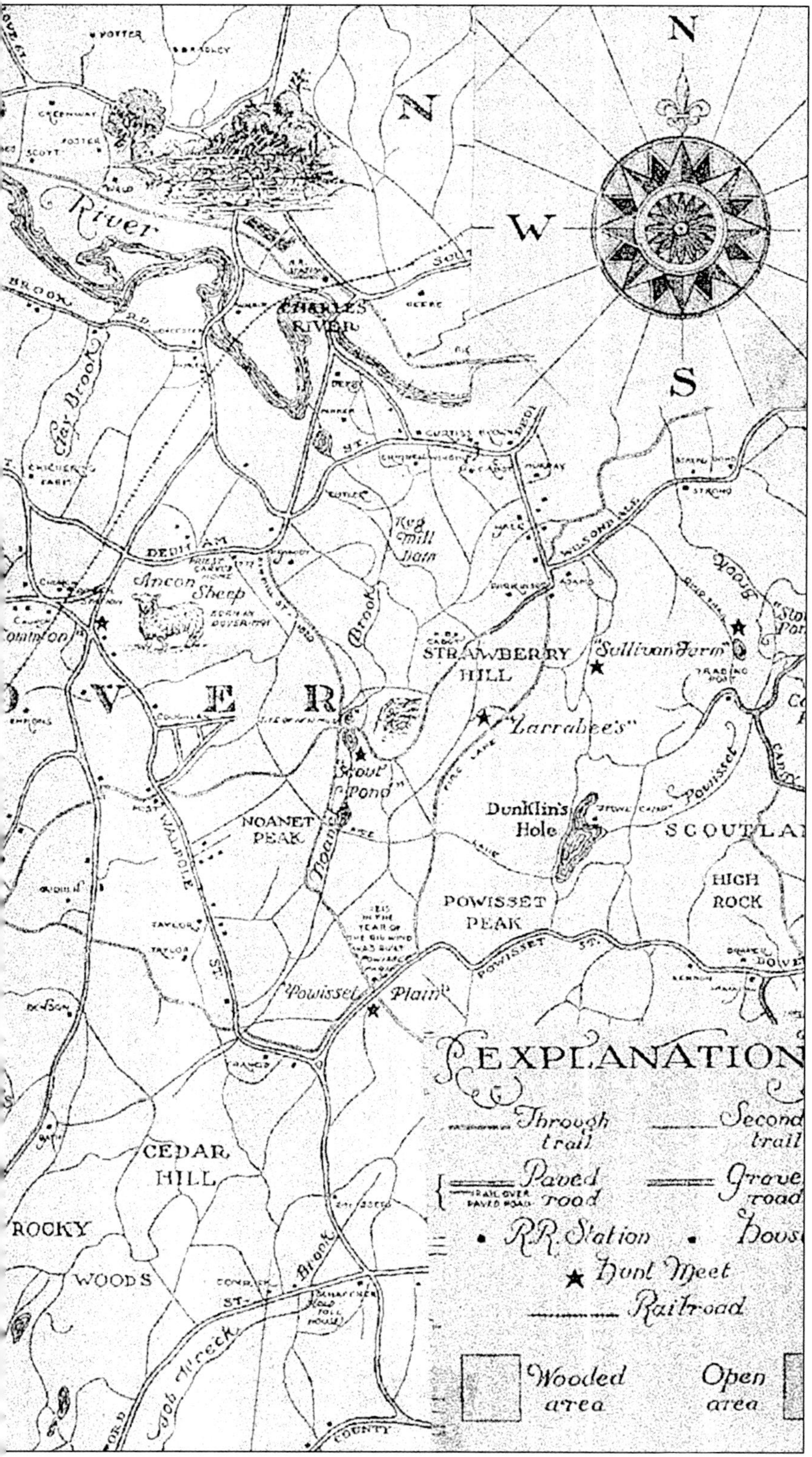

This map, delineated by Dwight Shepler in 1934 from a survey of ten neighboring towns by E. Worthington, is beautifully colored in the original. An excellent framed copy hangs in the Dover Town Library, courtesy of the Dover Historical Commission.

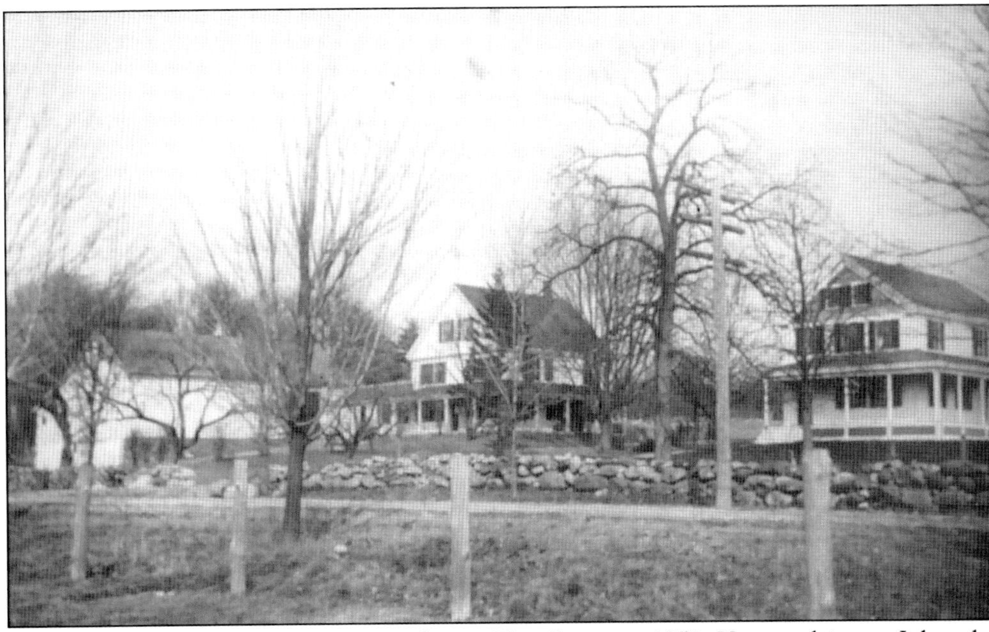

William McClure built the house at right on Glen Street in 1858. He gave his son, John, the land on the left to build a house in 1910. John McClure was the first superintendent of streets in Dover. (George Newcomb.)

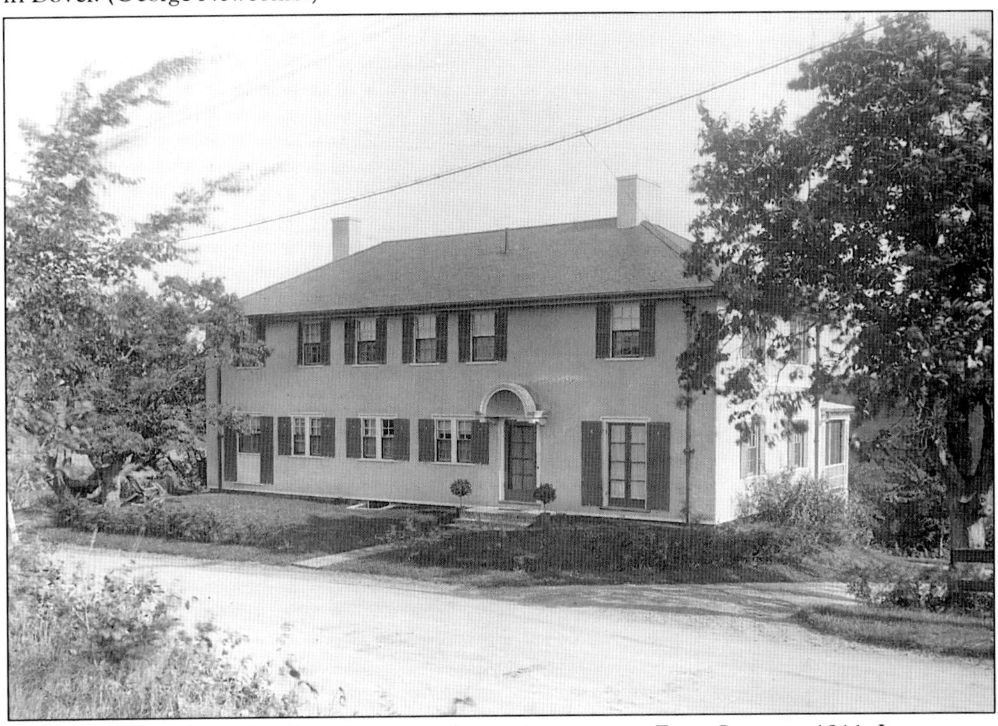

James W. Austin built this French country house in stucco on Farm Street in 1911. It was once owned by Charles Greenough, who was appointed by Governor Sargent to the Massachusetts Bay Transit Authority. The house also belonged to one of the first groups built before WWI, from which Dover acquired its reputation as a town of country estates.

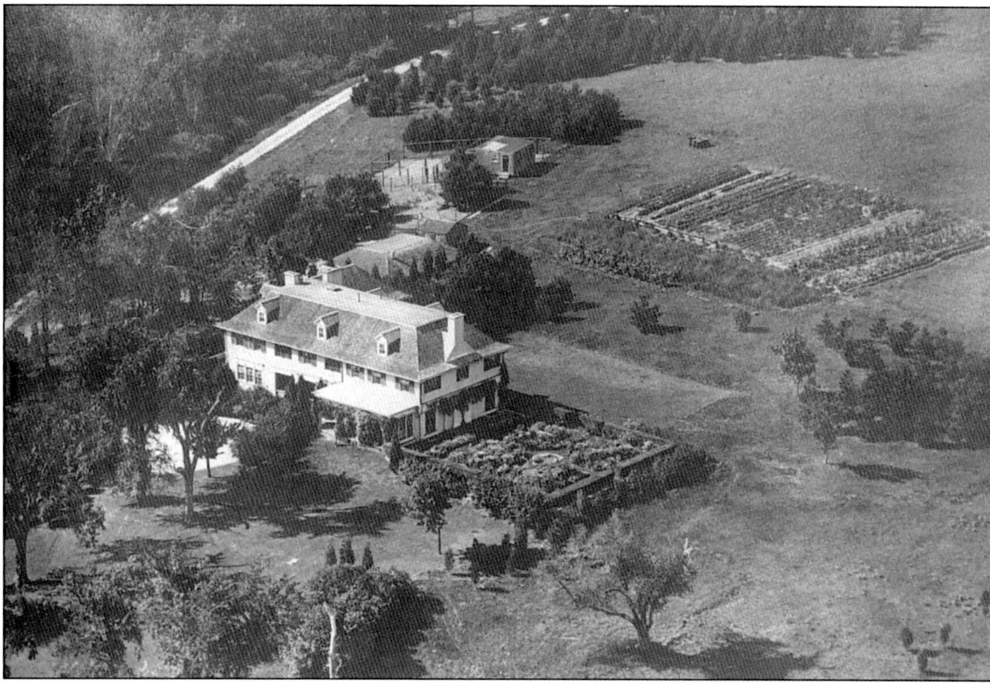

The Robert Fuller house on Pegan Lane was built in 1909–1910. This aerial view taken in the summer of 1919 clearly shows the surrounding landscaping and the large vegetable garden in the upper right corner. Similar gardens were common in the WWI period. Mrs. Fuller, although difficult to see in this view, is waving from the door in the center. (Robert Fuller.)

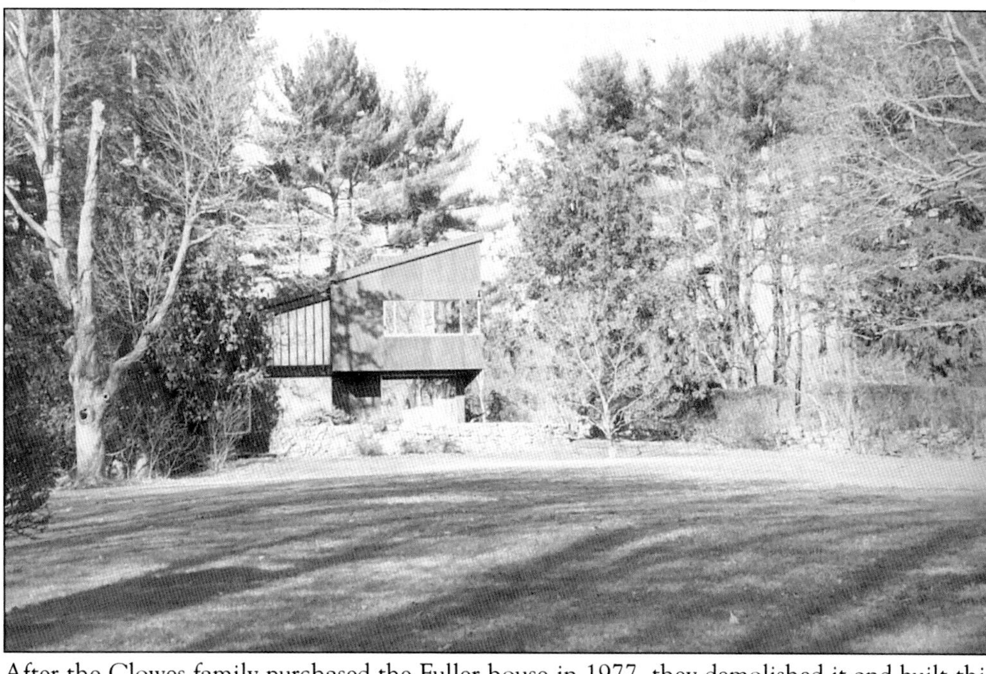

After the Clowes family purchased the Fuller house in 1977, they demolished it and built this smaller and more modern home. It is interesting to note that today, the reverse is happening: smaller houses are being torn down and replaced with much larger structures.

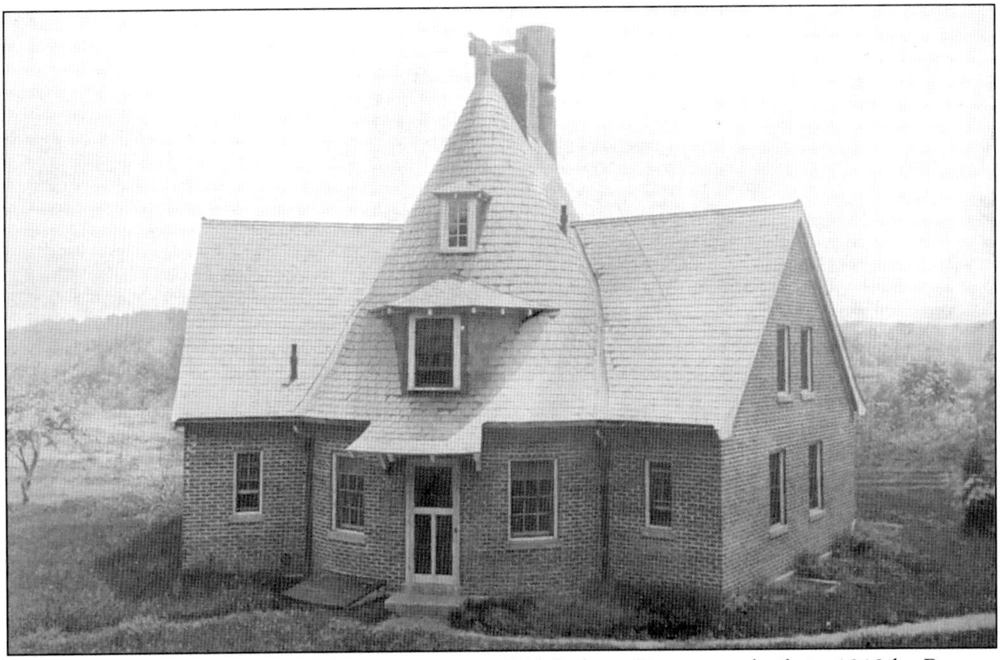

The "tepee house" on Springdale Avenue, now Old Colony Drive, was built in 1912 by Boston mayor Andrew J. Peters for his mistress, Starr Faithful. Faithful's body washed up mysteriously on shore at Long Beach on Long Island, New York, in 1931. The seven-room English cottage of poured concrete had a main circular room 24 feet across and 33 feet high; the house was one of the first houses to be heated entirely by electricity.

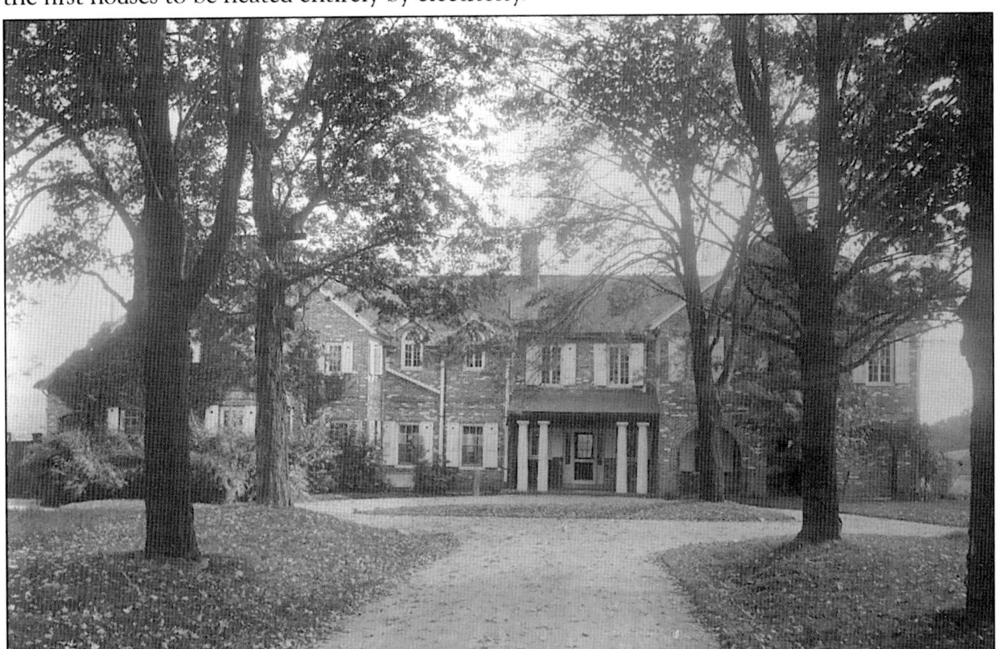

Boston real estate developer Walter Channing influenced the development of Farm Street and was active in town politics. He built this 1914 English Georgian building on Farm Street. It was another of the first group of country estates built before WWI.

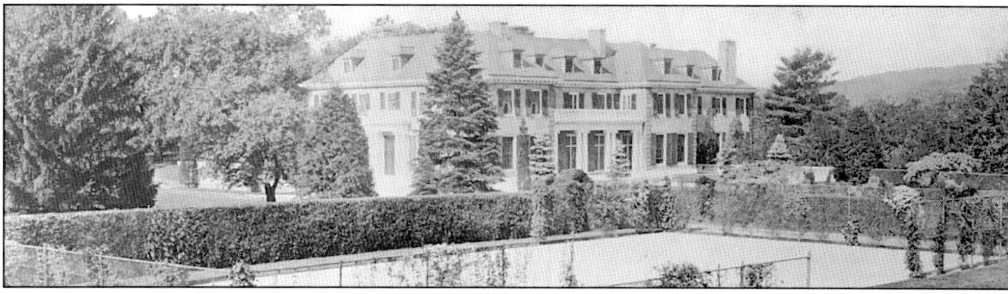

Benjamin Pierce Cheney, who helped found the American Express Company, created Elm Bank, an elegant estate in Dover that bordered the Charles River. The elm trees planted by Colonel Jones in the 1740s gave the property its name. The current mansion was built by one of Cheney's daughters, Alice Cheney Baltzell, in 1907.

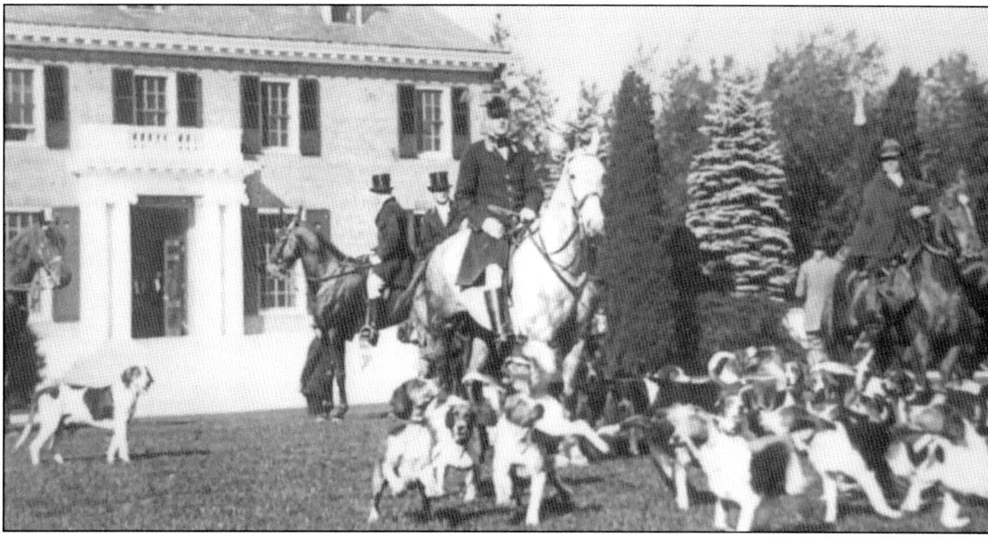

This 1926 view of the Norfolk Hunt Club hunt in front of Elm Bank paints an active picture. The Massachusetts Horticultural Society has taken responsibility for 36 acres of the 188-acre Elm Bank reservation. The only Dover property currently listed on the National Registry of Historic Places, Elm Bank was designated one of "America's treasures" by the White House in 1999. One can access the property by a bridge over the Charles River from Wellesley. (Norfolk Hunt Club.)

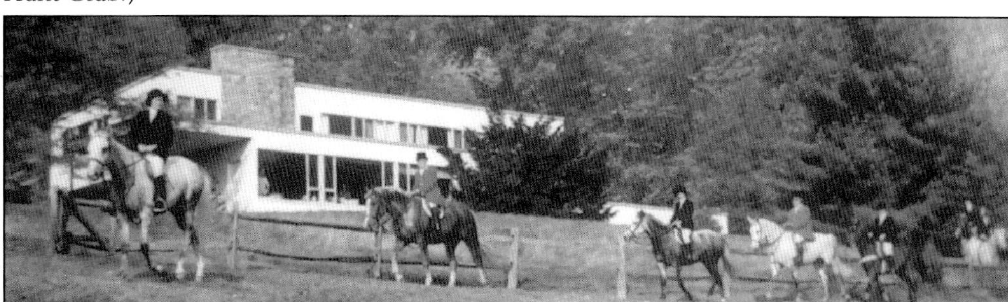

The 1973 Norfolk Hunt Club hunt passes through the front yard of the 1941 Jackson house on Farm Street, the first contemporary house built in Dover. This sight is common in Dover as the Norfolk Hunt Club works with property owners to maintain access and open trails. (Molly Jackson.)

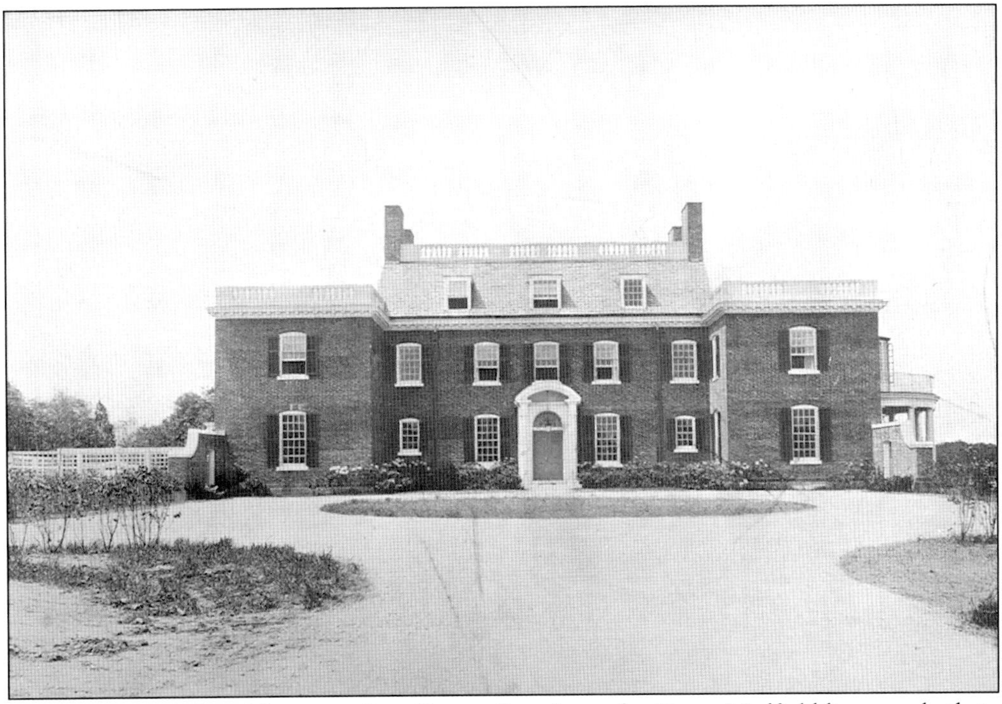

This Georgian Colonial house on Pine Street, directly on the Dover-Medfield line, was built in 1906 on farmland owned by Ebenezer Mason of Medfield. In 1960, a group in the Pine Street, Riga Road, and Cedar Hill area attempted, without success, to turn the house into a family club. Currently, the house is being restored as part of a development on neighboring Snow Hill land.

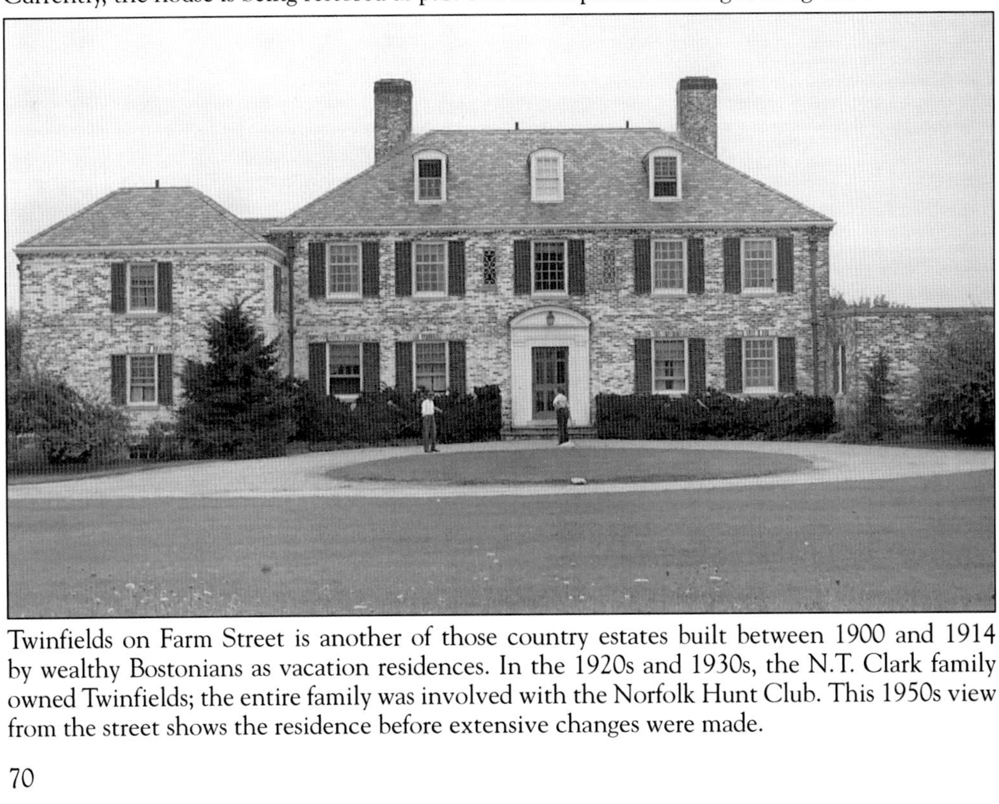

Twinfields on Farm Street is another of those country estates built between 1900 and 1914 by wealthy Bostonians as vacation residences. In the 1920s and 1930s, the N.T. Clark family owned Twinfields; the entire family was involved with the Norfolk Hunt Club. This 1950s view from the street shows the residence before extensive changes were made.

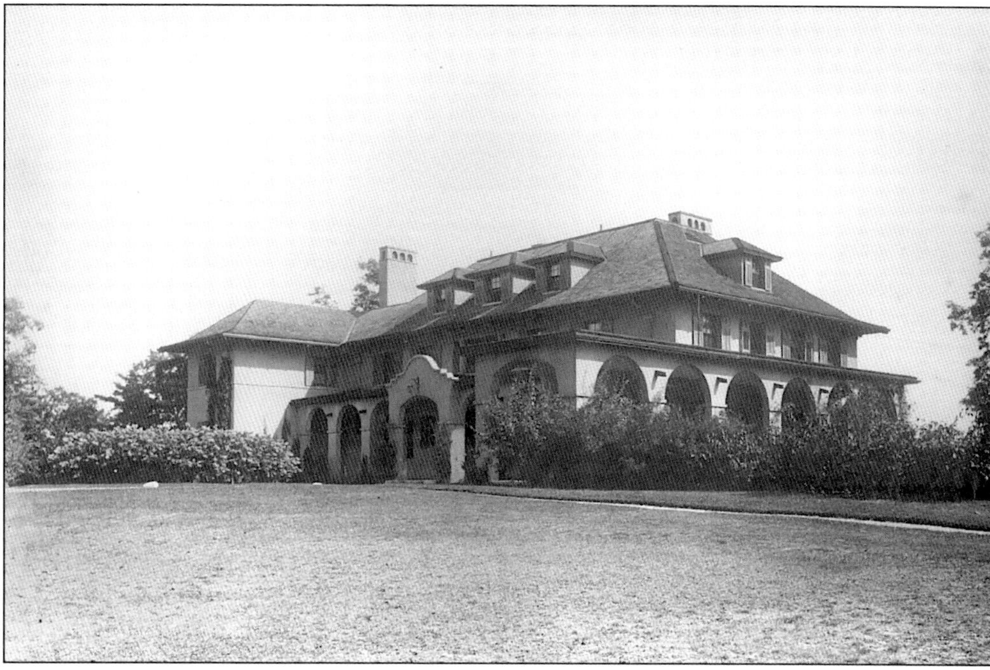

A member of a wealthy Boston family, A. Grant Forbes built this 1910 stucco house off Pleasant Street; the architectural design was unique in Dover. Mrs. Forbes, a Winthrop from the North Shore, was active in Boston society and the Norfolk Hunt Club.

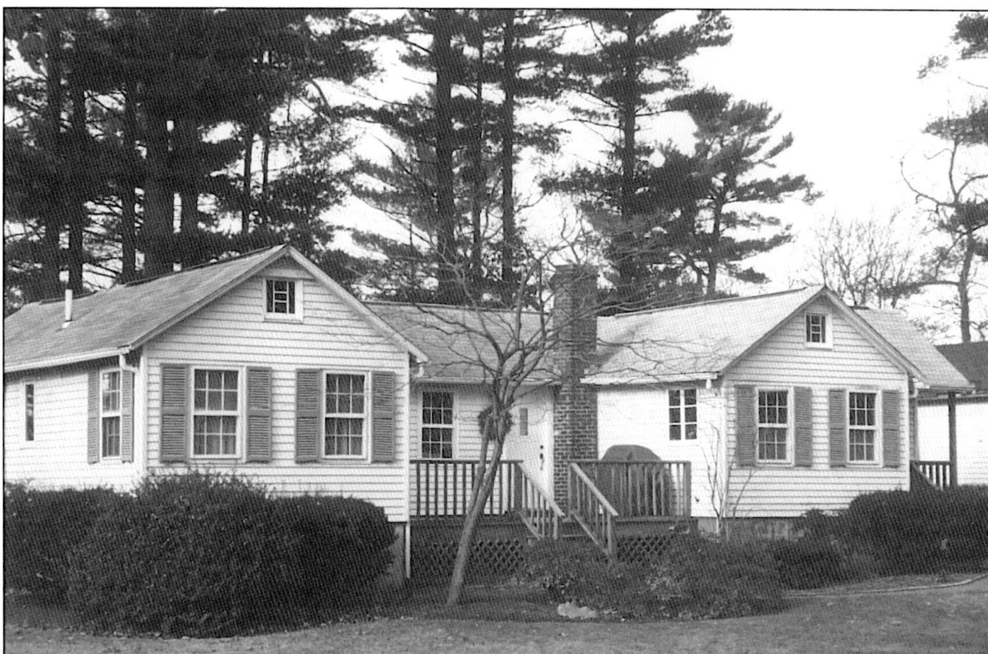

The area around Church Street and Meetinghouse Hill Road has a large number of Hodgson houses still in use, some with all of the company's house products collected on one property. This Meetinghouse Hill Road house shows the versatility of the basic prefabricated house, as well as the signature H windows at the gable ends. The H windows were crafted in stained glass.

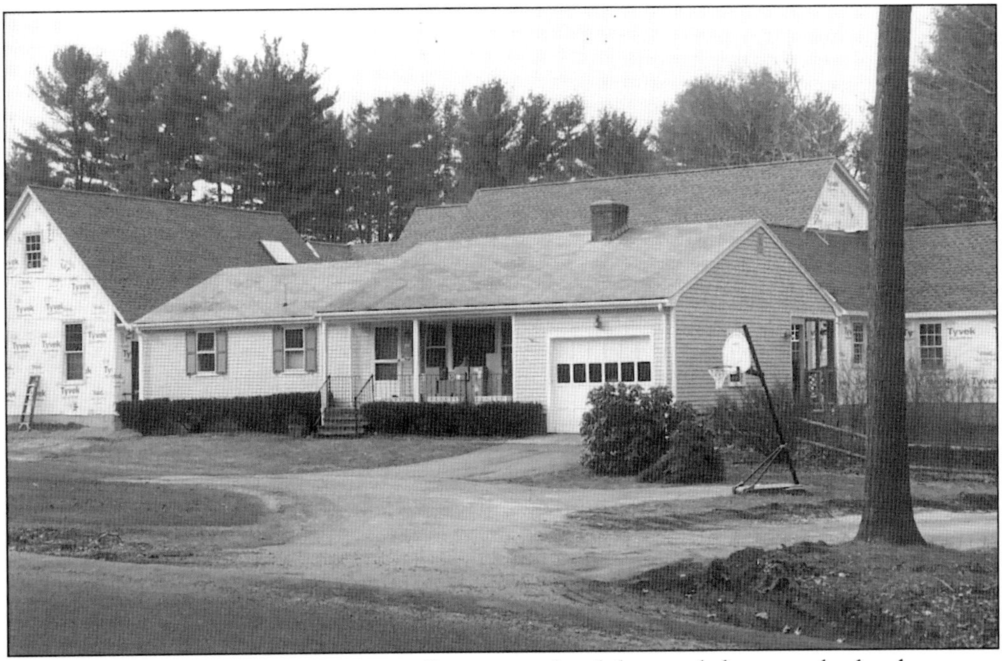

This Church Street property is an excellent example of the ranch house style that became a large part of new house development after 1945. This image also demonstrates how smaller houses were being replaced by larger structures in the expansive 1990s. You can clearly see new insulation being applied to the house walls.

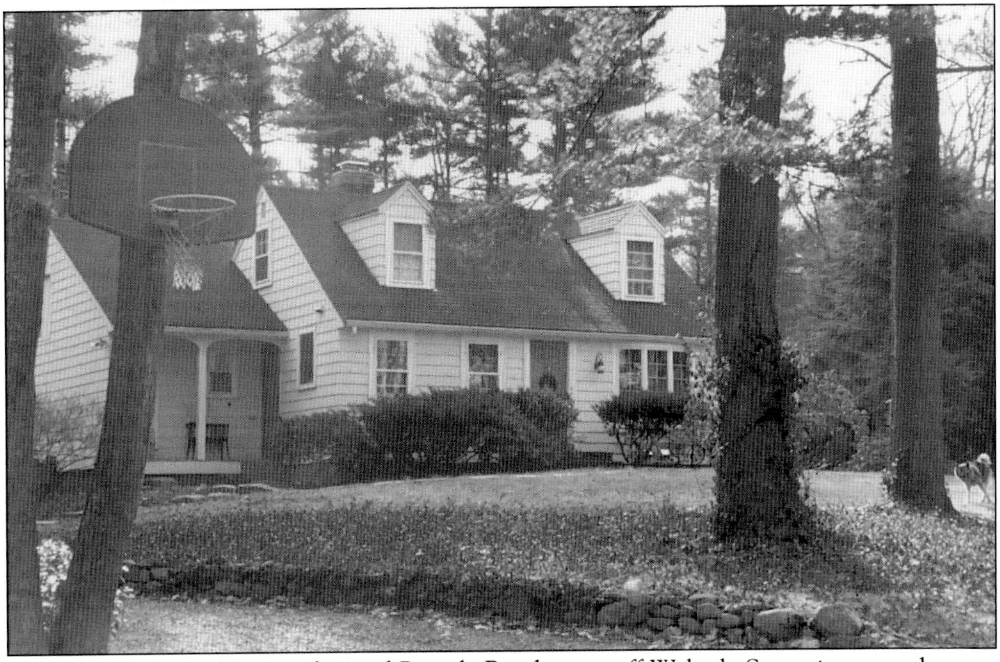

The Abby, Bretton, Normandie, and Picardy Road areas, off Walpole Street just past the new post office, were first developed just before WWII. This Bretton Road Cape is representative of the houses built in this area. The structure is also representative of the houses developed just after the war to fill the demands of returning veterans.

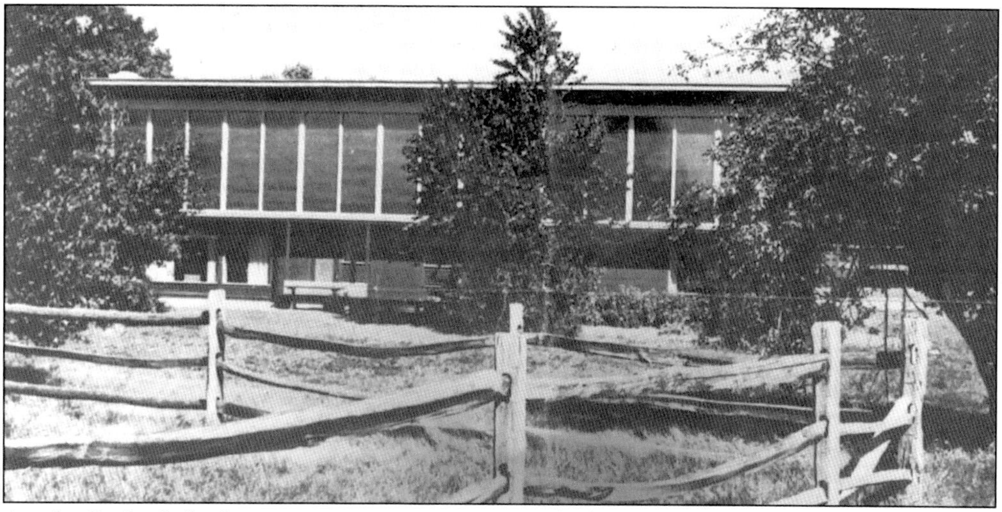

Amelia Peabody had a great many interests, one of which included solar energy. As a solar house pioneer, she commissioned architect Eleanor Raymond to design the first solar house in New England. The Sun House on Powissett Street was built and occupied by a family in 1948. The ten-foot-high windows ran the entire length of the house and faced south. The house was enlarged five years later and the experiment was concluded. The house is now conventionally heated.

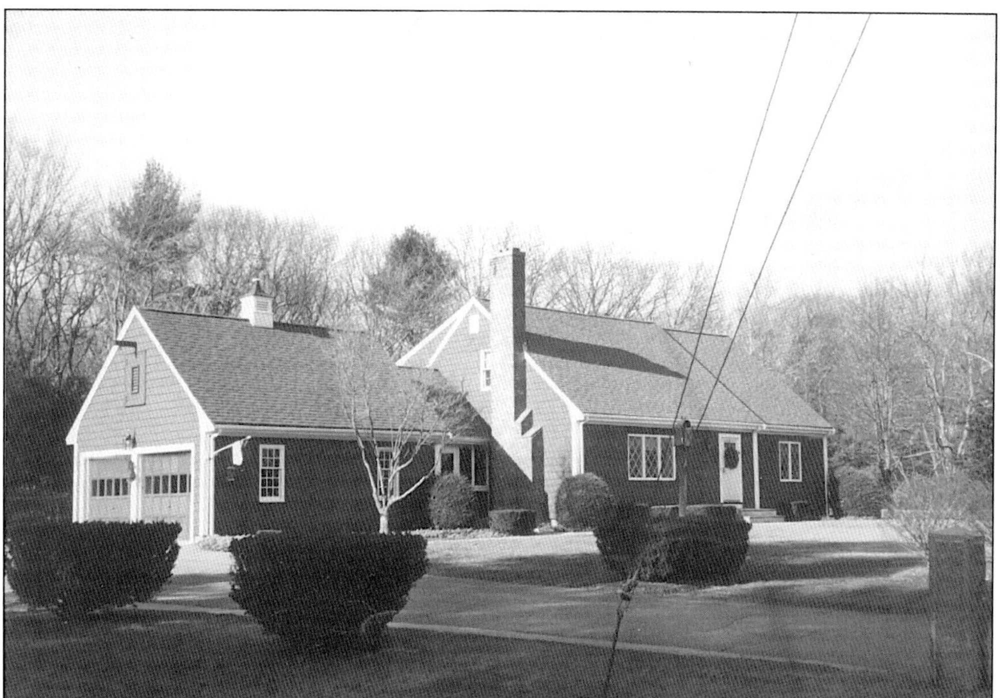

This house, located about two miles from Dover Center on Valley Road, is an example of the response to the increasing population in the 1960s. Expanded Capes can be seen in other areas of the town. The increase in population and house sizes are raising serious concerns, since Dover relies completely on septic systems and over 95 percent of the houses utilize wells.

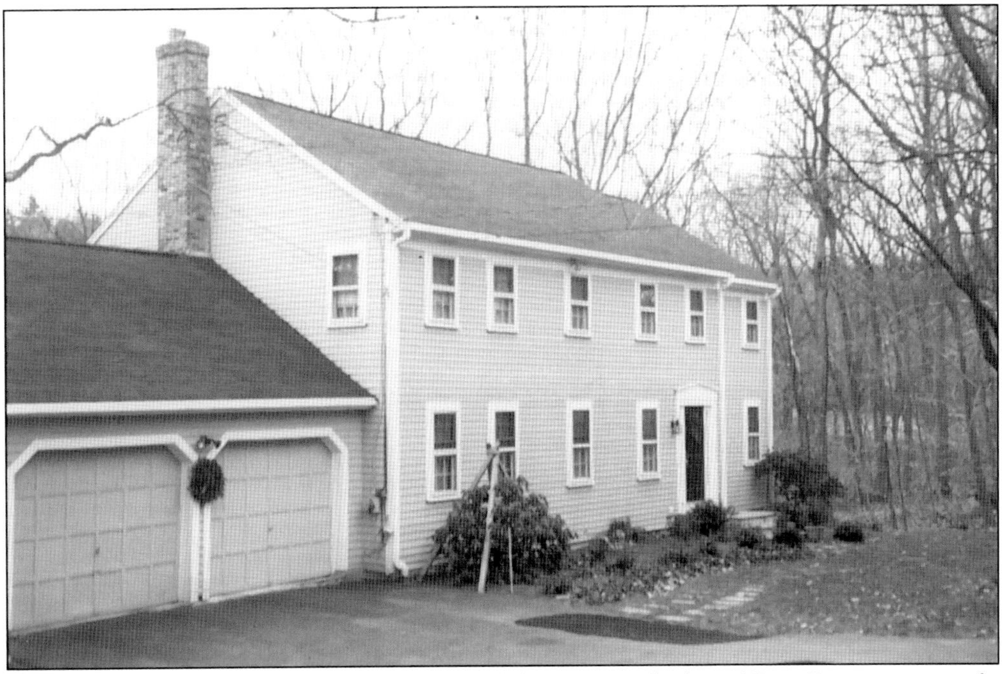

This 1967 Federal Colonial house on Riga Road, between Walpole and Pine Streets, is part of a development that is being serviced by the nearby Dover Water Company. This particular house and its neighbors sit across a former bridle path. The town is trying to link the trails from the Trustees of Reservations property on Walpole Street to its Rocky Woods property in Medfield at the end of Pond Street.

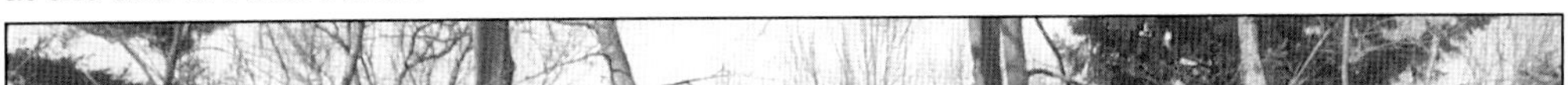

The Natick town line, the Charles River, St. Stephen Priory, and Glen Street define the Glen Ridge area. The upper houses draw their water from Natick's system, but still use septic systems. This house on Raleigh Road, which has its own well, is typical of the expanded Capes and split-levels of the area. Even though construction occurred between the late 1950s and the 1970s, the grounds are heavy with trees and mature foliage.

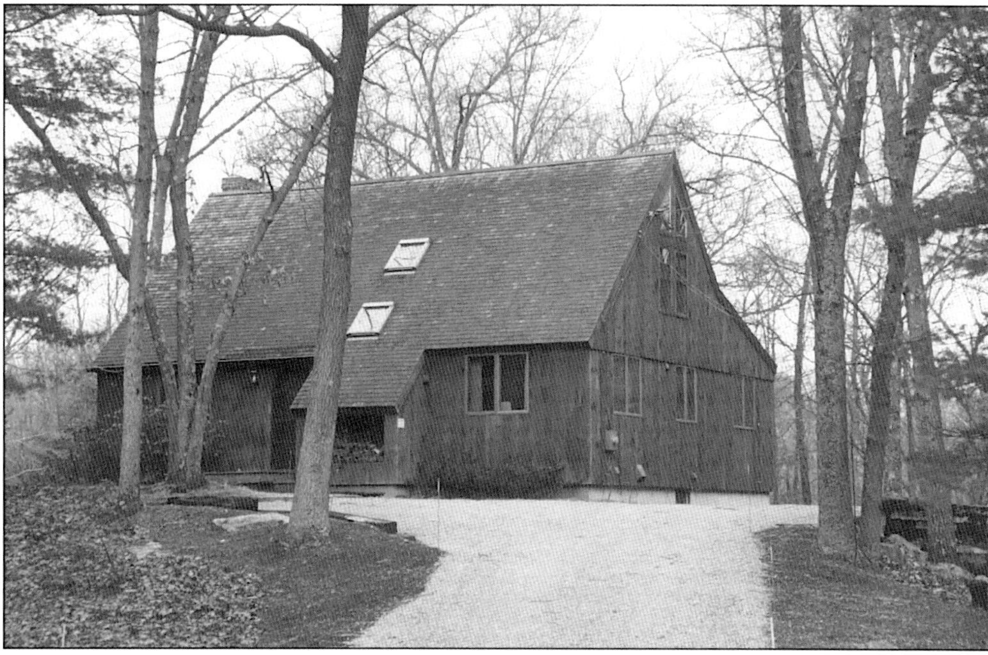

Dover's architecture has generally been traditional. However, this contemporary house on Wilsondale Street reflects the changing architectural styles that slowly crept into various areas of the town, primarily during the 1970s and 1980s. Deck houses and other contemporary styles, including the Copper House on Main Street, dot the landscape.

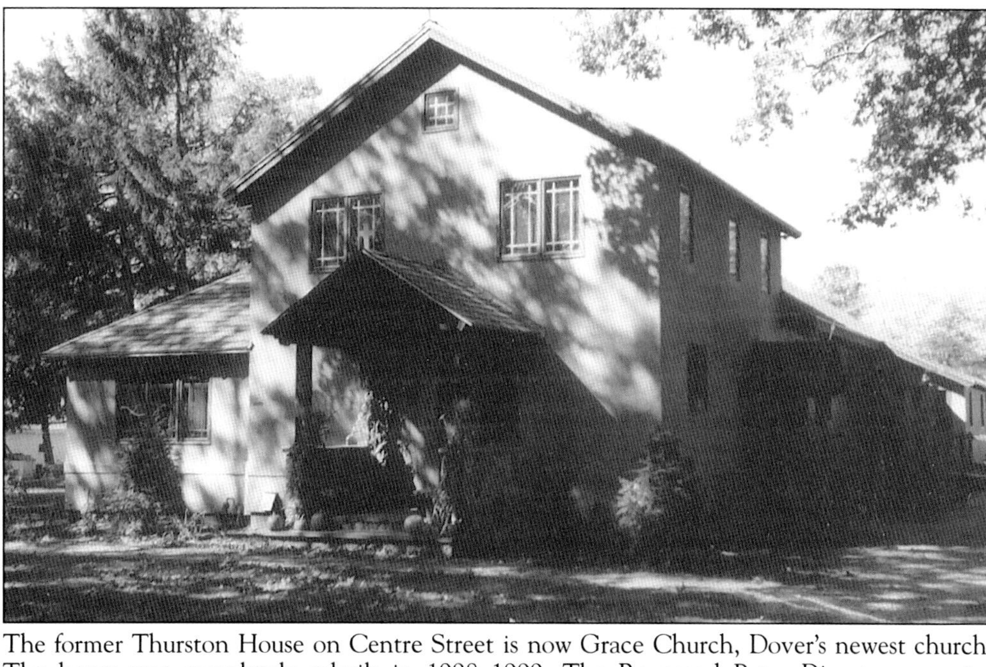

The former Thurston House on Centre Street is now Grace Church, Dover's newest church. The house was completely rebuilt in 1998–1999. The Reverend Peter Disanto, a master woodworker, did all the work himself. No nails were used in the construction inside the main part of the building. Reclaimed wood from old pews and other sites were used in the rebuilding. Reverend Disanto even built the furniture. (Peter Disanto.)

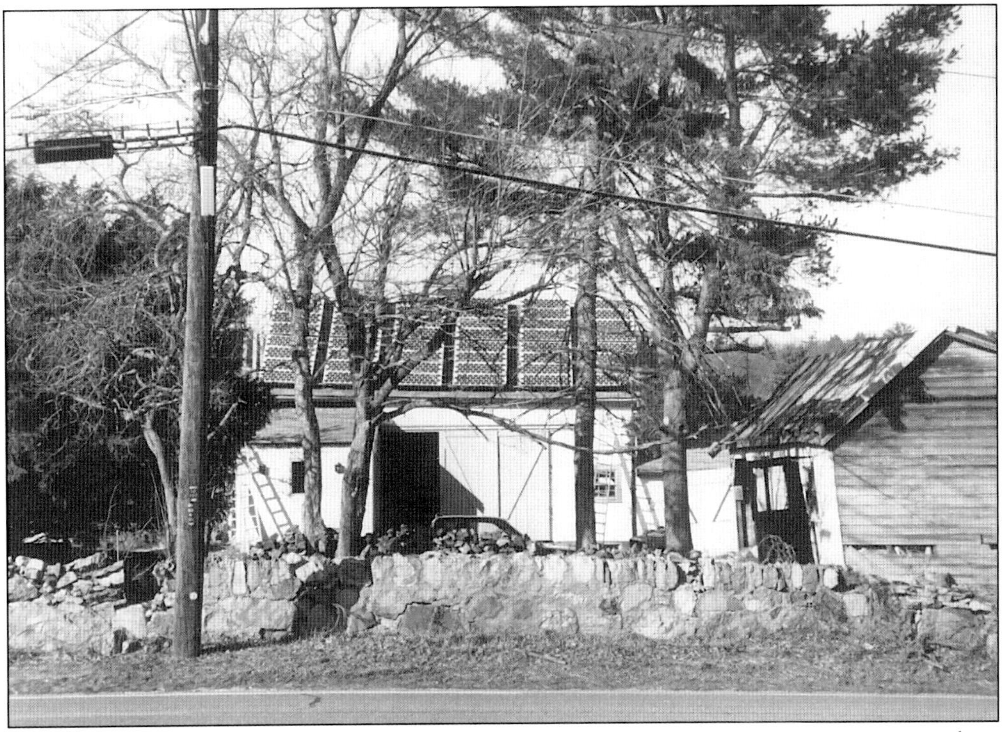

Solar panels can be seen with increased frequency in the town, as interest in environmentalism is high today. Amelia Peabody's solar house seen on page 73 might have failed, but the sun still shines. The panels being installed on the barn roof of a Dedham Street horse farm are much more open to the sun than the Peabody's house on Powissett Street was. As evidence of changing technology, the barn is being wrapped in state-of-the-art insulation materials.

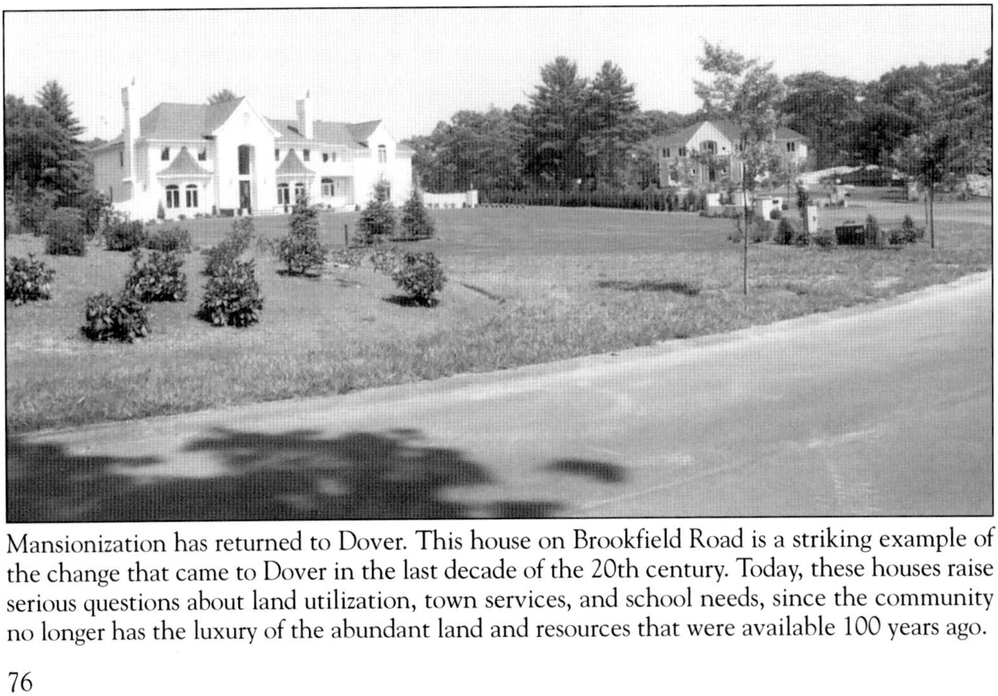

Mansionization has returned to Dover. This house on Brookfield Road is a striking example of the change that came to Dover in the last decade of the 20th century. Today, these houses raise serious questions about land utilization, town services, and school needs, since the community no longer has the luxury of the abundant land and resources that were available 100 years ago.

Six

Celebrations and Disasters

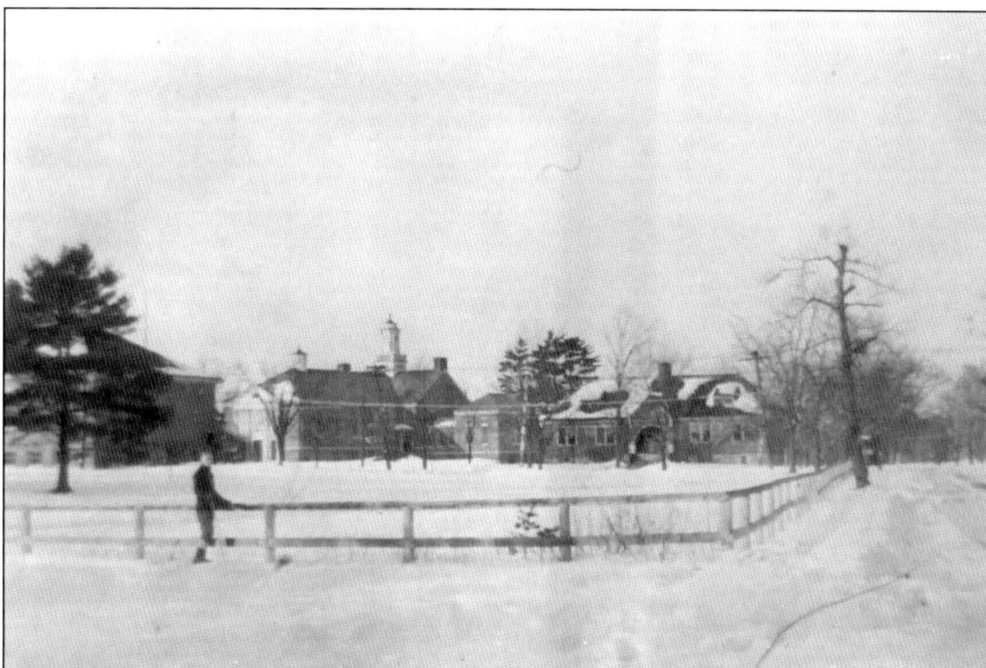

Dover Center with the Dover Town House in the rear looks like a college campus after a snowstorm in this 1920s image. The wood fence and the Sanger School to the right are long gone. The Caryl School is to the left.

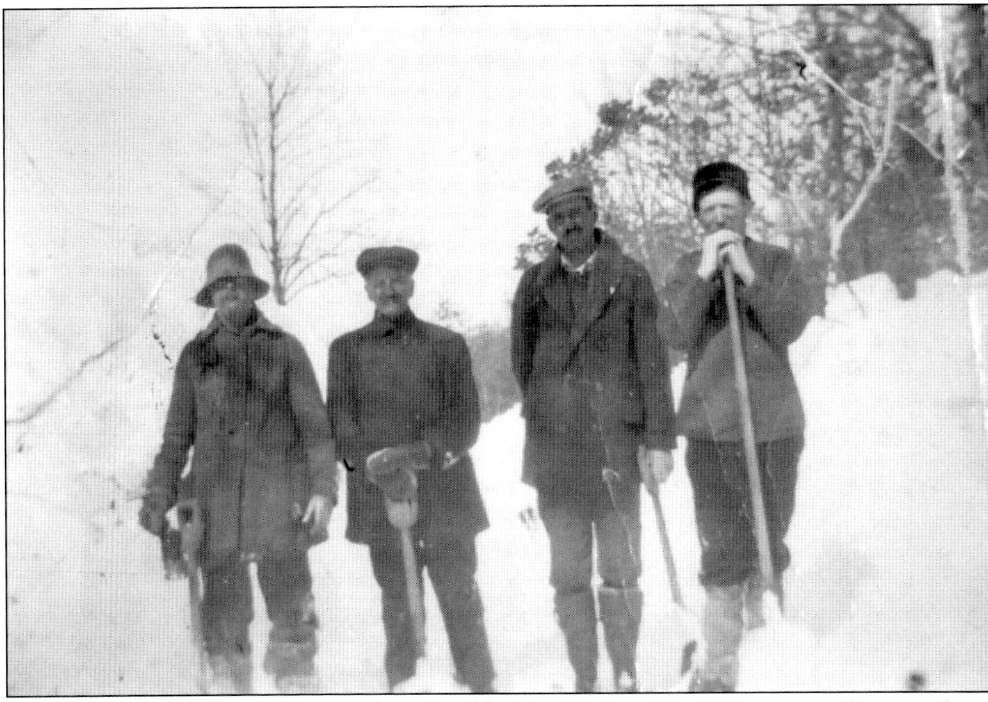

New England weather is both the bane and beauty of the region. Here, a road crew takes a break from working to free Walpole Street after a storm on Washington's Birthday in 1926. Third from the left is Jason Neale, who owned a farm on Hartford Street. Despite advances in machinery, human power was still needed to help clear snow after a storm. (Harry Neale.)

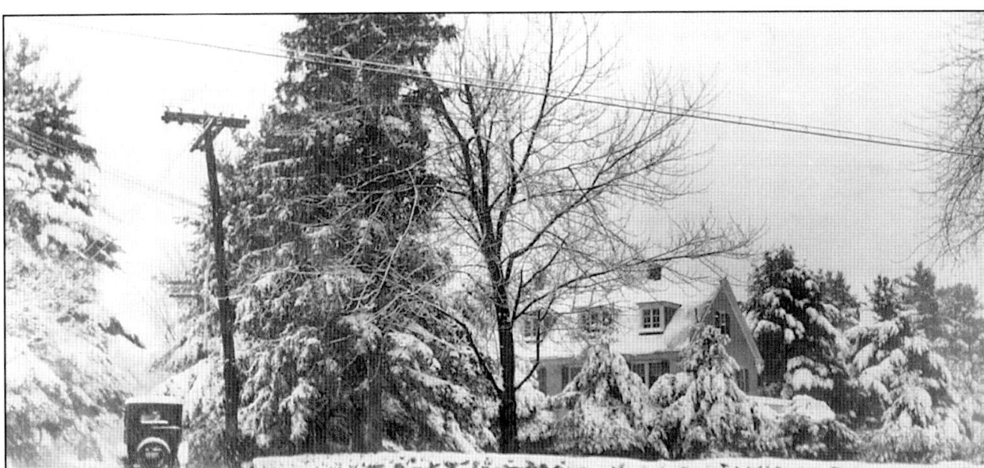

This February 1926 storm covered the Frost House at the junction of Walpole and Centre Streets. Trees always suffer great damage from such storms. Since the introduction of electricity, downed wires are a perpetual problem. Notice the advantage the old Model T Ford had in snow.

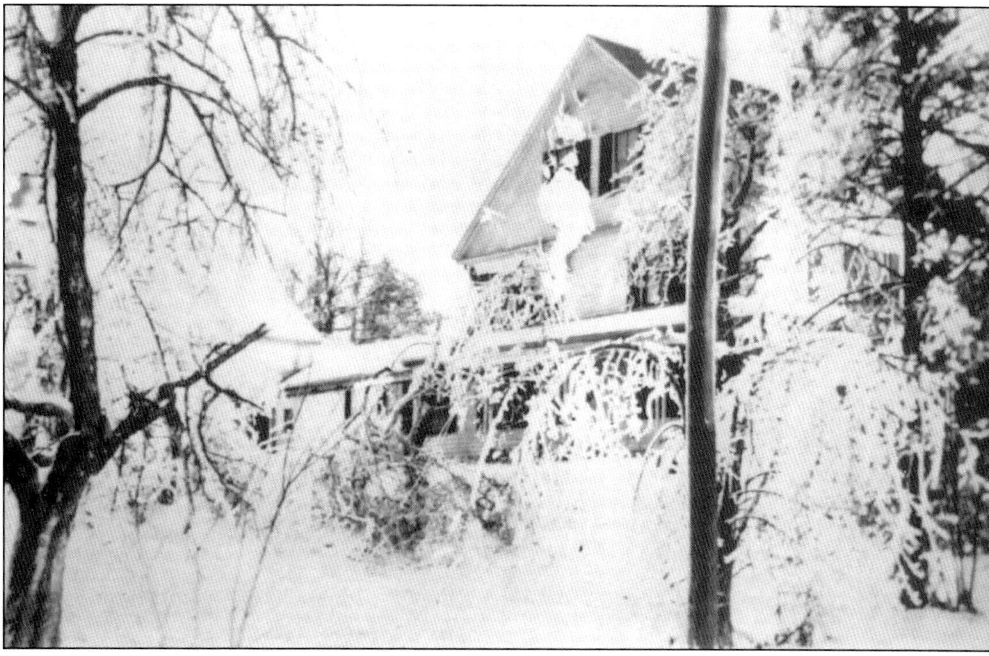

Weather is a subject that concerns most of us. Ice storms can be both dangerous and disruptive. The Newcomb house on Glen Street looked like this after a fierce ice storm in 1921. (George Newcomb.)

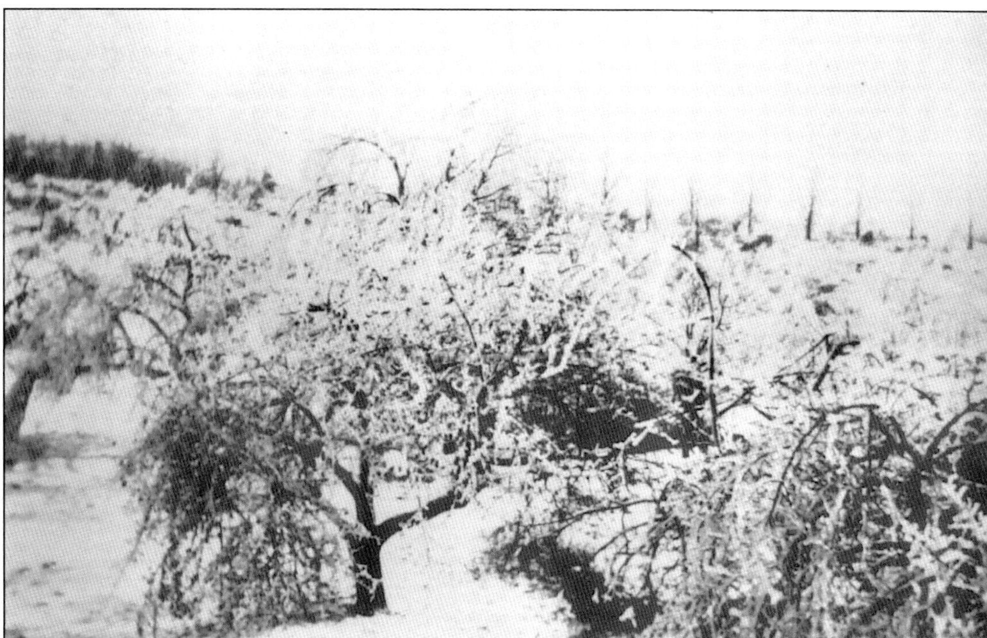

When George Newcomb looked out from the second floor of his parent's house on Glen Street, he saw the orchard in this condition after a 1921 ice storm. People close to the land learned to live with the havoc these events created. (George Newcomb.)

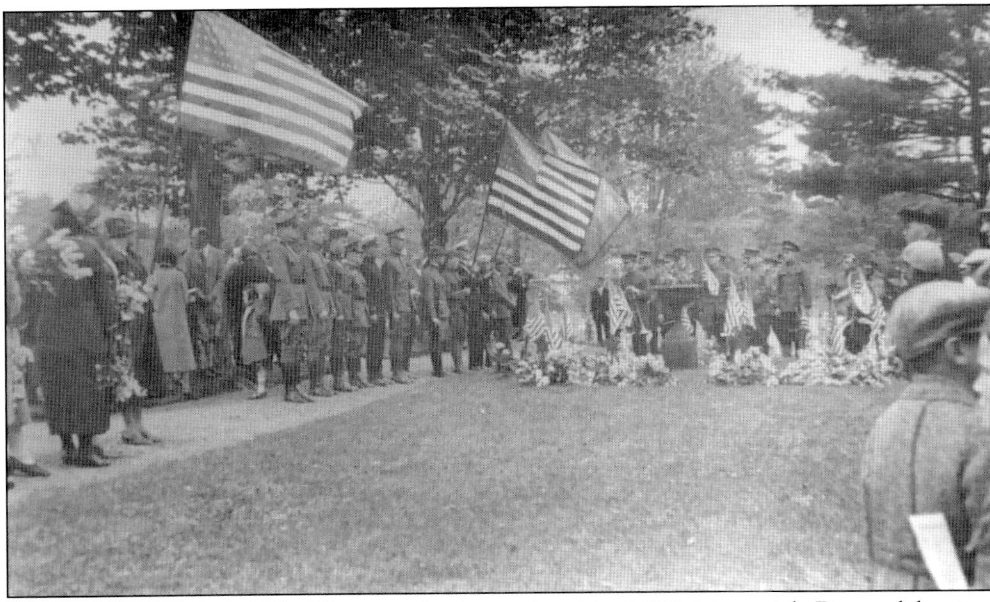

WWI uniforms and Old Glory predominate in this 1926 Memorial Day celebration. Communities made much more out of such celebrations in an era that was still close to 1918 and the "war to end all war." Dover still celebrates veterans with honor and glory on Memorial Day.

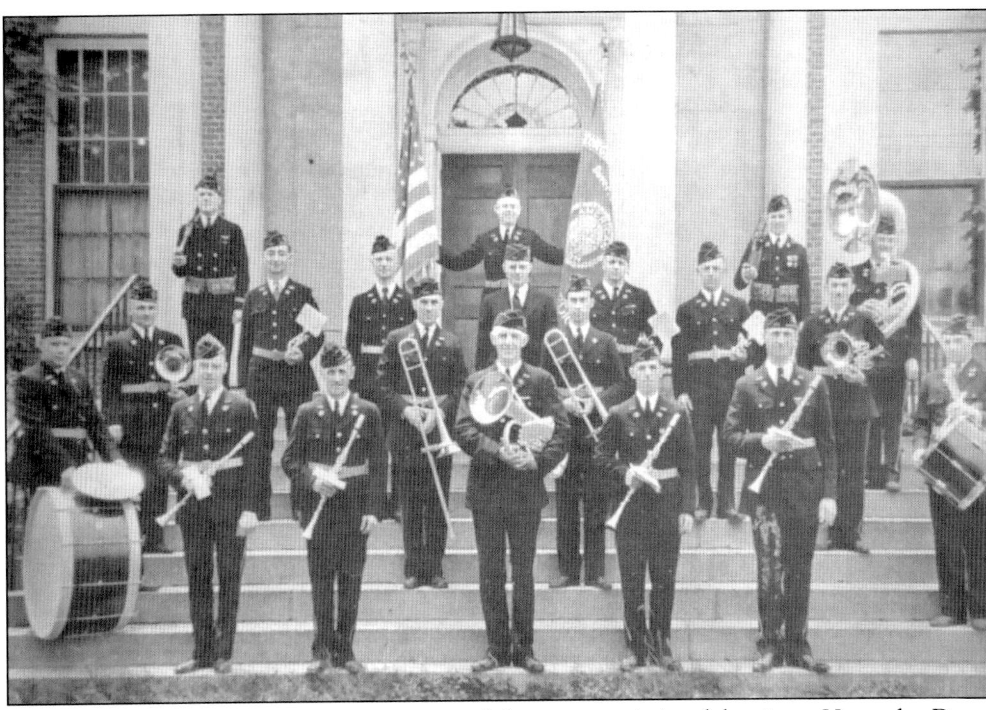

The American Legion is an important part of the community's celebrations. Here, the Dover Legion Band, Post No. 209, poses on the Dover Town House steps in 1931. Seen in the front row, from left to right, are Herbert Bond on the bass drum, Russell Higgins, Harold MacKenzie, Arthur Glidden, Joe Miele, and Leon Bean. (Janet MacKenzie.)

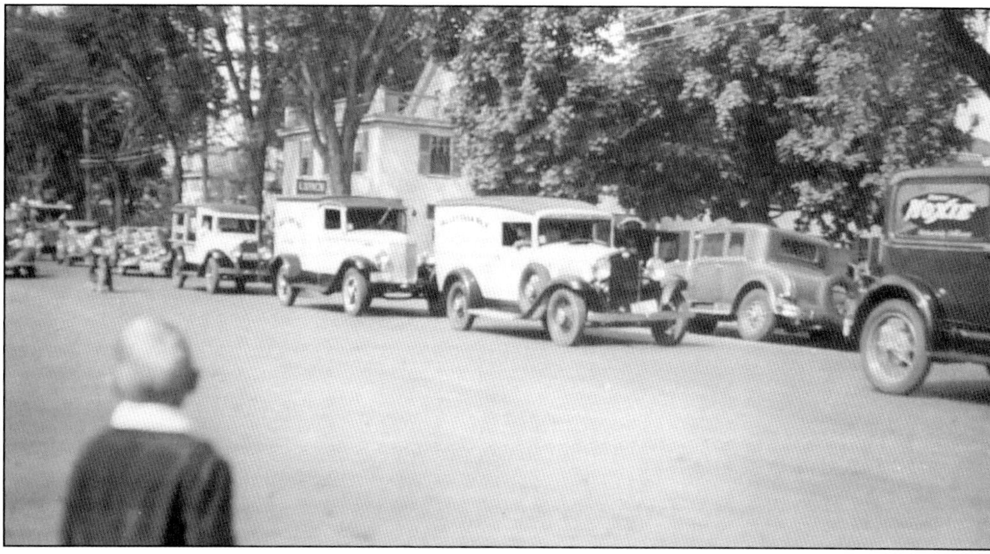

The town celebrated its centennial in 1936 with a great parade, complete with bands, floats, and marching groups. Valley Farm Dairy, one of the more popular businesses, paraded its fleet of delivery trucks. The vehicle in front displays another famous name: Moxie. (Robert Comiskey.)

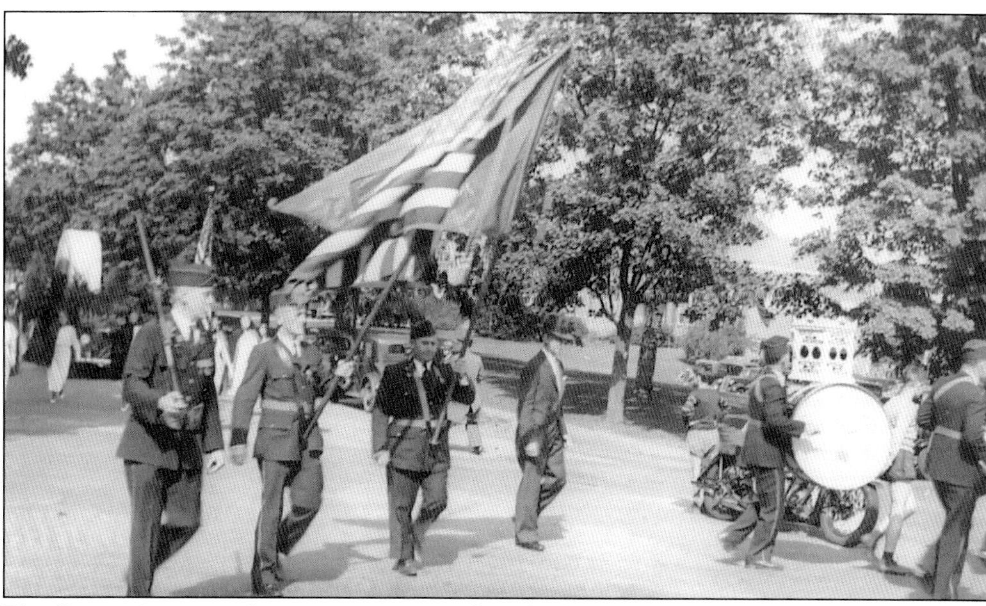

The Dover American Legion Honor Guard trails the band as the 1936 centennial parade winds its way through Dover Center. The parade ended at Highland Cemetery, where the town honored its founders and saluted all of its soldiers who gave their lives in defense of democracy.

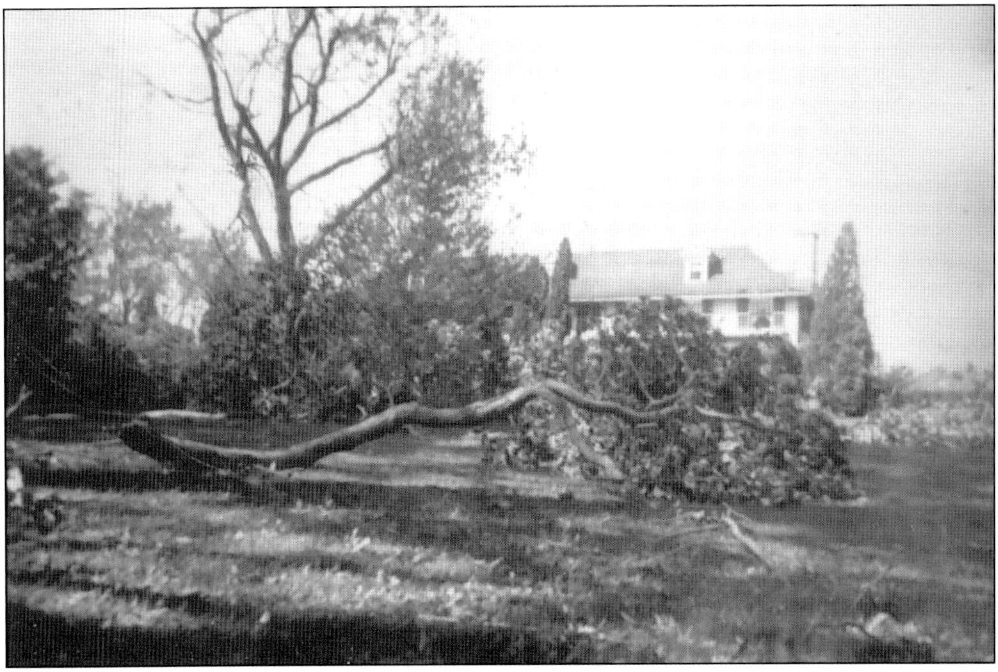

The Hurricane of 1938 came roaring through New England and Dover. The Fountain Farm—the Perry house, formerly the Fuller house, on Pegan Lane—was photographed on September 21, 1938. Trees were scattered all over Dover in the wake of the storm, causing great inconvenience and changing the landscape drastically. (Perry scrapbook.)

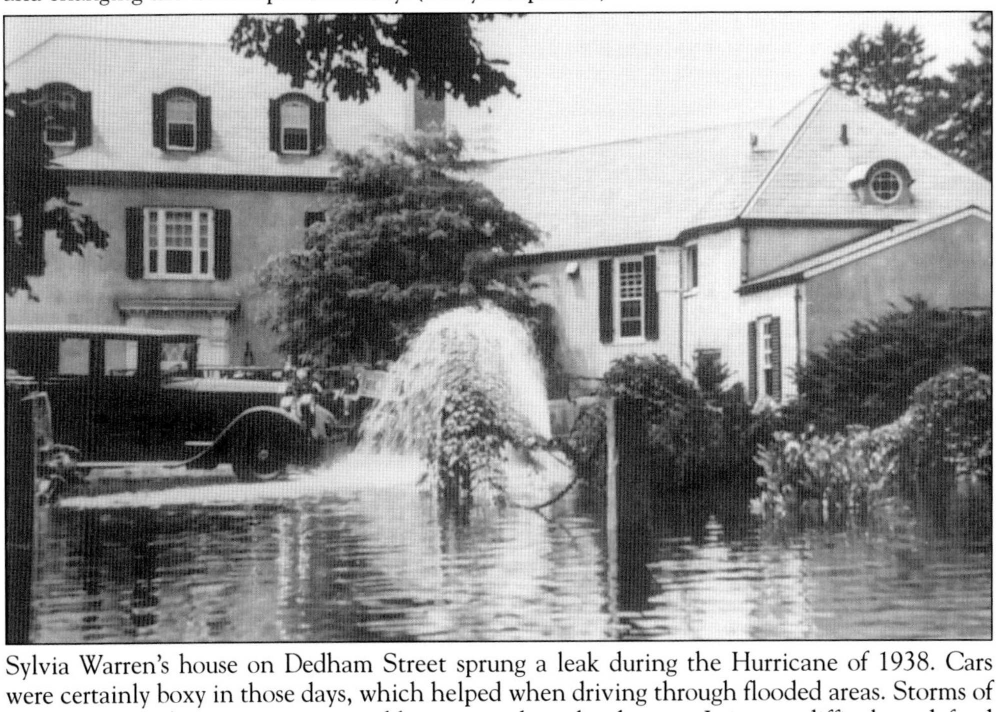

Sylvia Warren's house on Dedham Street sprung a leak during the Hurricane of 1938. Cars were certainly boxy in those days, which helped when driving through flooded areas. Storms of this proportion have come again and have caused similar damage. It is very difficult to defend against nature.

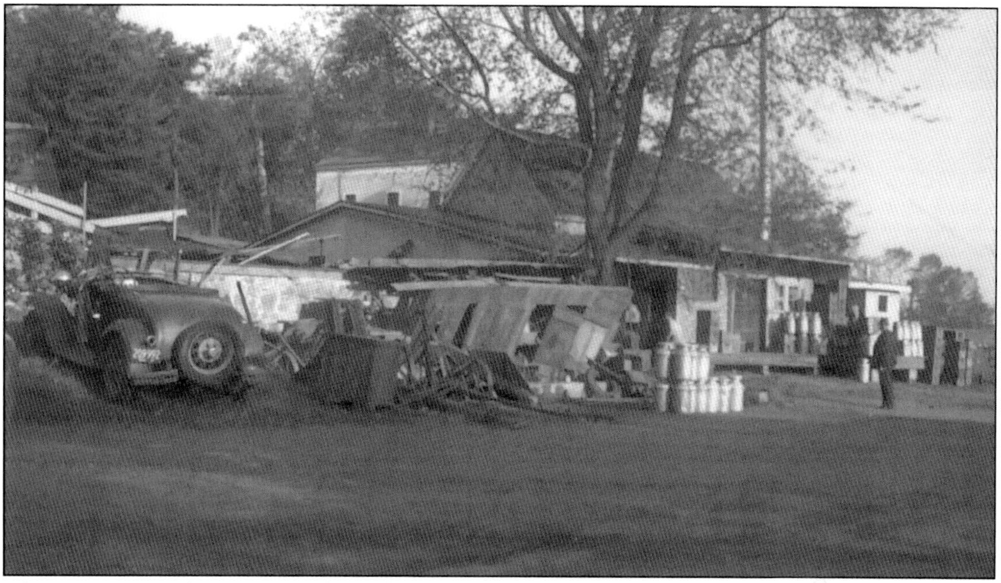

The Hurricane of 1938 went through Valley Farm, located on the corner of Haven and Main Streets, with the greatest of ease, flattening a number of buildings on the property. The trees did serious damage to various vehicles parked near them. (Robert Comiskey.)

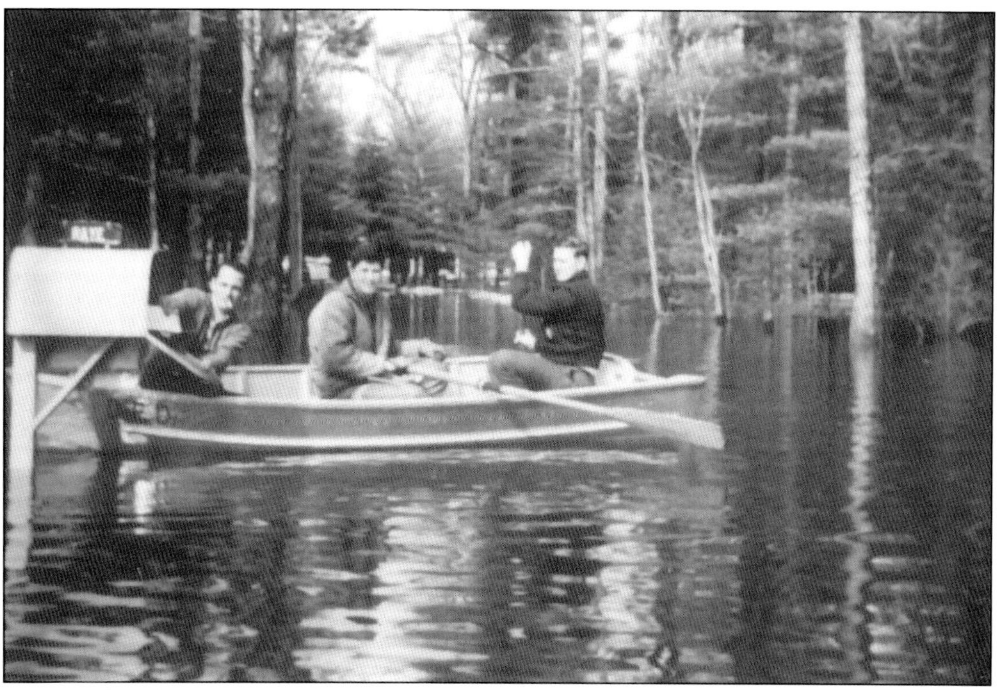

One wonder of Dover is that the Charles River partially serves as the town boundary. However, it also means that flooding happens in certain areas of the town, especially on the Needham-Dover line. During this 1968 flood, Jim MacTavish, Dexter Andrews, and Dave MacTavish deliver the mail by rowboat on Turtle Lane. (Dave MacTavish.)

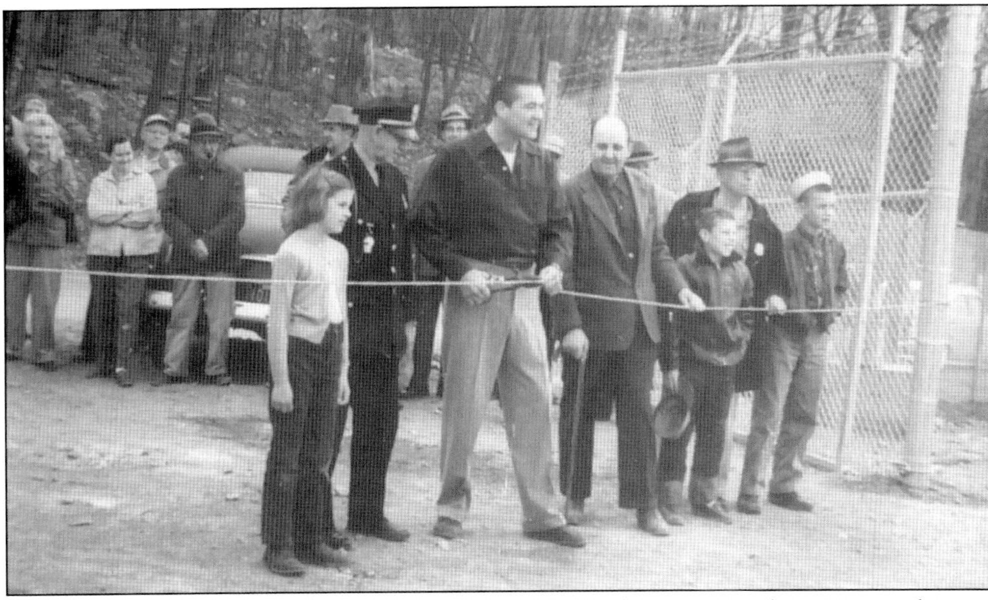

In 1958, Dover opened a solid waste recycling center. The town was beginning to become more conscious of environmental needs, especially in regard to the handling waste materials. Chief Chester Heinlein is in the center with George Sargent, chair of the board of selectmen; selectman Thomas McGill; and Dover's famous poet dump master, George Ryder. Myrtle Clough and Janet and Harold MacKenzie can be seen in the background.

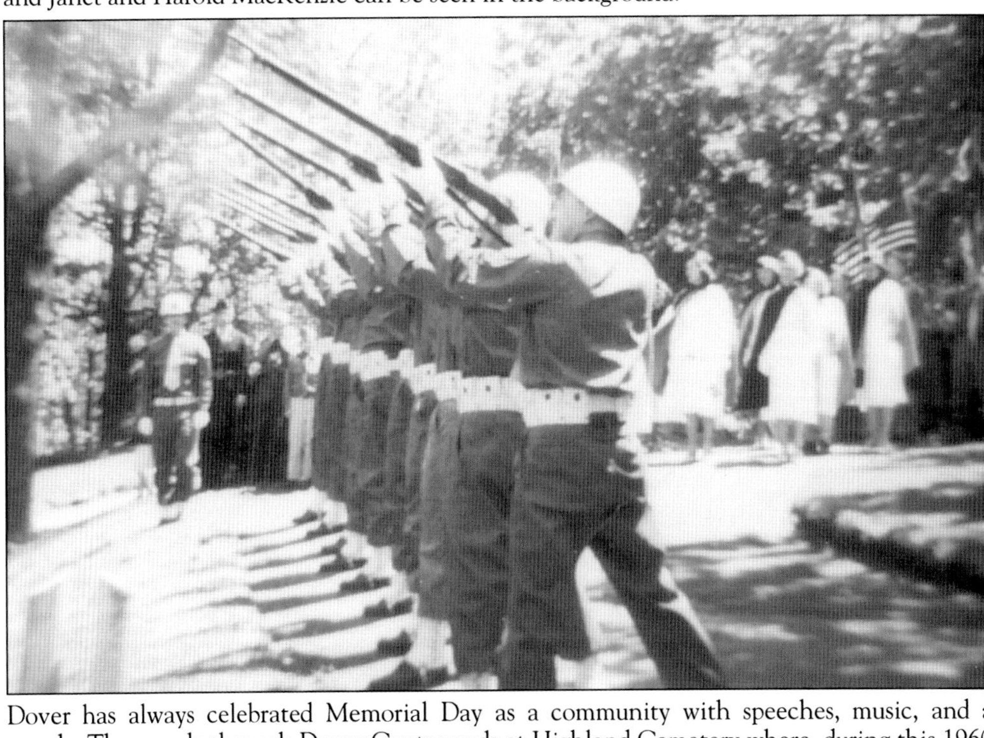

Dover has always celebrated Memorial Day as a community with speeches, music, and a parade. The parade through Dover Center ends at Highland Cemetery where, during this 1960 Memorial Day ceremonies, the Dover American Legion firing squad rendered honors to our fallen heroes.

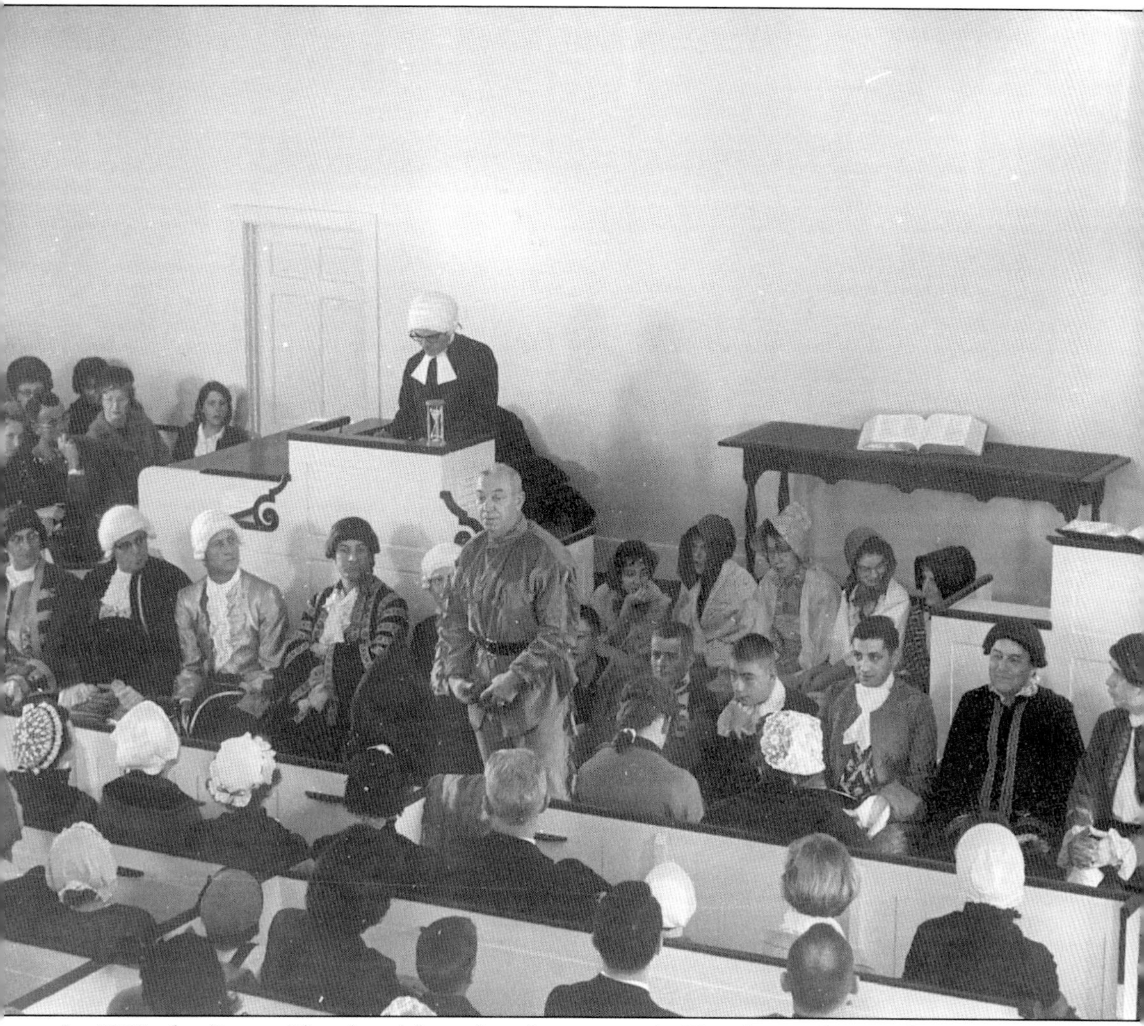

In 1962, the Dover Church celebrated its bicentennial. Church members and townspeople attended the celebration meeting in colonial dress. Between 1748 and 1762, Springfield Parish (as Dover was known then) had 21 ministers. The first permanent minister was Rev. Benjamin Caryl. Born in Hopkinton in 1732, he graduated from Harvard College at age 29 and was ordained here on November 10, 1762.

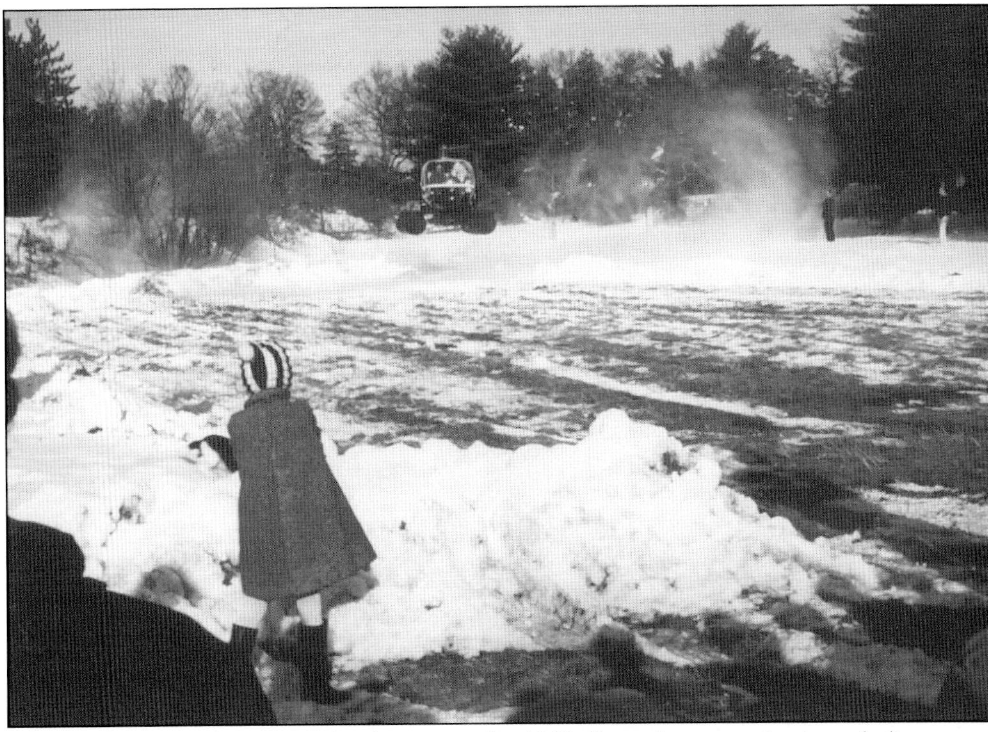

Christmas is a wondrous time for the young. By 1969, Santa has started using a helicopter to make his rounds. Here, Santa lands his vehicle in the field behind the American Legion Post, where a child waits in great anticipation for him and his bag of gifts.

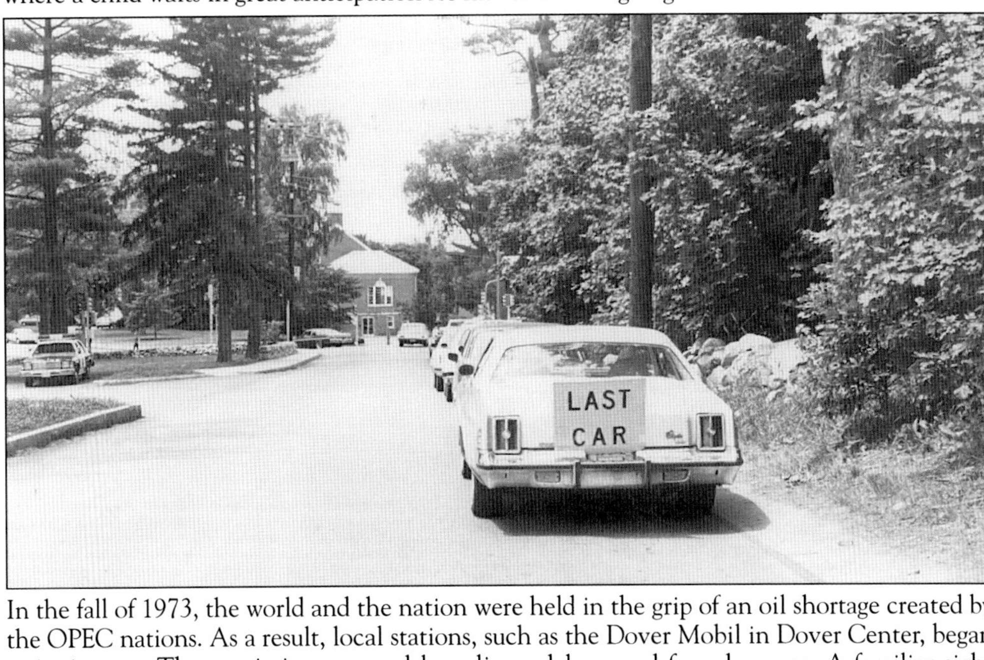

In the fall of 1973, the world and the nation were held in the grip of an oil shortage created by the OPEC nations. As a result, local stations, such as the Dover Mobil in Dover Center, began rationing gas. The restrictions created long lines, delays, and frayed nerves. A familiar sight during this period was this sign on a gas-guzzler, as the line to the pumps snaked up Walpole Street past the new protective services building.

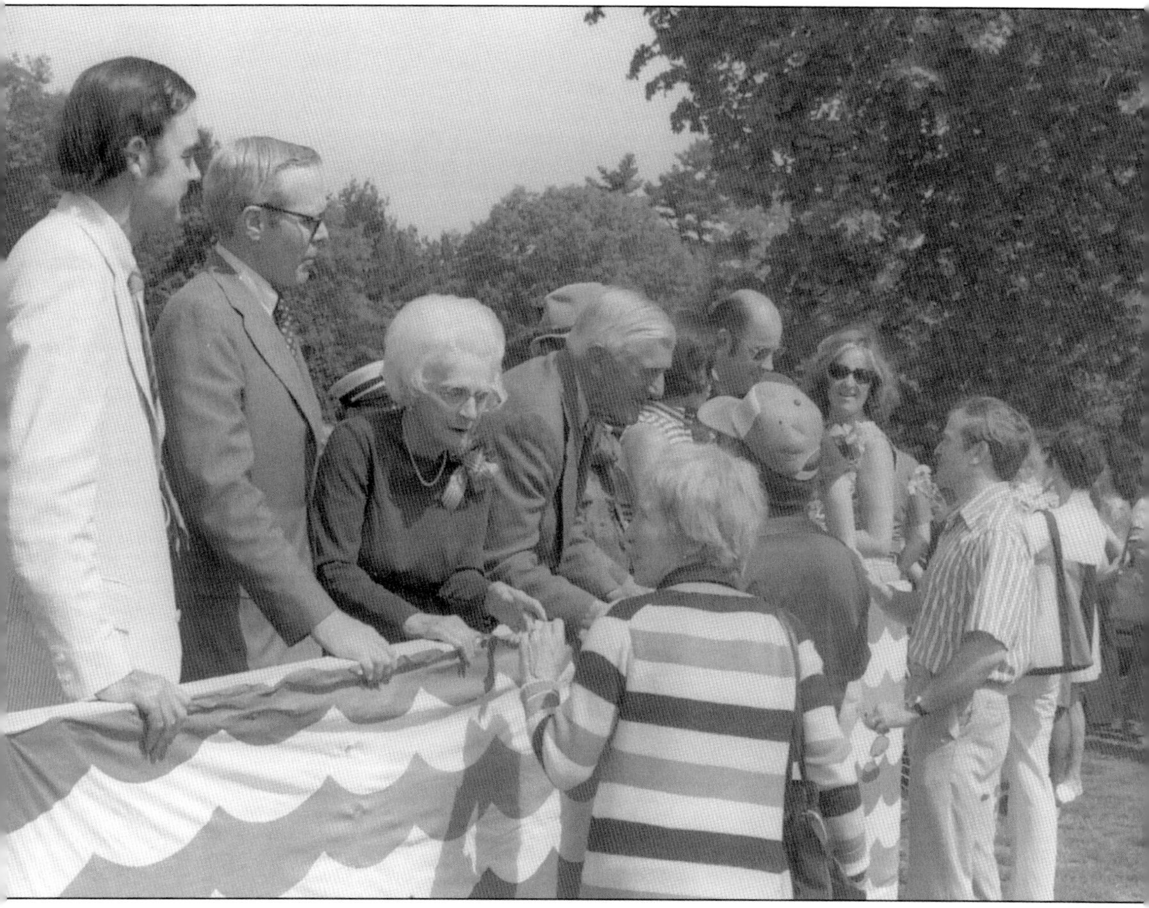

The Dover Days Fair celebrated America's 1976 bicentennial. Shown greeting people on the reviewing stand, from left to right, are the following: Charles C. Cabot Jr. (chair of the Dover selectmen), Charles Long (state representative from Dover), Margaret Quinlan (longtime Dover elementary teacher), Sen. Leverett Saltonstall (Dover's most famous national politician), Ann Wise (first selectwoman in Dover), Fred Maier (Dover selectman), and Martha Lawrence (chair of the Dover bicentennial celebration). Just behind Senator Saltonstall's head, Amelia Peabody's felt hat is visible; she was also a member of the committee.

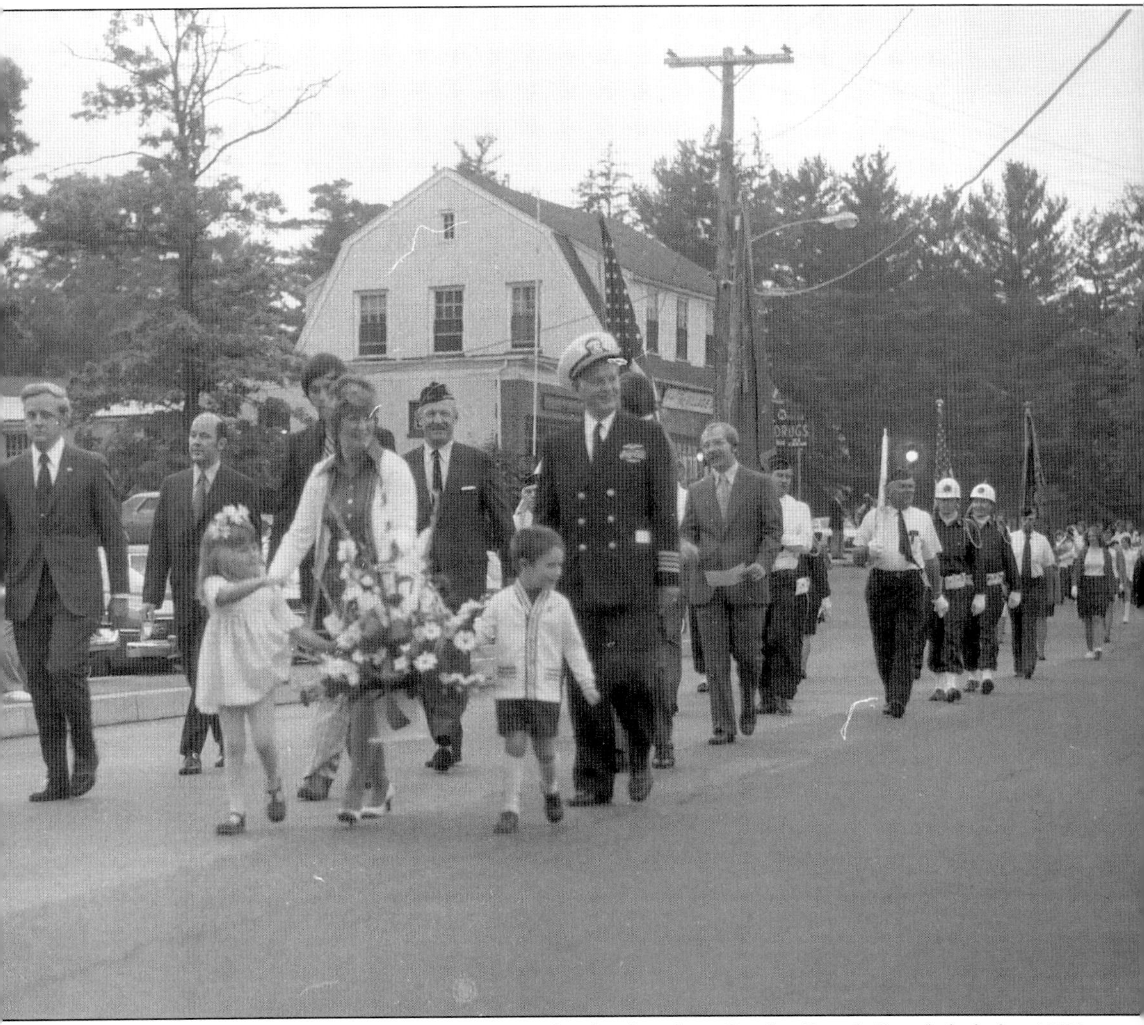

Capt. Joseph F. Enright, U.S. Navy Retired, who lived on Rocky Brook Road, led the 1976 Memorial Day parade. Enright was the commander and captain of the submarine *Archer-Fish*. On November 29, 1944, the submarine under his command entered Tokyo Bay and sank His Imperial Majesty's Ship *Shinano* (72,000 tons), a super battleship converted to an aircraft carrier. For sinking the largest warship in history, Enright received the Navy Cross, and his crew received the Presidential Unit Citation.

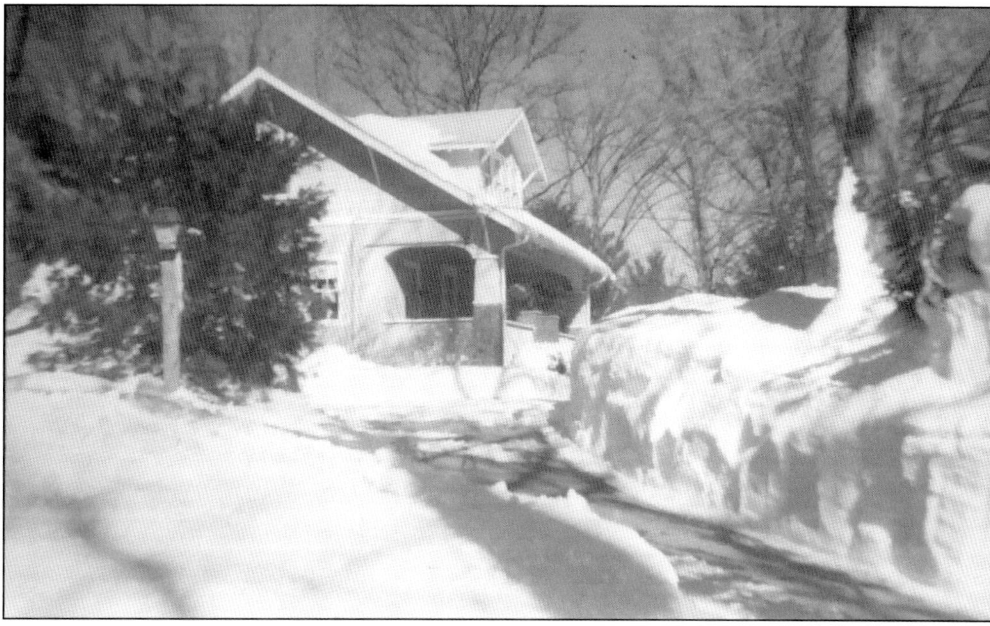

On February 5–7, the Blizzard of 1978 buried Dover. After it ended, the town was covered with more than 8 feet of snow. Here, the MacKenzie house on Centre Street can be seen after digging out of that wonderful stuff. (Janet MacKenzie.)

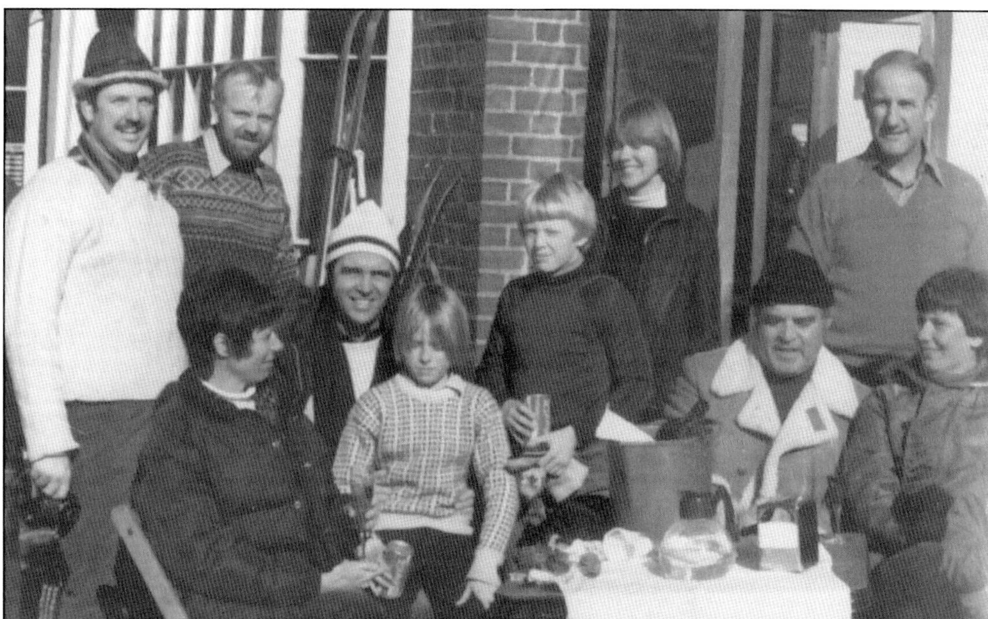

Gov. Michael Dukakis declared a state of emergency following the Blizzard of 1978. Everybody stayed home and dug out, since automobiles were not allowed on the roads. On February 8, townspeople walked to Dover Center for supplies and celebrated clean streets, sun, and good fellowship in front of the Dover Drug. Seen here, from left to right, are Dave Stapleton, Bob Smith, Sue McGill, Jim Quinn, an unidentified child, Dave Stapleton III, Wendy Wharton, Dick McGill, Don Ball, and Gene Richards. (Don Ball.)

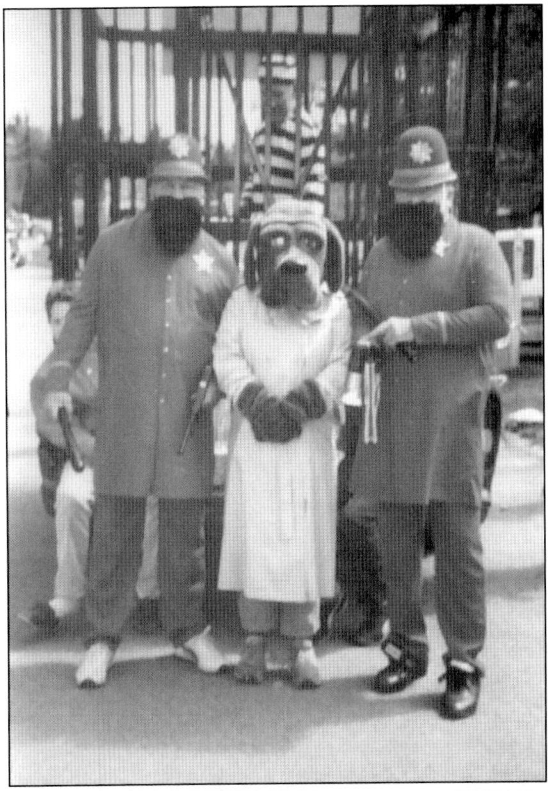

The Dover Police Association float in the town's 1986 sesquicentennial celebration featured, from left to right, George Michel, "Crime Dog" (Martha Campbell), and James McGill. Guess who was in the cage. It was none other than Don Ball.

Each year, children and parents alike enjoy the Dover tree lighting in front of the Dover Town House. This ceremony took place on December 16, 1997. (*Dover-Sherborn Press.*)

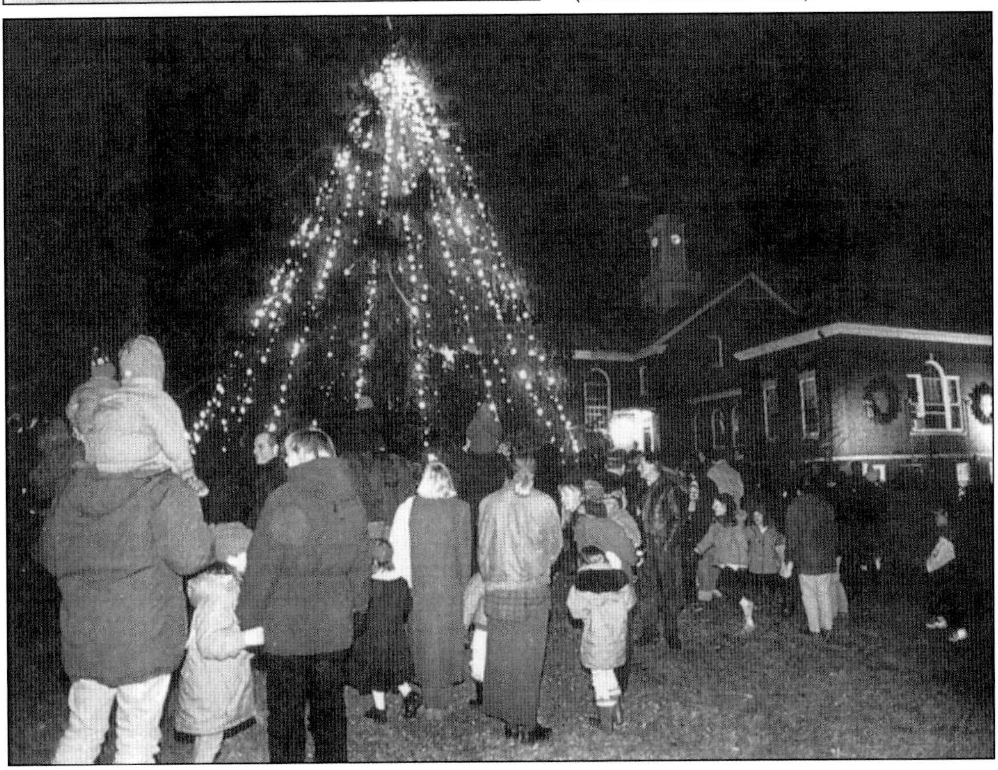

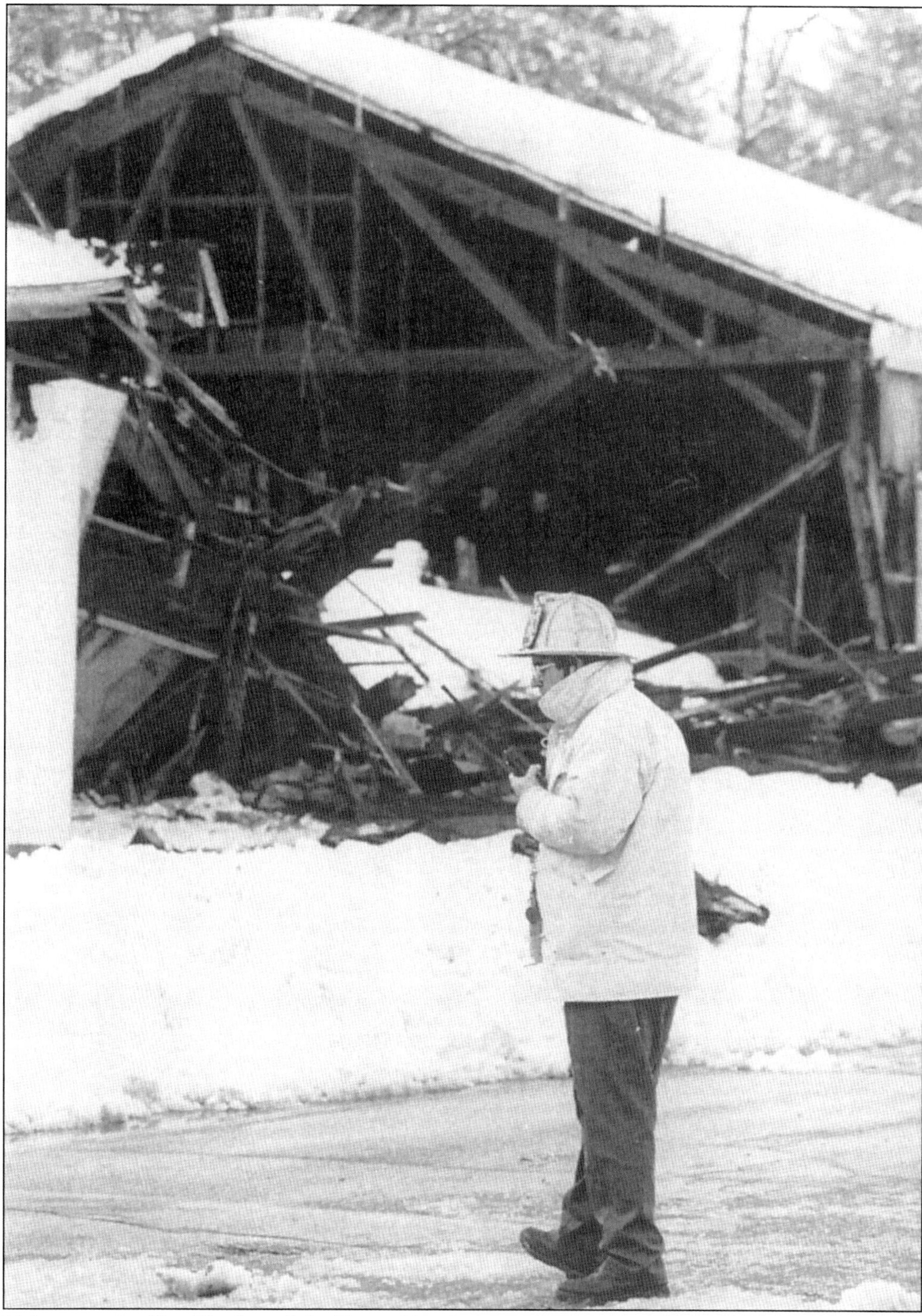

Volunteer chief Jay Hughes of the Dover Fire Department stands in front of the collapsed town highway garage. A snowstorm on March 31 and April 1, 1997, overwhelmed the old building. Hughes is also the proprietor of Dover Country Properties. (*Dover-Sherborn Press.*)

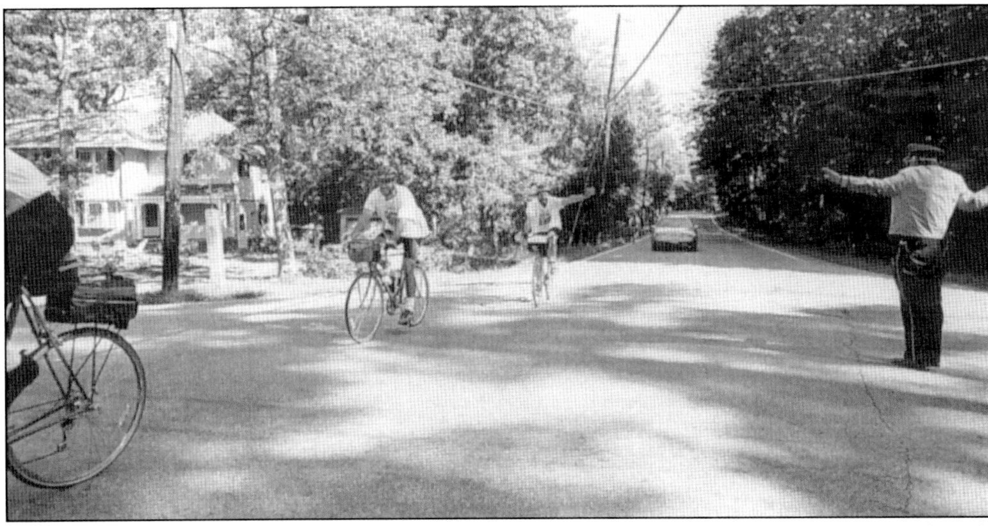

Officer Bill Jones directs traffic at Haven and Main Streets as the AIDS benefit bicycle race—3,800 strong—passes through Dover on the way to New York City on September 21, 1995. Dover is a favorite destination for cycling enthusiasts in all seasons. (*Dover-Sherborn Press.*)

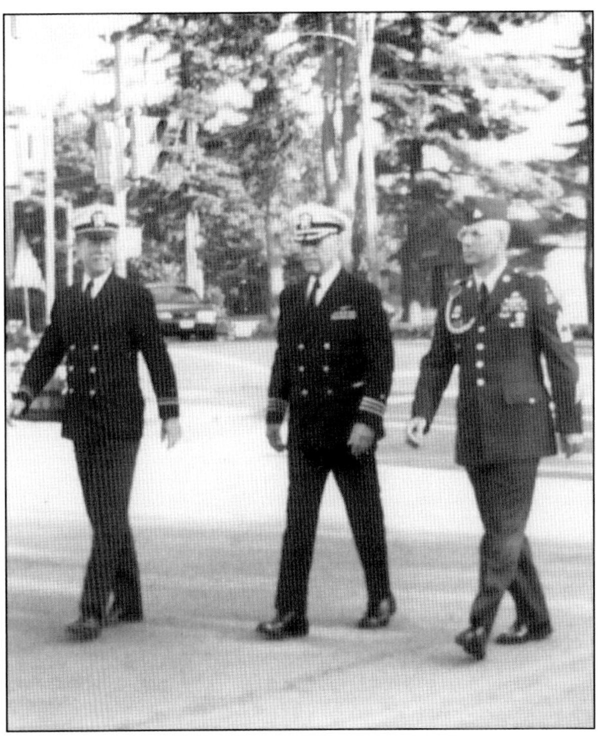

The 1999 Memorial Day speakers step off as the line of marchers heads for Highland Cemetery. Traditionally, speakers are members of the community who have served in the armed forces. Seen here, from left to right, are Curt Anderson, Roland Young, and M. Sgt. Stephen Ball of the U.S. Army. Sergeant Ball is the son of Don Ball, proprietor of the Dover Store.

Seven

SCHOOLS AND SPORTS

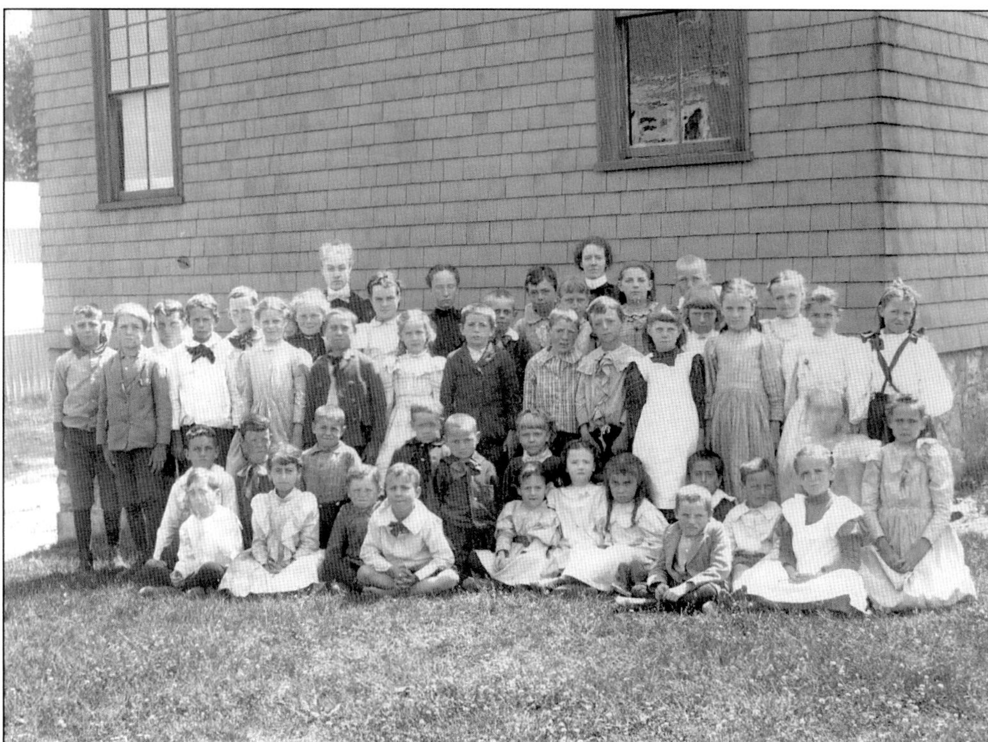

The Dover School on Springdale Avenue had all grades present for this 1898 photograph. The teacher was Marion Spring, and the assistant teacher was Martha Colburn. This school was built in 1888 to replace the much used Old Center School, which stood facing Springdale Avenue across from the present Dover Store.

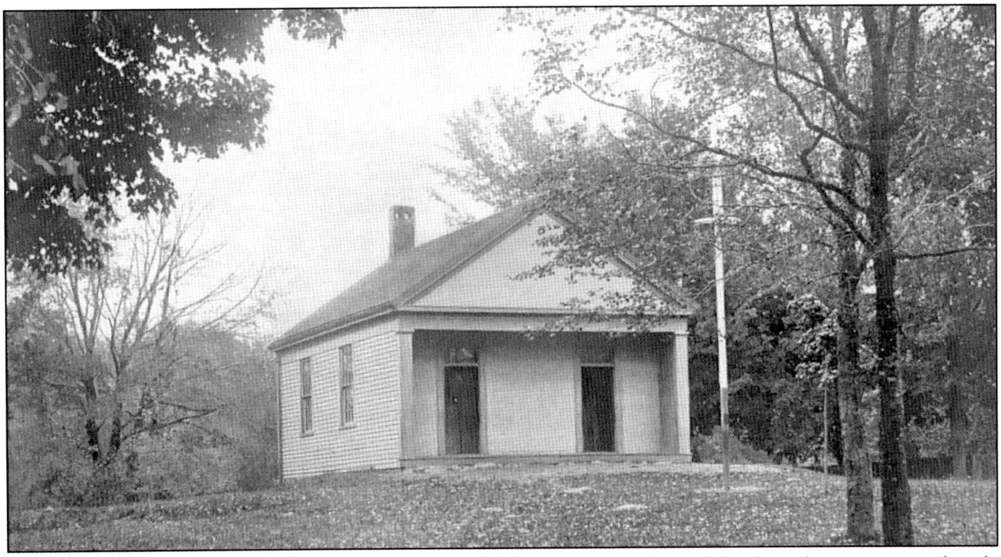

At the beginning of the 20th century, Dover children attended neighborhood one-room schools like the East School on Strawberry Hill. This concept of education formed the base of the American system. Between 1900 and 1910, the East, West, and North Schools were closed, and all children were educated at the 1888 Dover Center School.

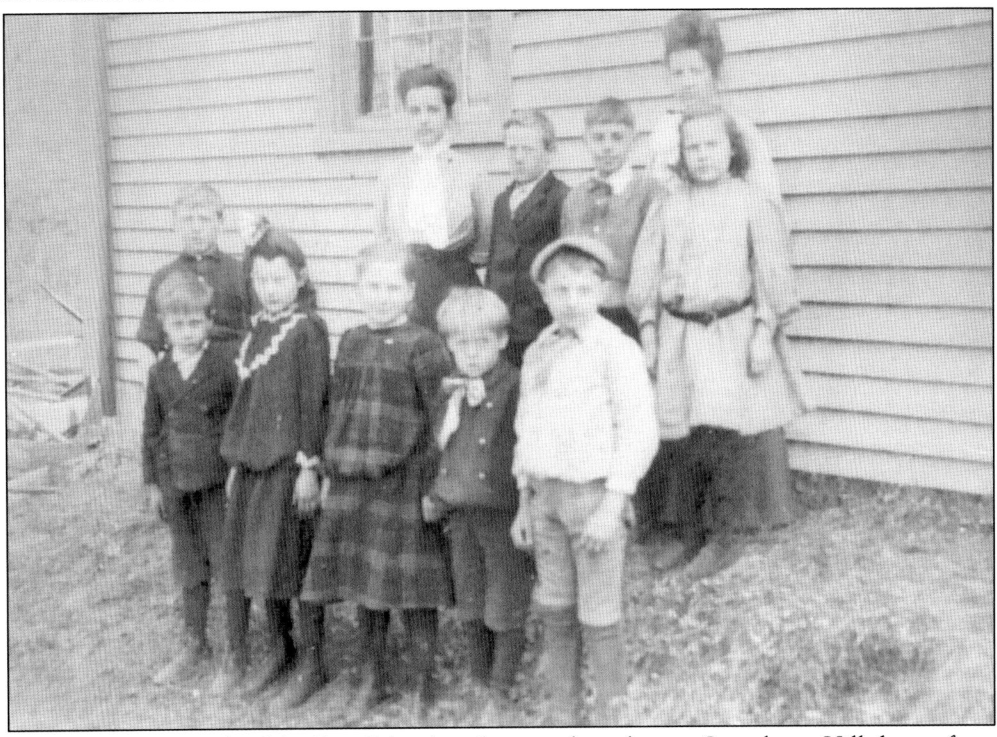

This 1904 photograph of the East School students and teacher on Strawberry Hill shows, from left to right, the following: (front row) Leon Bean, Herbert Bond, Lucy Brown, Esther Bond, Payson Woodward, and "Jessie" Brown; (back row) Elizabeth Woodward, Lee Rayme, Teacher Loring Woodward, and ? Rayme. After the school closed in 1910, Richard Hale bought the building and attached it to his house on Strawberry Hill Street as his library.

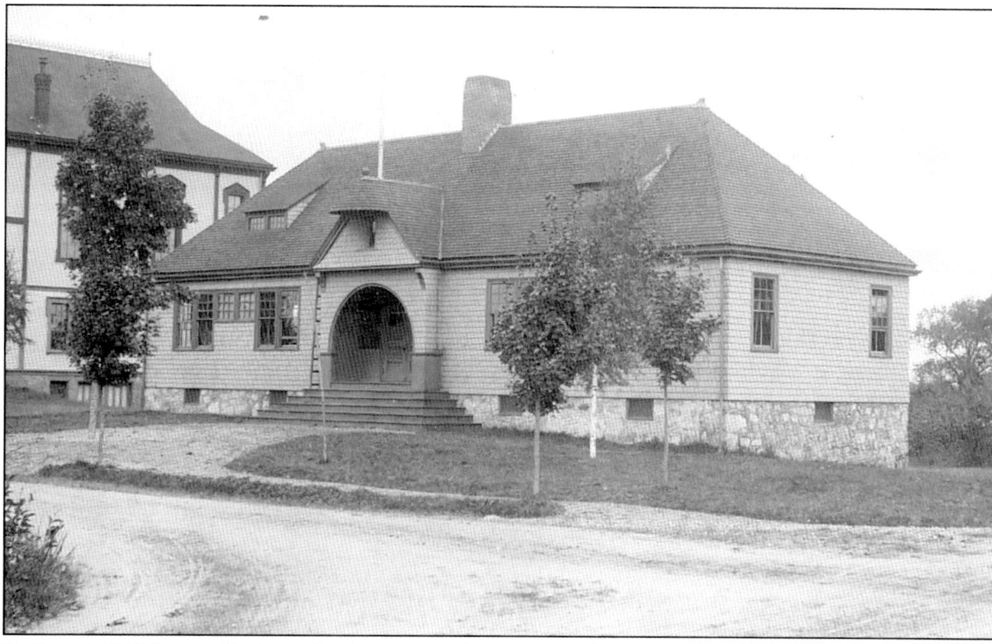

Built in 1888 facing Springdale Avenue at the corner of Centre Street, the Sanger School was named after Dr. Ralph Sanger, the town's second minister. The school became a four-year high school after the Caryl School was built across the street in 1910. In 1931, a rear wing annex to the Caryl School building became the junior and senior high school.

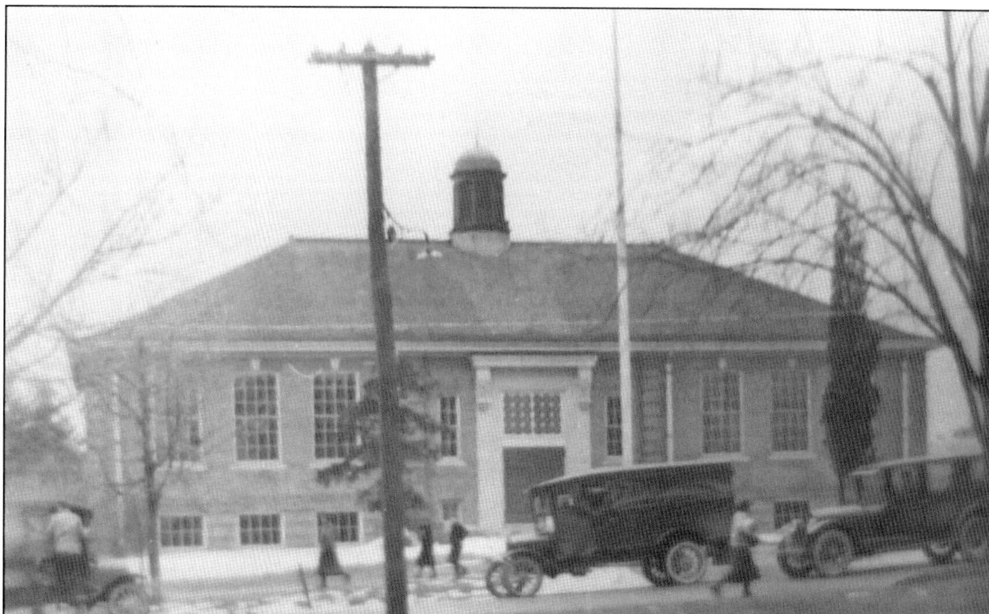

Built in 1910, the Caryl School on Springdale Avenue at Centre Street commemorates Dover's first minister, Benjamin Caryl. Reverend Caryl's house on Dedham Street is owned by the town and managed by the Dover Historical Society. Notice the ruggedness of the cars and trucks parked in front of the school.

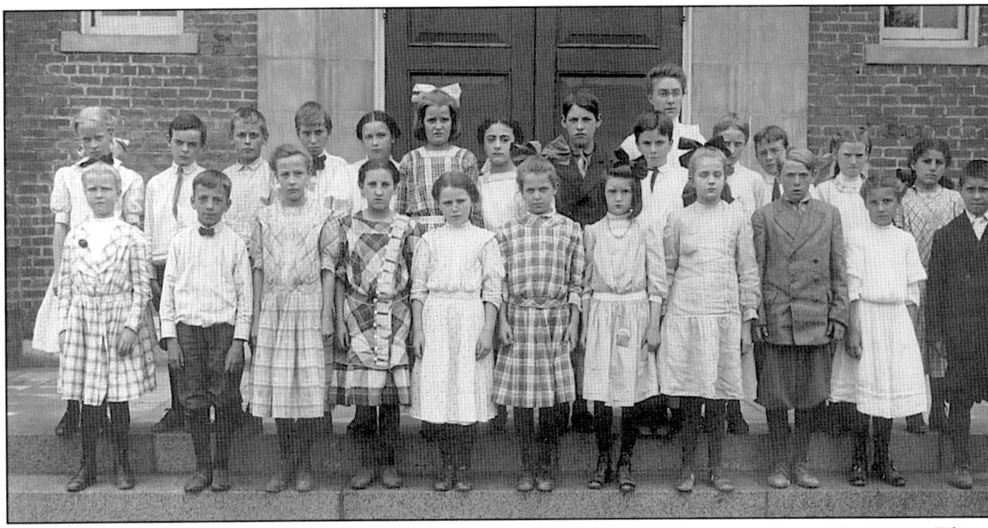

Grades five and six of the Caryl School pose for their class picture on June 27, 1911. Those identified in the picture are the following: (front row) Edith Locke, third from left; Evelyn Fletcher, fourth from left; Margaret Wall, fifth from left; and Kathryn Wheeler, sixth from left; (back row) Wendell Higgins, second from left; Hester McGill, sixth from left; and Willard Fletcher, eighth from left. Why do we all seem to look grim on such occasions?

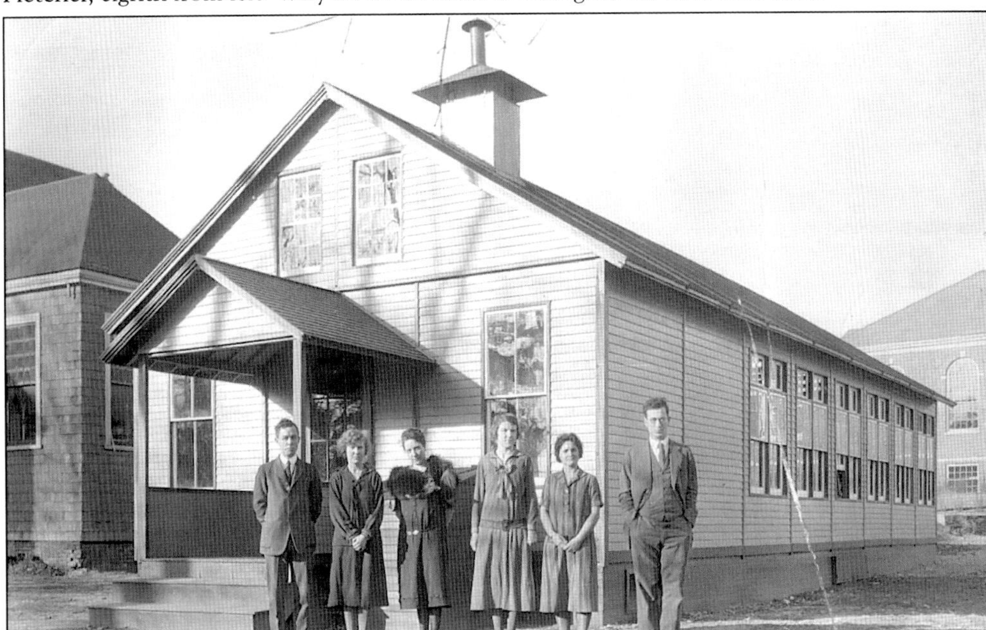

Population pressures necessitated the use of this portable schoolhouse made by the E.F. Hodgson Company. It was used as a junior high school. This 1926 photograph shows the faculty in front of the school, which stands behind the Sanger School facing Centre Street. Seen here, from left to right, are George Durgin (principal and math teacher—Harvard); Helen Thompson McGill (English—Wheaton); Madam Allen (French war bride who taught French at the Charles River School in the morning and the junior high in the afternoon); Doris Fish Schaffner (commercial); Marion Stark Robinson (Latin and history—Boston University); and Lawrence Harris (sciences—MIT). (Shirley McGill.)

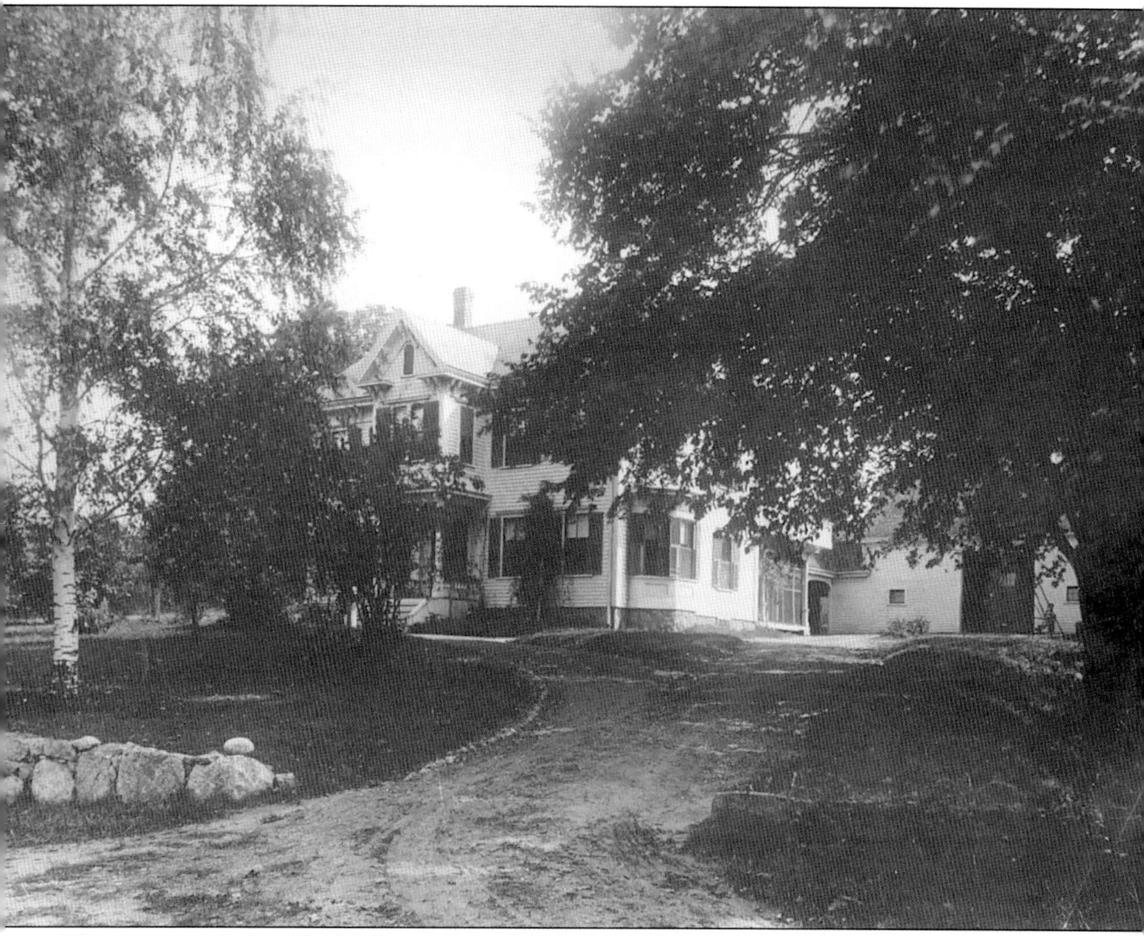

The trustees of the Charles River School (CRS) bought the Allen Smith House, an 1877 Victorian structure, at 56 Centre Street in 1917. A country day school, CRS was a reflection of the desires of many old and new Dover residents who wanted a different form of education for their children. Similar schools had been established in neighboring Wellesley, Newton, and Dedham.

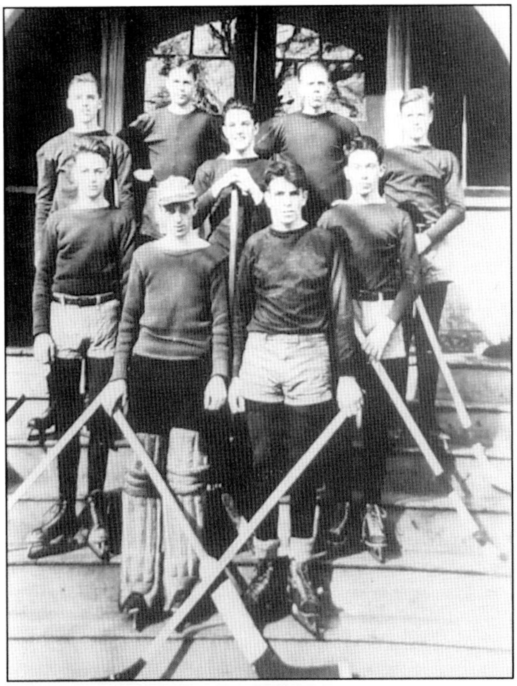

Hockey is a sport particularly popular in New England. This late 1920s photograph seems as though it may have been staged out of season with pick-up uniforms. Shown, from left to right, are the following: (front row) George Hinbaugh and Paul Schaffner; (middle row) Mel Hinbaugh, K. Boudin, and Kilburn Treadwell; (back row) Gerald Casey, unidentified, Bill Quinn, and Carl Walden.

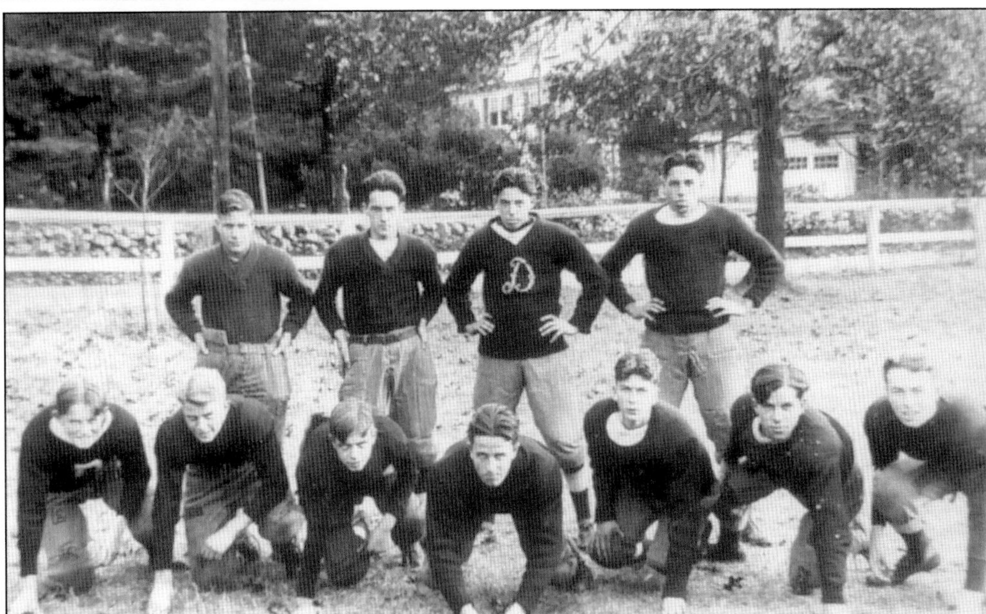

Sports have always been an essential part of the Dover community spirit. This was the 1925 Dover football team. Note the equipment, the numberless jerseys, and the hair styles. Known to be in the photograph, in no particular order, are Richard Treadwell, C. Corriveau, L. Corriveau, J. Walker, Roger McGill, Paul Schaffner, J. Heard, W. Brown, A. Francesco, and George Walker. (Shirley McGill.)

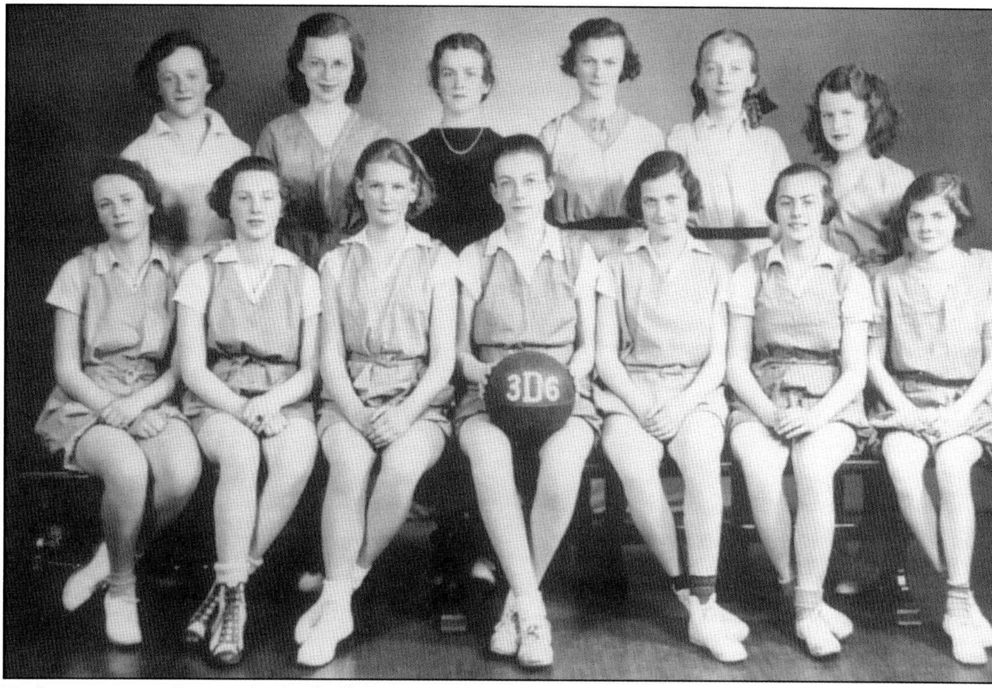

Today, women playing basketball have reached the professional level. This is the 1936 Dover High School girl's basketball team. How many remember those uniforms? The coach wears the traditional strand of pearls. Shown, from left to right, are the following: (front row) Gertrude Burbank, Evelyn Flynn, Betsy Humphries, Mary Schaffner, Elena Gibbs, Audrey Goucher, and Marion Heinlein; (back row) Charlotte Glidden, Eleanor Monroe, Miss Kenney, Cynthia Gibbs, Elena Schaffner, and Ruth Murray. (Marion Gerrity.)

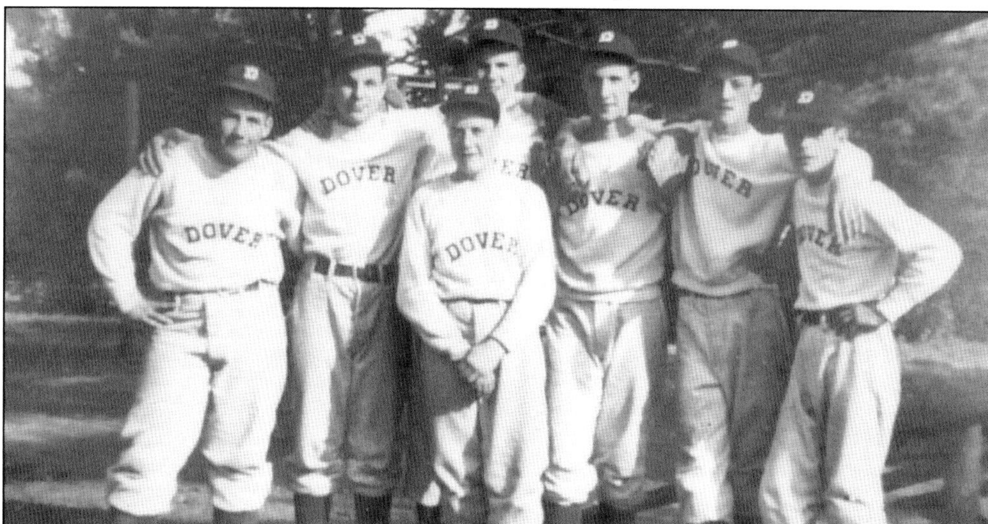

Baseball, the national pastime, has been and continues to be very popular in Dover. The members of the 1941 Dover baseball team are, from left to right, Harry Goucher, Kenny DeLong, Fred Roach, Jim Middleton, George Michel, Bob Rafter. John Goucher stands in front. Harry Goucher, Kenny DeLong, Jim Middleton, George Michel, and John Goucher all served in WWII.

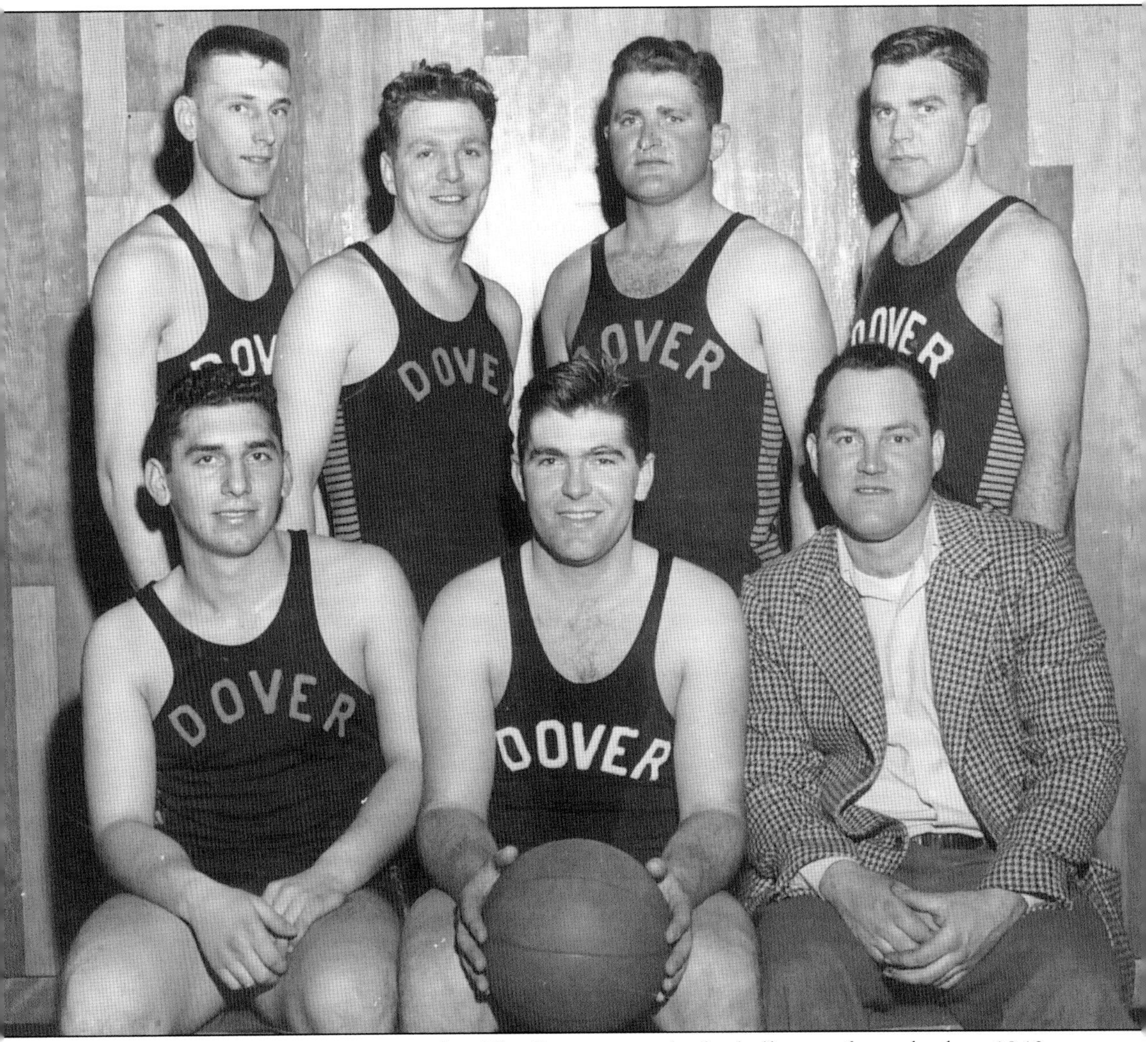

Dover town teams are very popular. The Dover town basketball team from the late 1940s to 1950s, from left to right, are as follows: (front row) Ray Luttazi, Jim McGill, and George Michel; (back row) Jim Bertschy, Skippy Tripp, Bill McGill, and Dick McGill. Maybe it should have been called the McGill town basketball team. (Don Ball.)

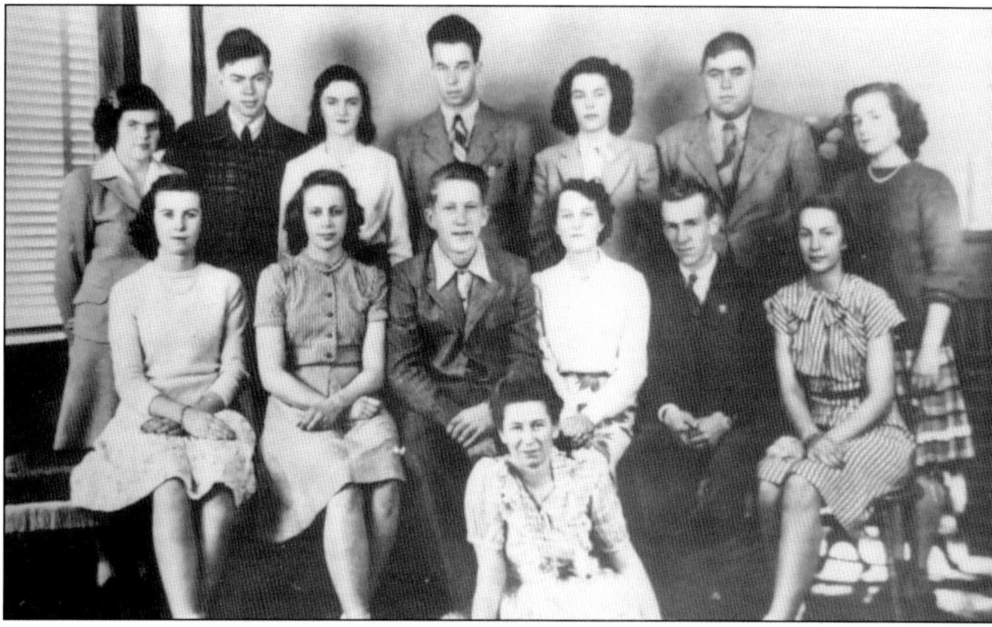

In the good old days, classes were small. The members of the Dover High School Class of 1945, from left to right, are as follows: (front row) Gloria Lloyd; (middle row) Marjorie Maker, Betty Piper, Gerald Fitzpatrick, Violet Lockhart, Carlton Sherman, and Elva Goucher; (back row) Mildred Horsford, Roger Monroe, Madeline Francesco, Derrick Fowler, Dorothy Sprunt, Alden Kennet, and Shirley Bond. Gloria Lloyd had joined the class after being discharged from the service. Where are these students now? (Shirley McGill.)

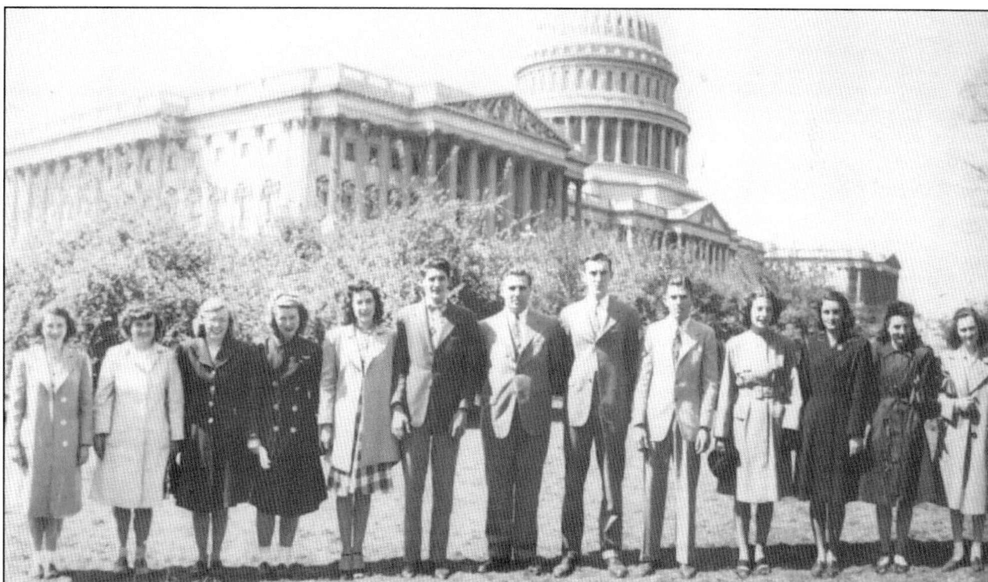

Senior class trips are nothing new. This 1946 senior class trip to Washington, D.C., was a popular event. Shown, from left to right, are the following: Margaret Thibedeau, Mary Comiskey, Peggy Hurst, Elaine Morris, Priscilla Gleason (chaperone), Ralph Cote, Robert Gleason (teacher), John Glidden, James McGill, Barbara Fowler, Grace Grandfield (teacher), Eleanor Sterling, and Janet MacKenzie. (Shirley McGill.)

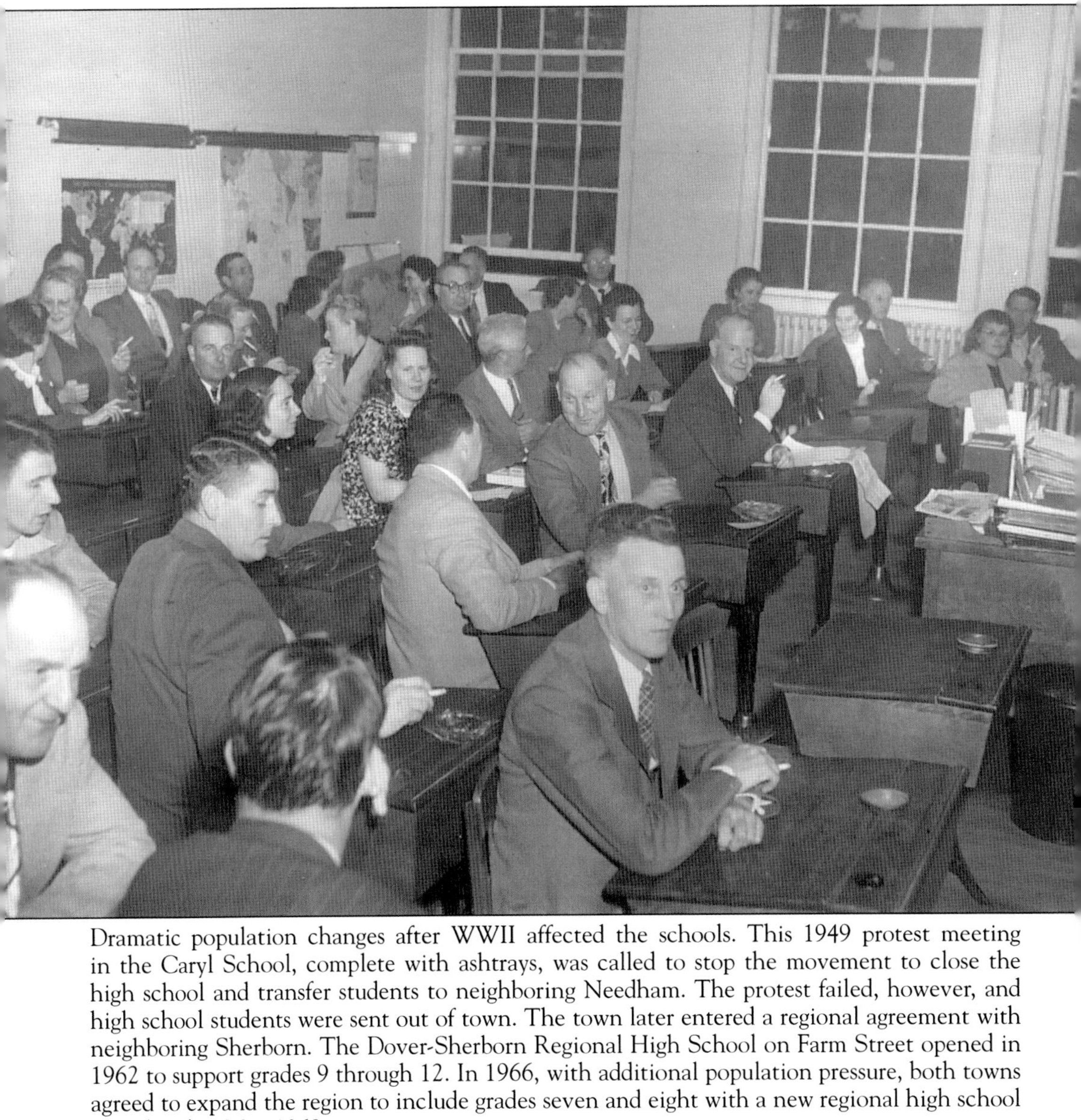

Dramatic population changes after WWII affected the schools. This 1949 protest meeting in the Caryl School, complete with ashtrays, was called to stop the movement to close the high school and transfer students to neighboring Needham. The protest failed, however, and high school students were sent out of town. The town later entered a regional agreement with neighboring Sherborn. The Dover-Sherborn Regional High School on Farm Street opened in 1962 to support grades 9 through 12. In 1966, with additional population pressure, both towns agreed to expand the region to include grades seven and eight with a new regional high school completed in May 1969.

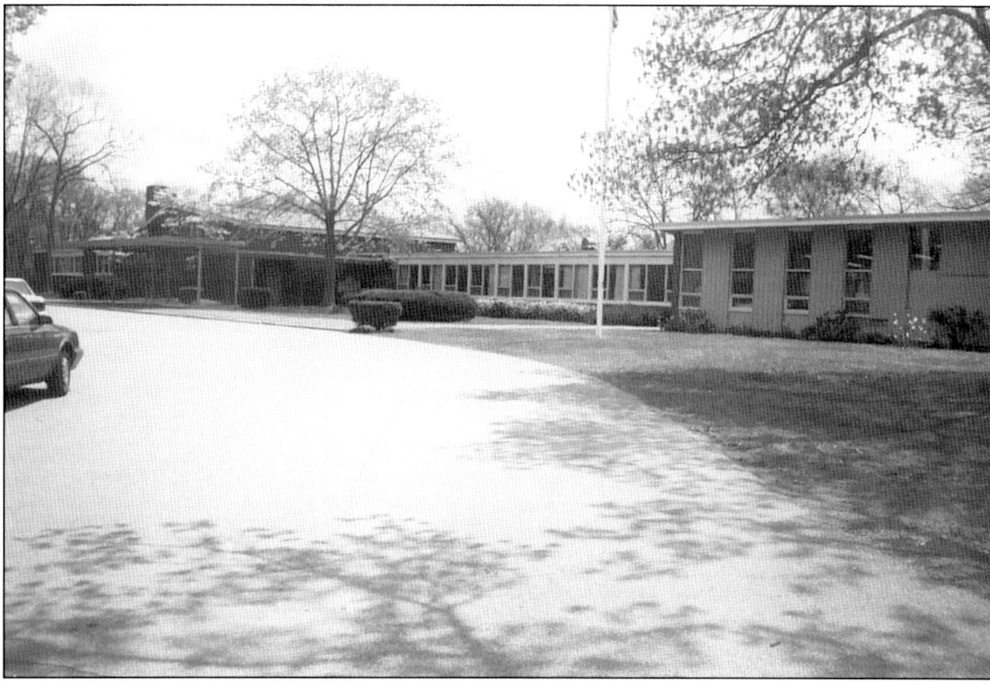

Opened in November 1956, the Chickering School on Cross Street was built to house kindergarten through grade four. School enrollment pressures required four additional classrooms in September 1961. With continued population demands, the 1999 town meeting voted to build a new school on the site which would house 750 students from kindergarten through grade five.

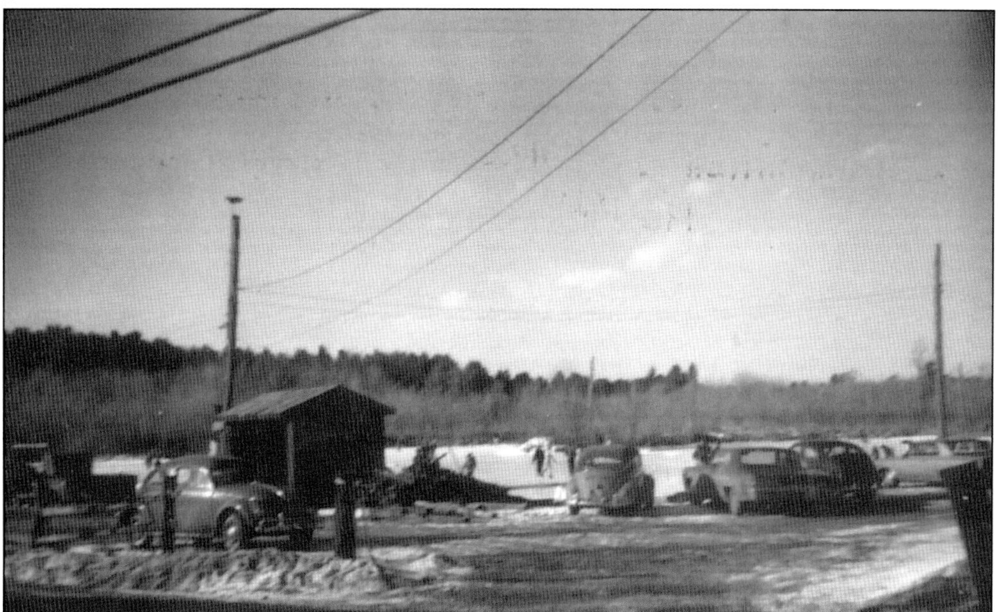

Channing Pond on Springdale Avenue supports important recreational and environmental activities in the town. This 1960 winter picture shows the pond being used for skating and hockey. Notice the Volkswagen Beetles in attendance. (Dave MacTavish.)

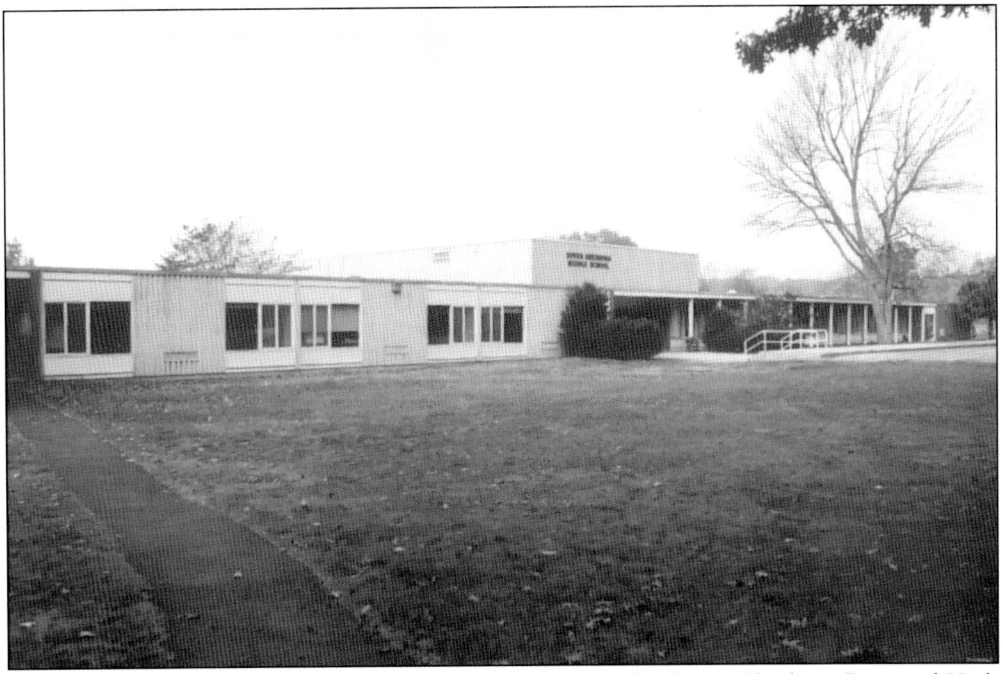

The Dover-Sherborn Middle School was originally built as the Dover-Sherborn Regional High School and opened in September 1962. The two towns voted that a new regional high school should be built beside this school in March 1966. By the time the grades shifted to the new high school in September 1969, when this school became the Regional Junior High School, some 795 students had squeezed into a building designed for 400.

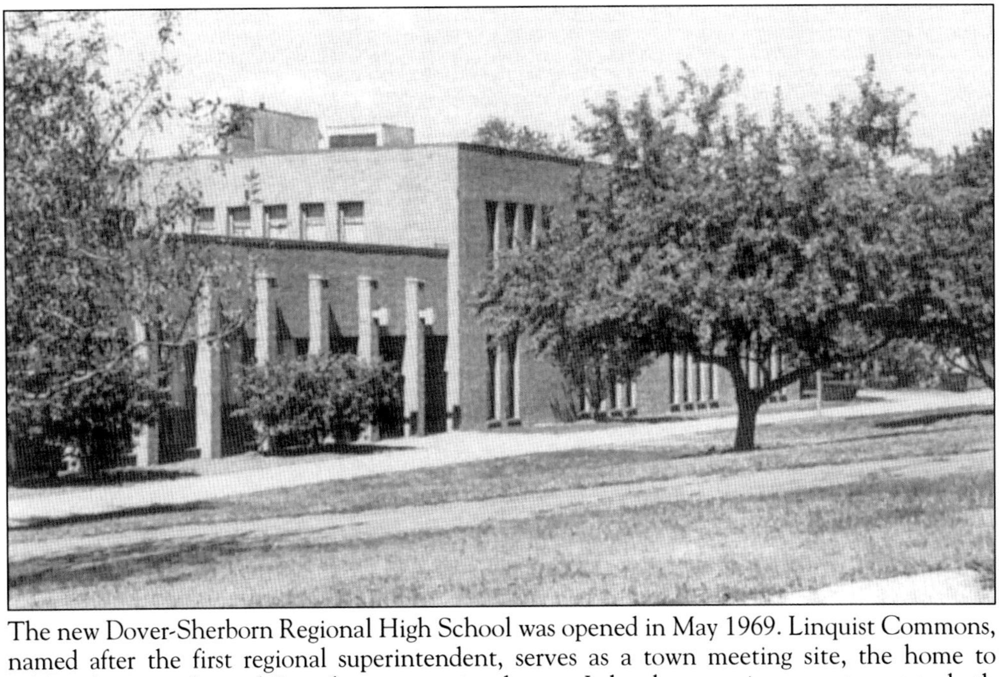

The new Dover-Sherborn Regional High School was opened in May 1969. Linquist Commons, named after the first regional superintendent, serves as a town meeting site, the home to cable television channel 8, and a community theater. It has been an important asset to both communities. (*Dover-Sherborn Press.*)

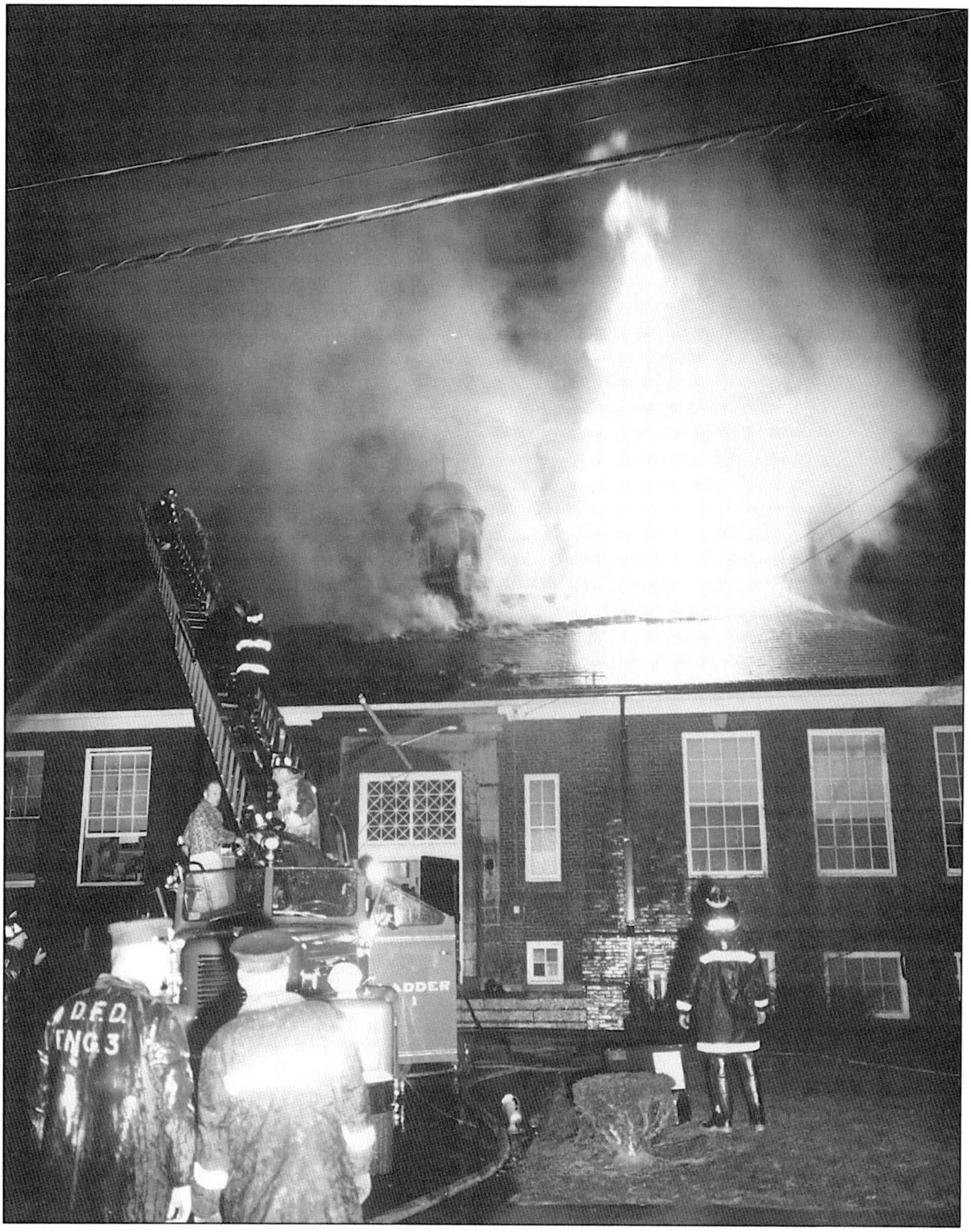

April 14, 1970, was a sad day for the Dover community. The 60-year-old Caryl School was gutted by a ten-hour blaze that was battled by firemen from five surrounding towns. The 275 fourth-, fifth-, and sixth-graders were moved to temporary school quarters at the Stigmatine Fathers Elm Bank property. The renovated school was reopened in April 1972.

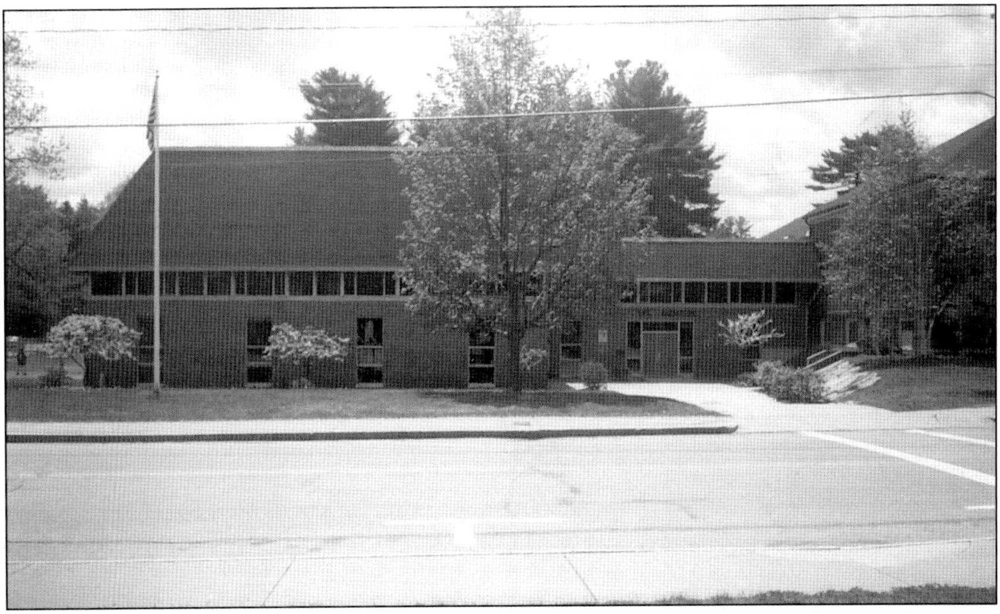

The rebuilt Caryl School on Springdale Avenue opened with an instructional materials center. Today, with the current state and national educational reform discussion, schools are under increasing pressure to validate their actions. The town population was 4,529 in 1970 when the new regional high school was fully open; a reasonable current projection is 6,200. In 1999, the town meeting voted to replace the Caryl School with a new Chickering School to house kindergarten through grade five and the increased student population.

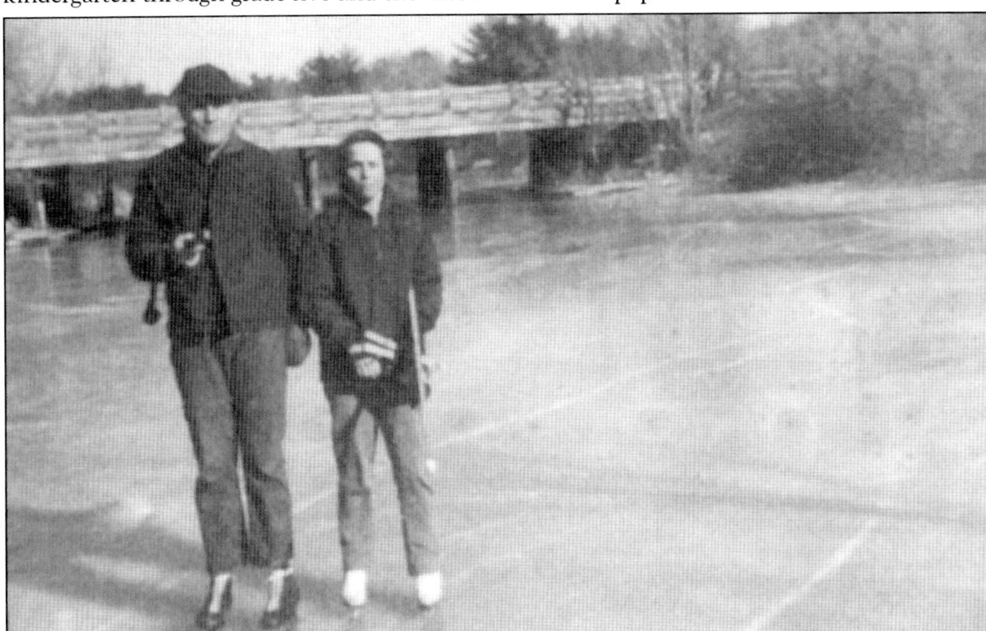

The Charles River continues to be an important part of our sports activities. One can boat, canoe, and fish on the river that is becoming less and less polluted with the efforts of the Charles River Watershed Association. Charles and Betsy Jackson enjoy skating on the river in this 1968 photograph. (Molly Jackson.)

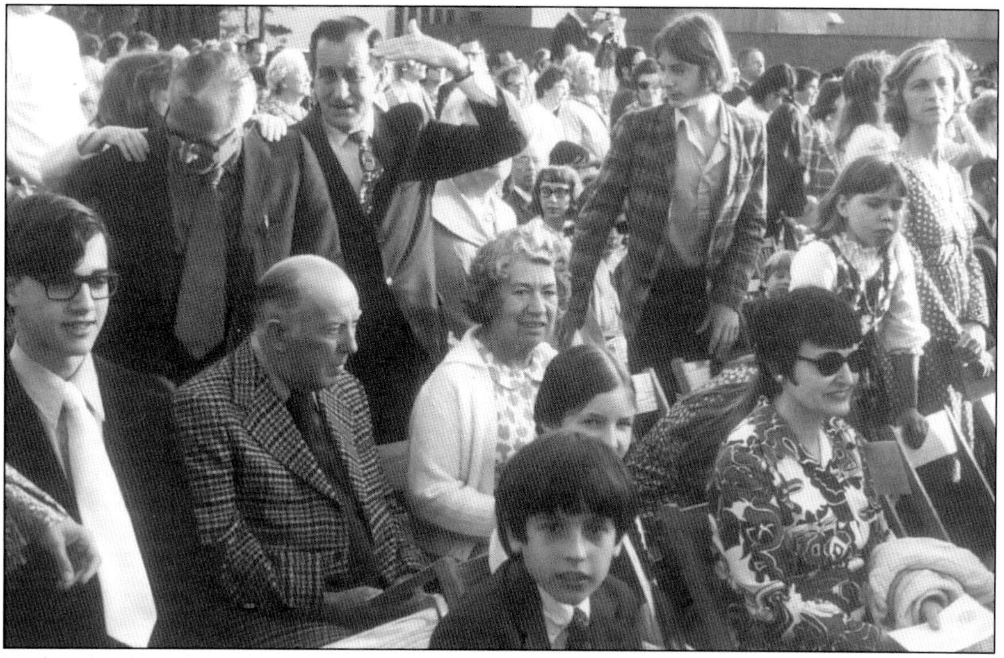

High school graduations are an important part of the community culture. Everybody gets dressed up for the celebration. Parents and family members wait expectantly for the Class of 1972 to march to the front. The quality of our schools is one of the most important concerns we have.

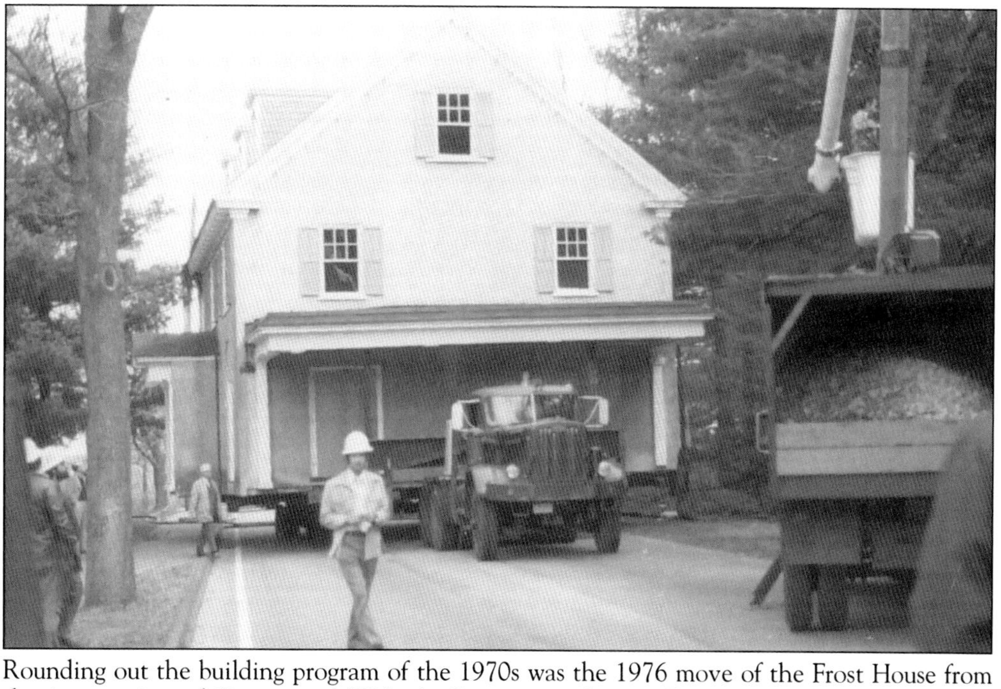

Rounding out the building program of the 1970s was the 1976 move of the Frost House from the intersection of Centre and Walpole Streets to a lot on Farm Street that was adjacent to the Dover-Sherborn Regional Junior and High Schools. The relocated building houses administrative offices. The structure had last been used for youth programs.

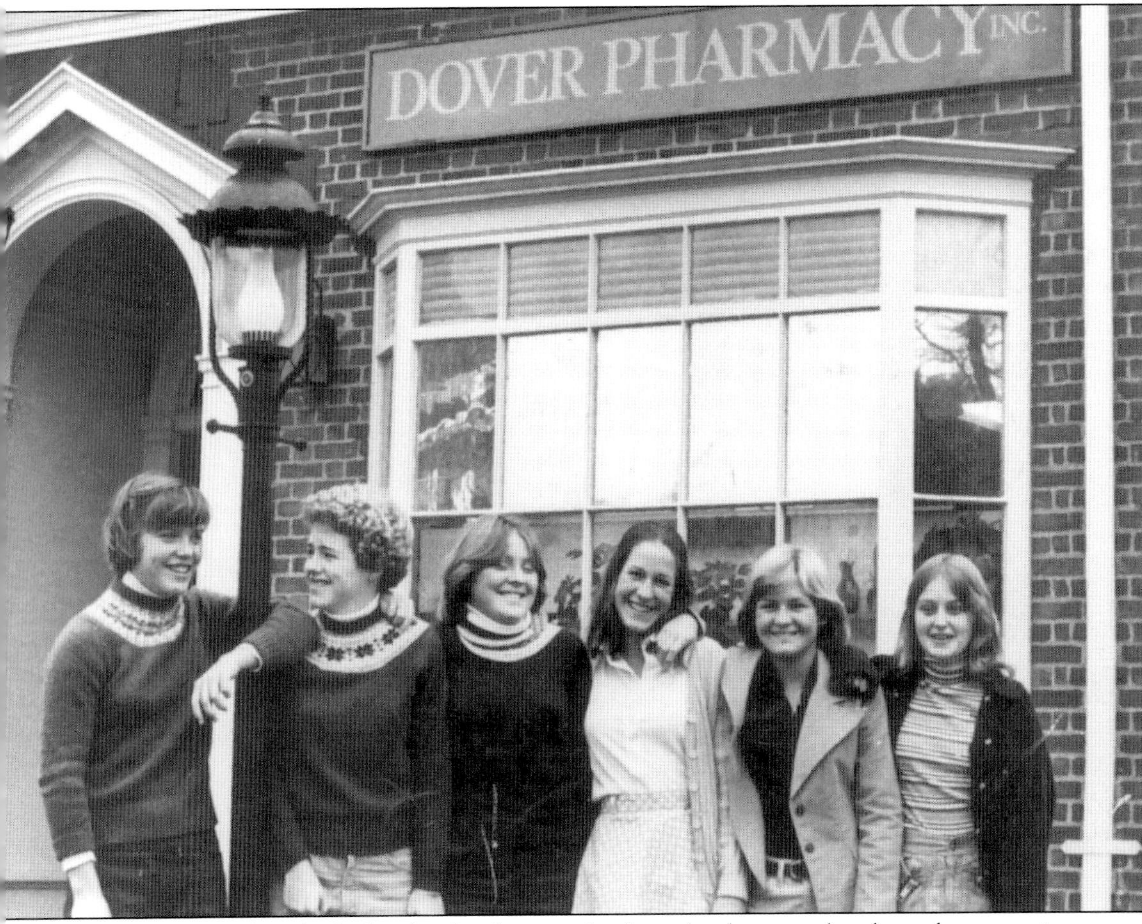

One popular place for high school girls to work after school, on weekends, and on vacations has been the Dover Pharmacy, now the Dover Store. In 1979, the girls working for the popular Ball brothers took out an advertisement using this photograph in the Dover-Sherborn Regional High School yearbook. The "soda fountain girls," as they called themselves, are, from left to right, Paige Duncan, Paula Murphy, Nancy Chandler, Alison Parry, Susan Parry, and Karen Lucy. (Don Ball.)

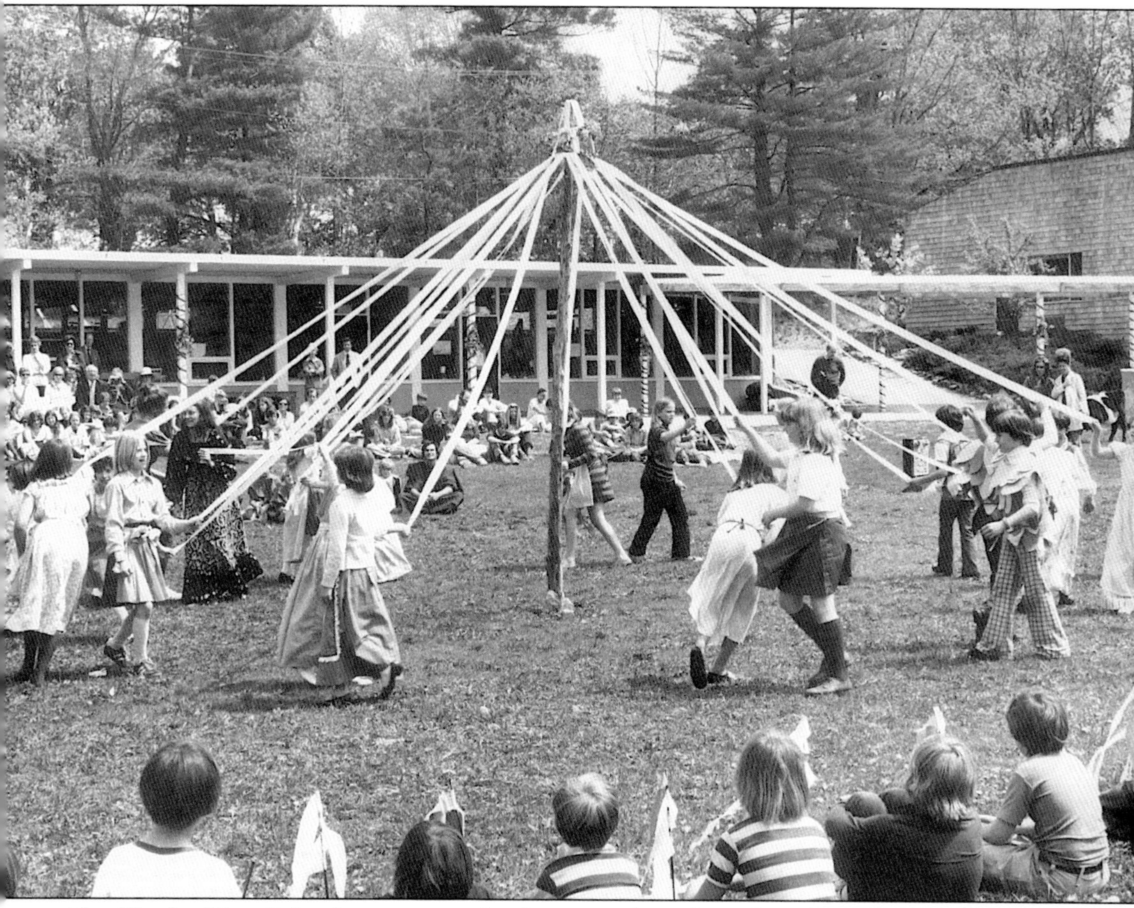

The Charles River School supports pre-kindergarten through grade eight and an enrollment of about 200 students from Dover and the surrounding area. The school prepares students for both day schools and boarding schools, such as Milton, Dana Hall, Andover, and Nobles. The 1977 May Day festival, shown here, is typical of the cultural activities that have made the school famous. (Charles River School.)

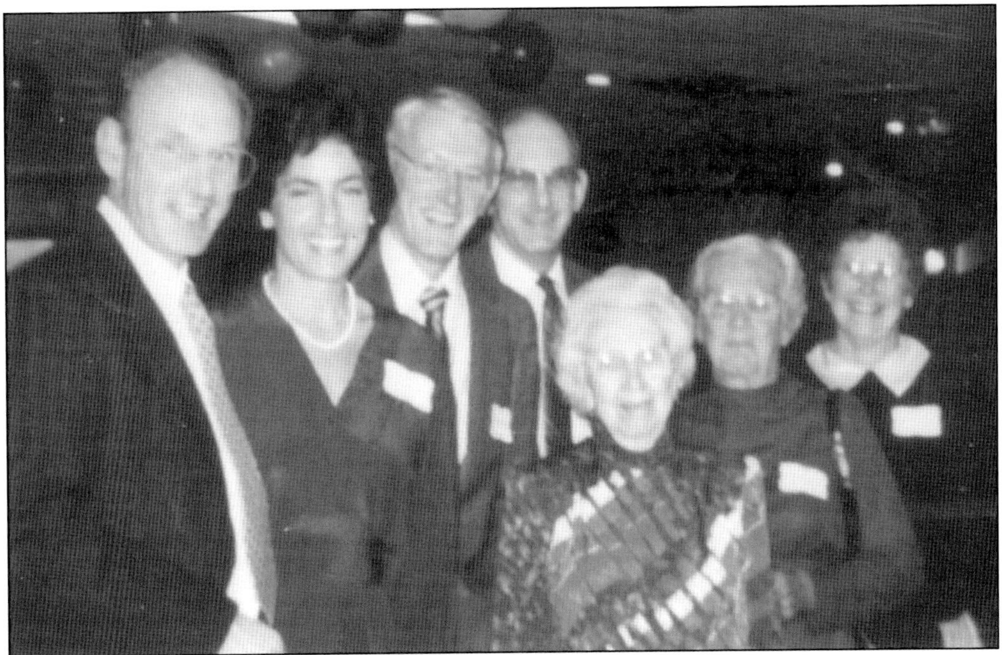

High school reunions are a wonderful time to greet old friends and share stories. Shown at the 1988 Dover High School reunion, from left to right, are Robert and Pat Bertschy, James Bertschy, Harry Bertschy, Antoinette (Chickering) Weathers, Emily (Chickering) Bertschy, and Joan Bowditch. (Janet MacKenzie.)

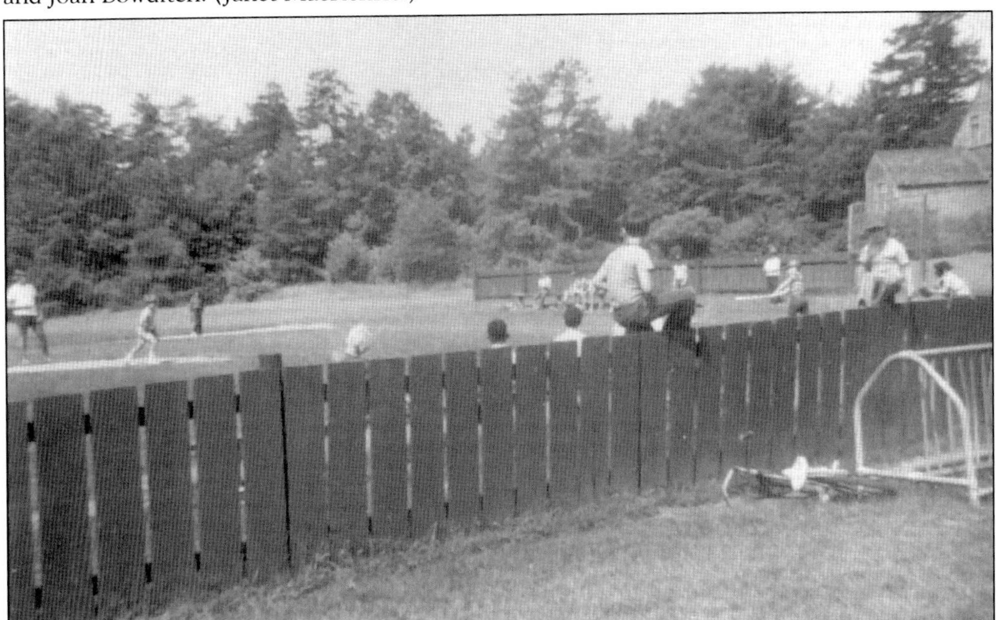

Kids enjoy the Caryl Park baseball diamond on a warm summer day. The Park and Recreation Commission facilities are an important part of the life of the community. In addition to this field, the town added the new Chickering Playing Fields in 1998. Each season has a different activity schedule: sports, the arts, and summer concerts on the common. At every level of activity, one can find a program for youths and adults alike. (Ford Spalding.)

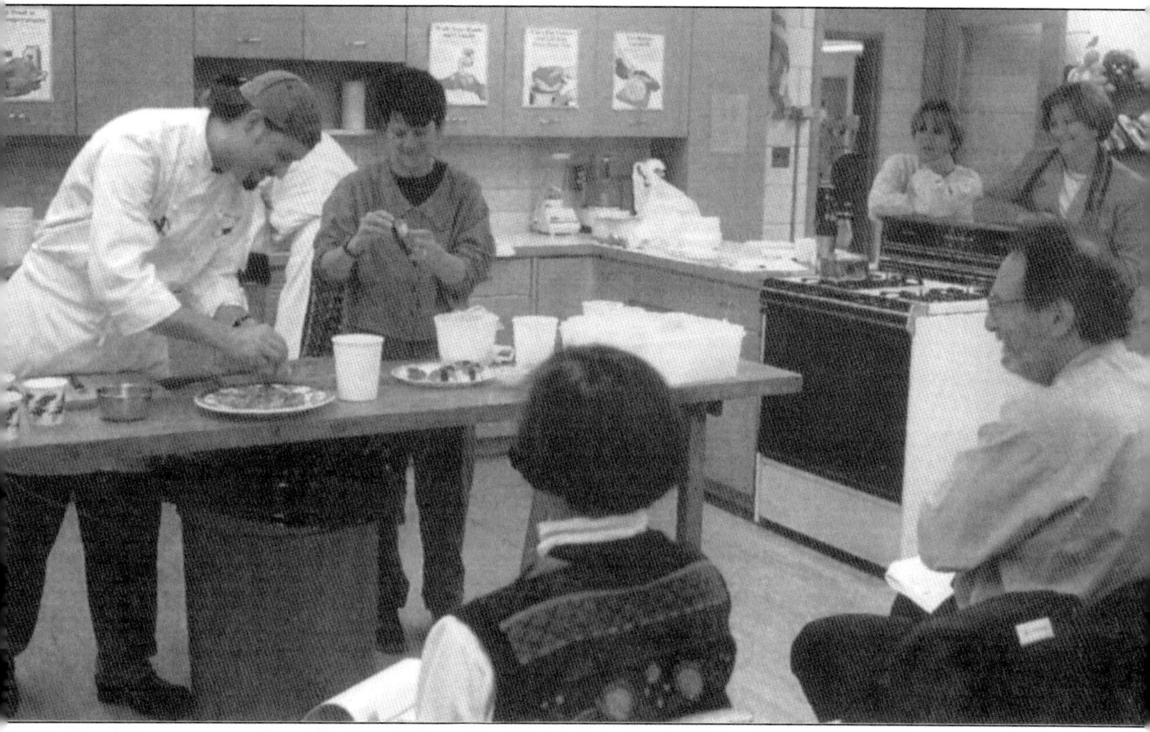

Cooking is a popular subject in the Dover Community Education Program. In this December 1998 photograph, the class watches chef James Scoon and Ellen Goldenberg work on some *hors d'oeuvres*. Other subjects offered include Orienteering, Building Stone Walls, Chair Seat Reweaving, and Creating an Herb Garden. (*Dover-Sherborn Press.*)

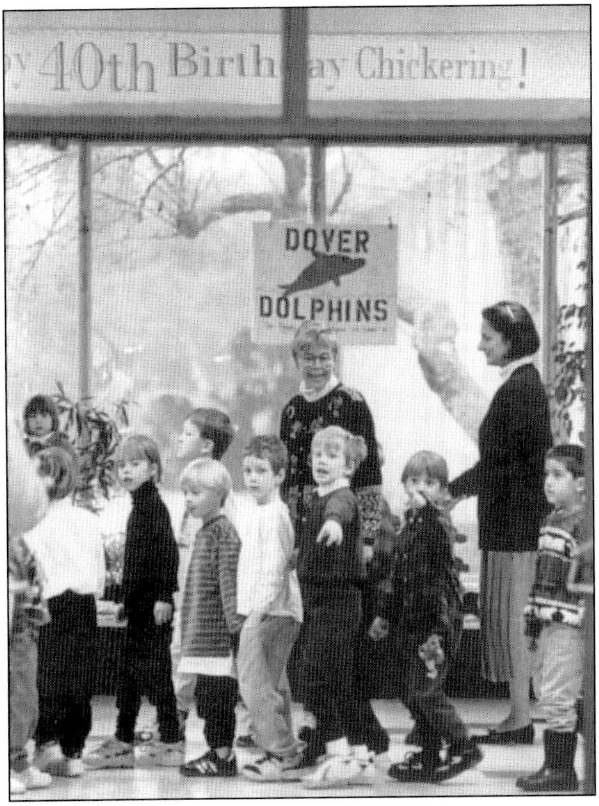

The Chickering School students celebrate the school's 40th anniversary with great spirit. This school will be razed after the construction of a new school for kindergarten through grade is built nearby. In 1999, the town meeting voted to build the new school for kindergarten through grade five. (*Dover-Sherborn Press.*)

The AIDS benefit bicycle race came through the town center on September 5, 1996. The fourth and fifth grades of the Caryl School stand on the roadside cheering the riders on. (*Dover-Sherborn Press.*)

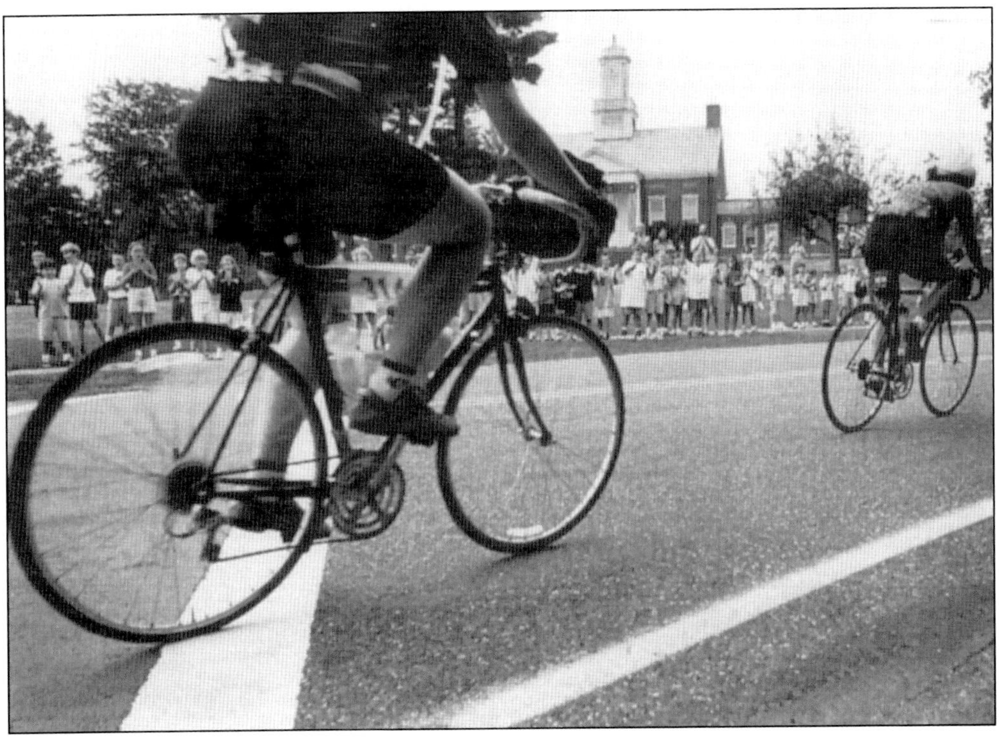

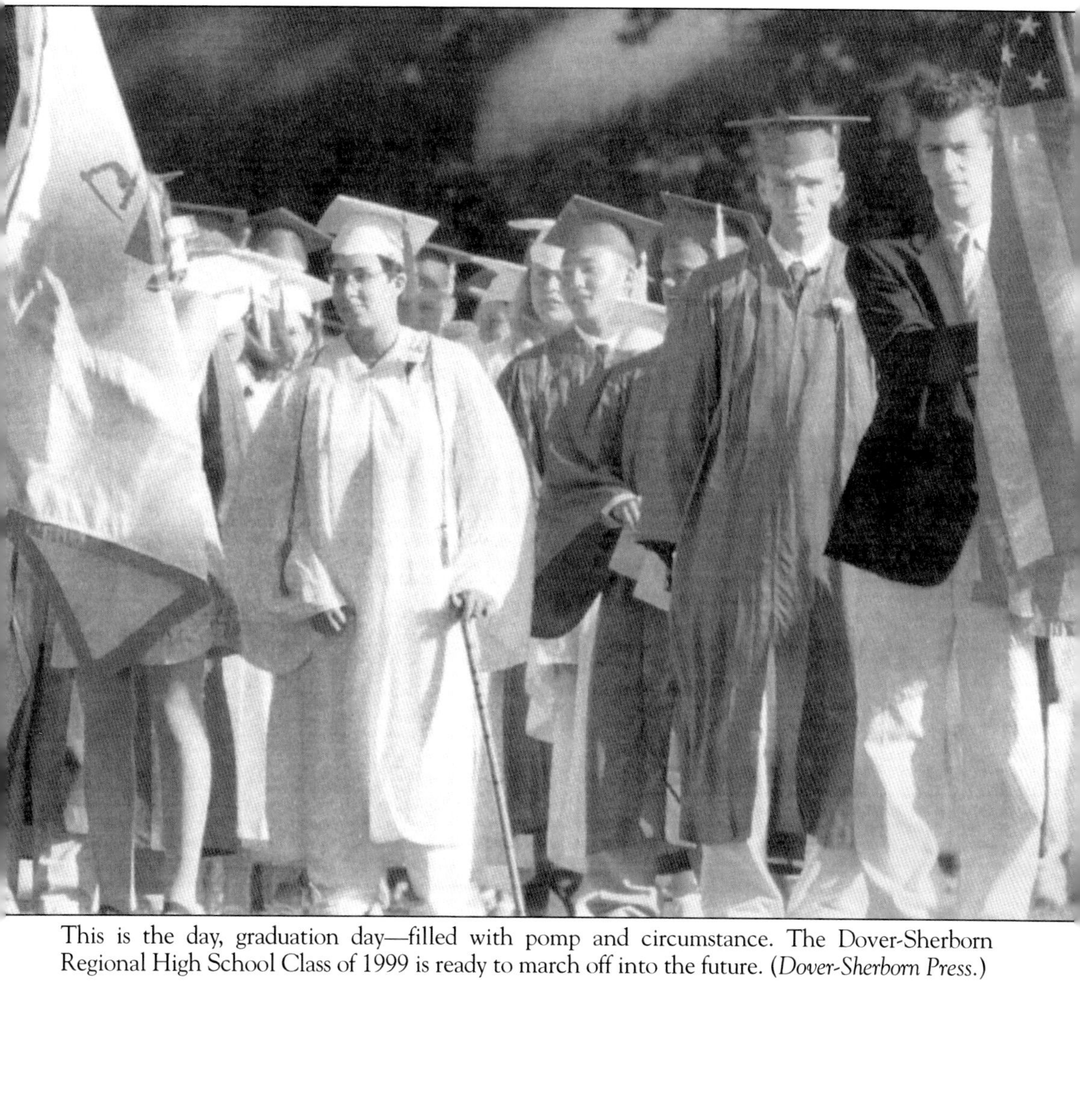

This is the day, graduation day—filled with pomp and circumstance. The Dover-Sherborn Regional High School Class of 1999 is ready to march off into the future. (*Dover-Sherborn Press.*)

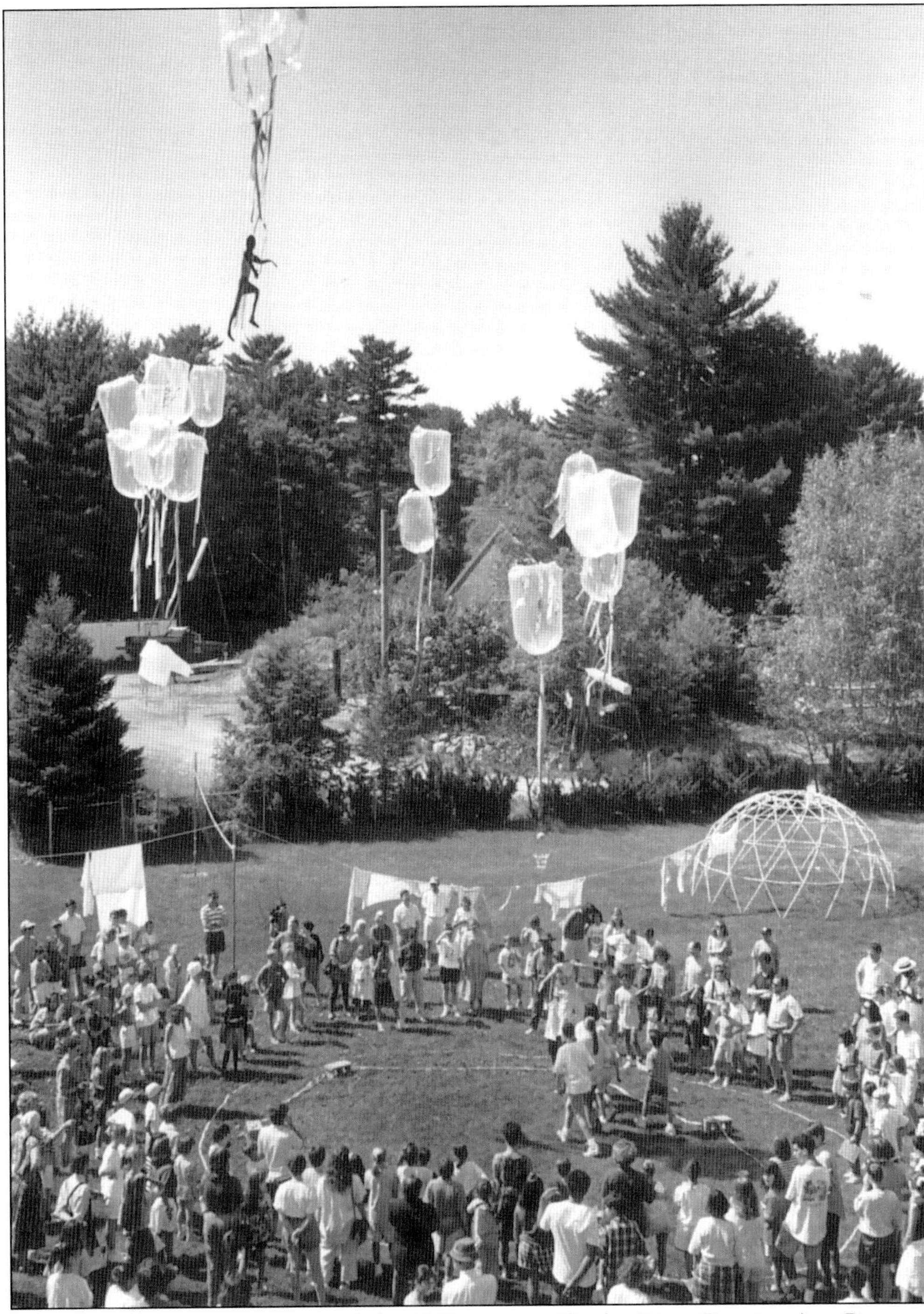

Shown is the opening ceremony of the 1992 summer Charles River Creative Arts Program. The program was founded in 1970 to provide an environment where youths pursue and develop interest in the arts as well as in gymnastics and sports. The program has earned national and international attention as well as federal and state funding. The Summer Festival is permanently housed on the campus of the Charles River School. (Joshua Levine.)

Eight

DOVER BY POSTCARDS

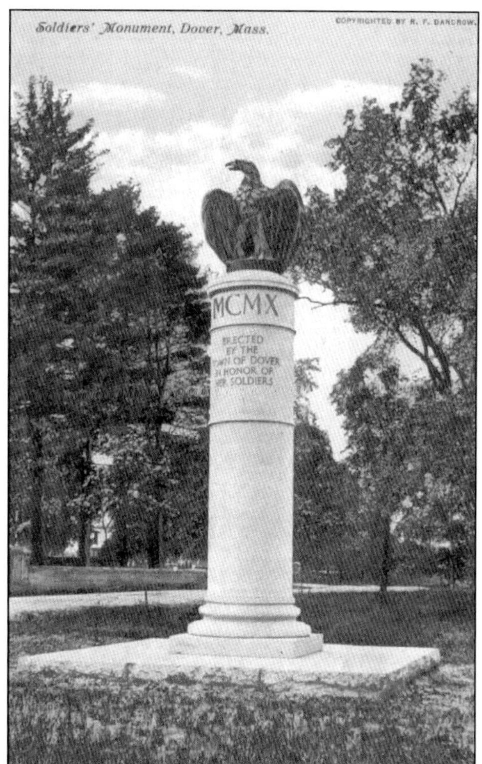

Postcards are a wonderful way for a town to show itself to others. The Soldiers' Monument was built by the Holt-Fairchild Company of Boston from Westerly granite on a base of Rockport granite. On the front of the column is the date of its erection in Roman figures that are engraved in granite. Below, in bronze letters, is the following inscription: "Erected by the Town of Dover in honor of her soldiers." The monument is sited on the Old Training Field; the field was used for military purposes from about the mid-18th century to the mid-19th century. (Robert Comiskey.)

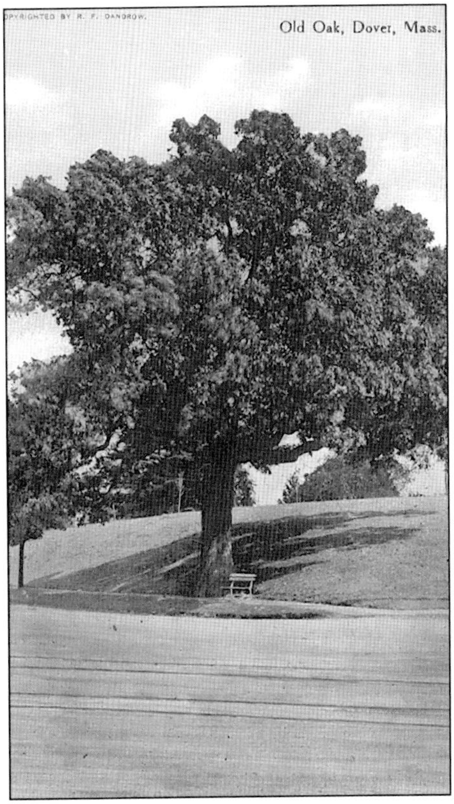

Every community has a symbol such as the old oak tree on the Dover Common. Trees, in particular, suggest the primeval nature of society and remind us of the process that surrounds us. For the town's people, this tree is a daily reminder of how close our lives are to nature. (Hope Hynes scrapbook.)

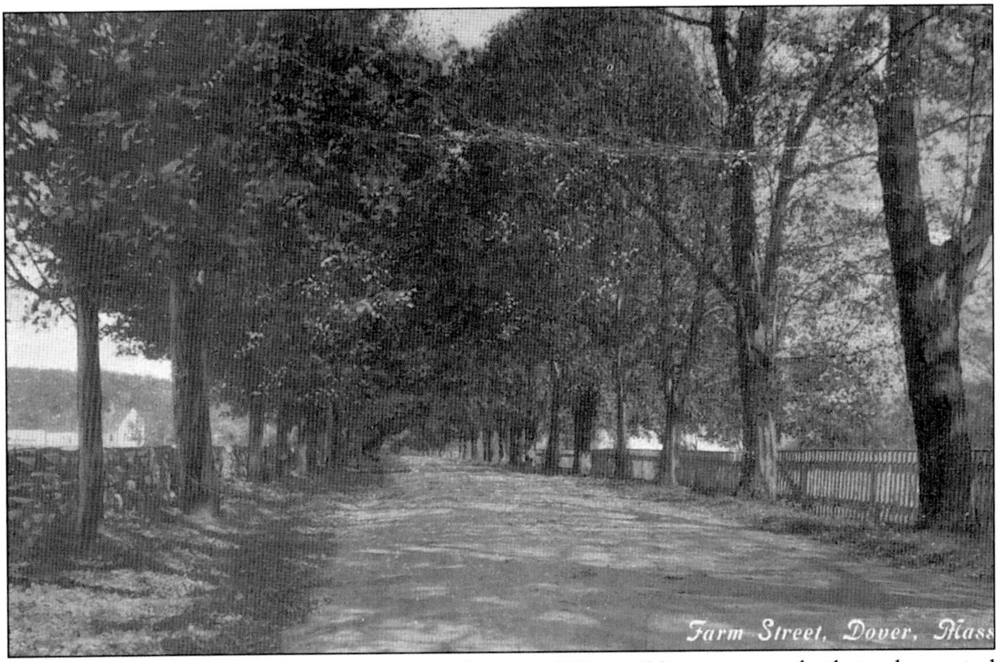

Many Farm Street country estates, some as large as 300 or 400 acres, were built in the period from 1900 to 1914. (Robert Comiskey.)

Every town has a lover's lane, and Dover is no exception. The pastoral nature of the community increasingly draws people to its boundaries. The exact location of this lover's lane is unknown. (Hope Hynes scrapbook.)

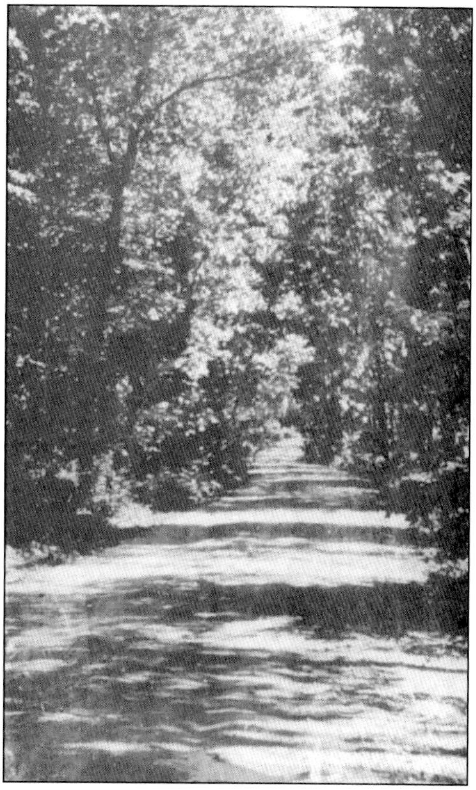

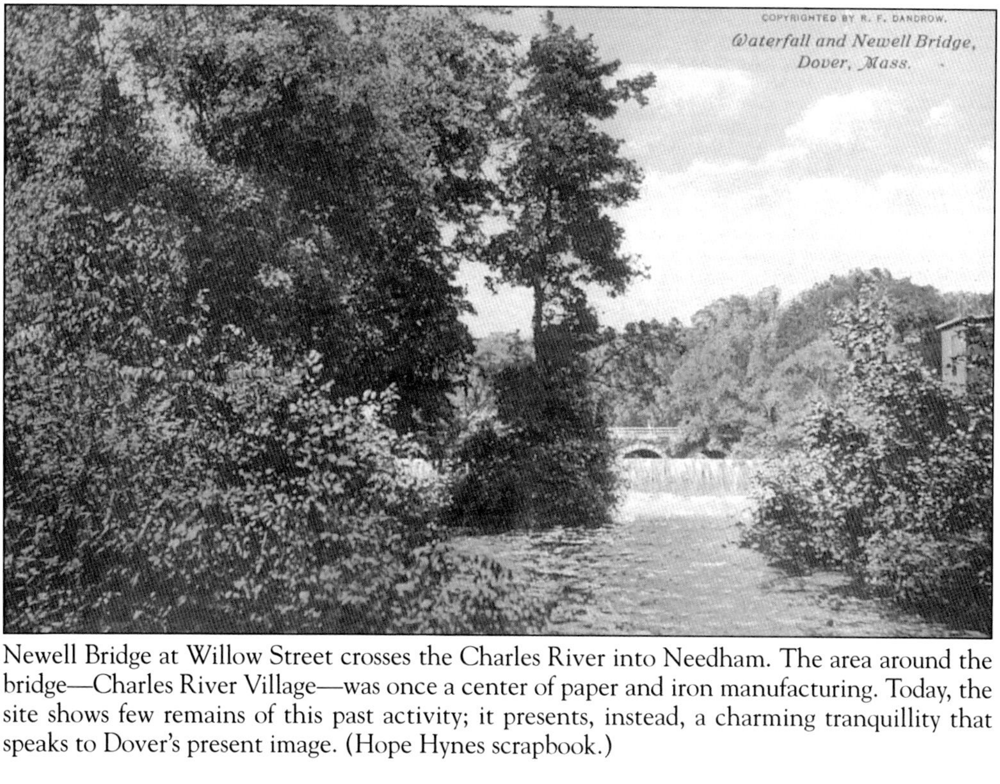

Newell Bridge at Willow Street crosses the Charles River into Needham. The area around the bridge—Charles River Village—was once a center of paper and iron manufacturing. Today, the site shows few remains of this past activity; it presents, instead, a charming tranquillity that speaks to Dover's present image. (Hope Hynes scrapbook.)

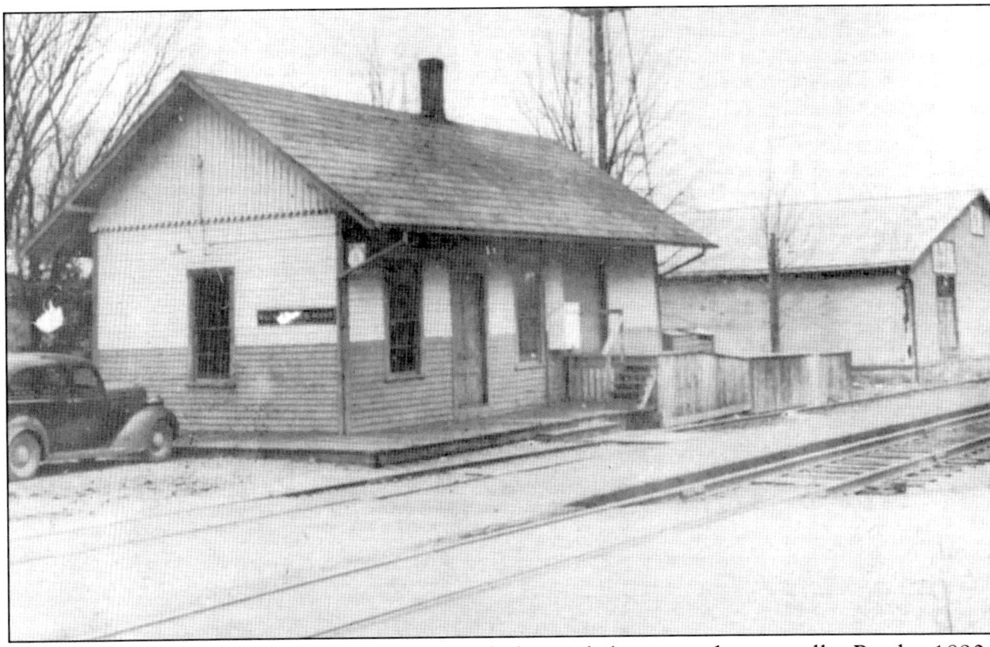

The railroad entered Dover in the 1850s and changed the town dramatically. By the 1890s, many wealthy Bostonians saw the convenience of the railroad and moved into the town, changing it into a suburban community. Service eroded over time and passenger service ceased in 1967. (Hope Hynes scrapbook.)

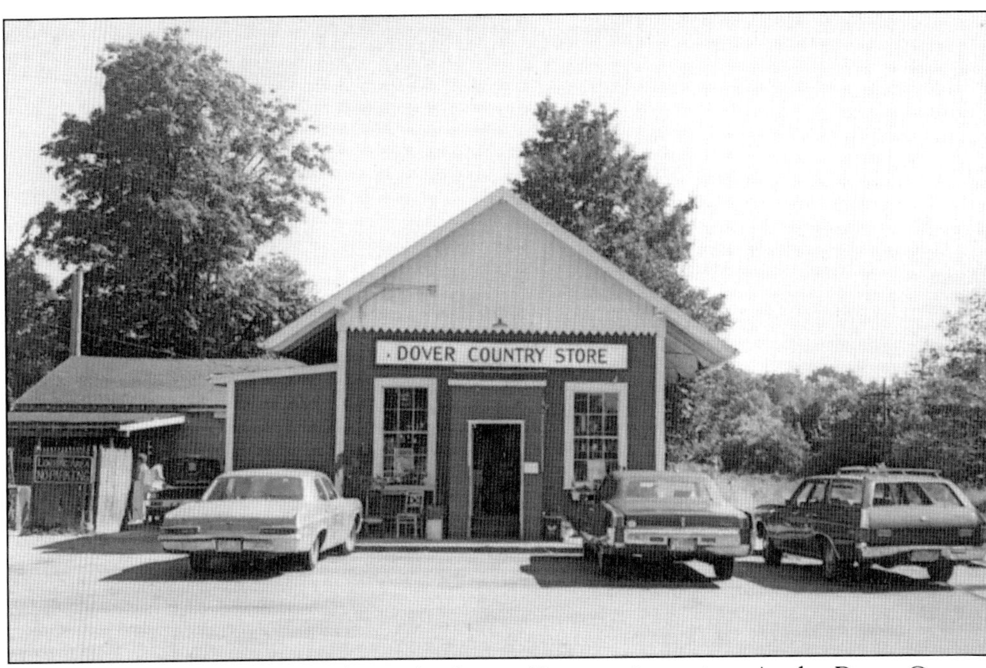

This more contemporary view shows the former Dover train station. As the Dover Country Store, people traveled here from all over New England in the pursuit of good junk. The car on the left makes the point about no more passenger service. Currently, the station houses the Whistle Stop, an antiques store, and Century 21 Realty. (Robert Comiskey.)

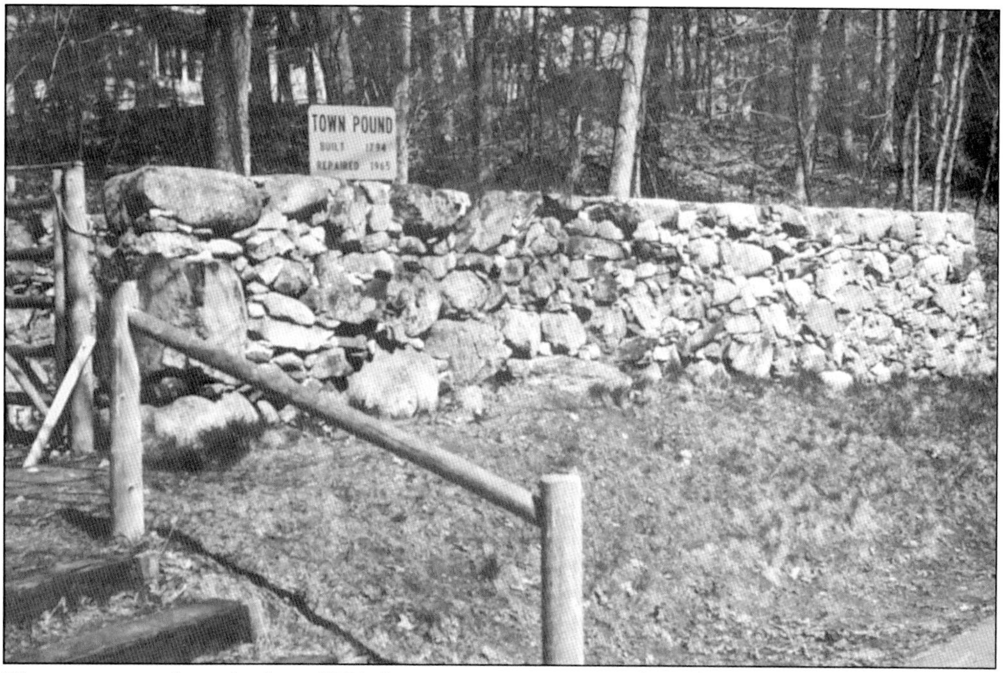

The town pound was built in 1794. Its purpose was to provide a place where straying livestock could be locked up. Such animals could become a nuisance in a farming community. The pound keeper would not release an owner's animals until a fee was paid.

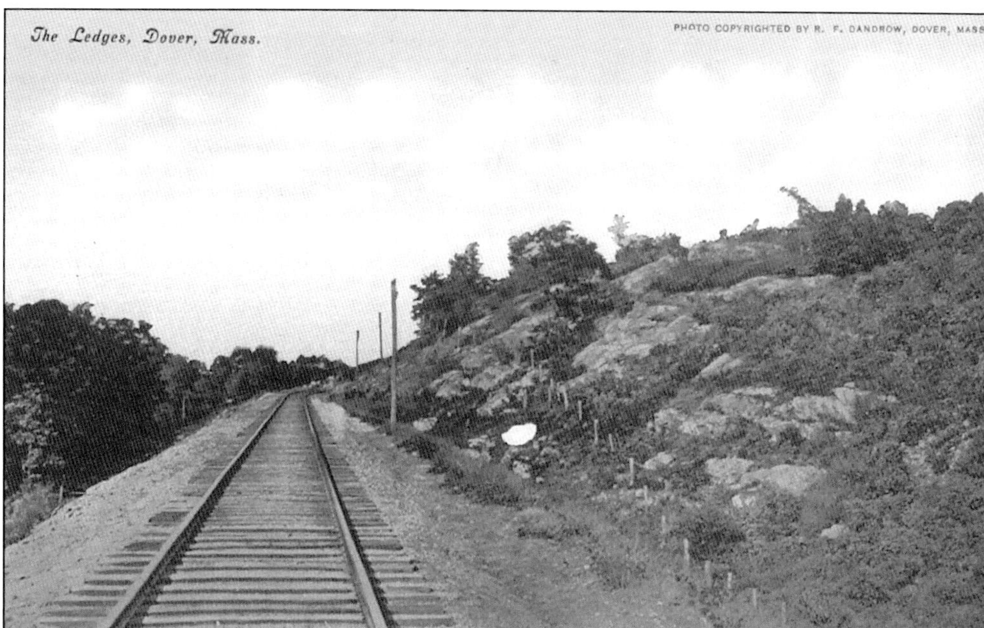

Railroad tracks have been in Dover since the 1850s, but today the residents do not normally see much of them. The area known as the Ledges is one place where the tracks remain behind the scenes. (Hope Hynes scrapbook.)

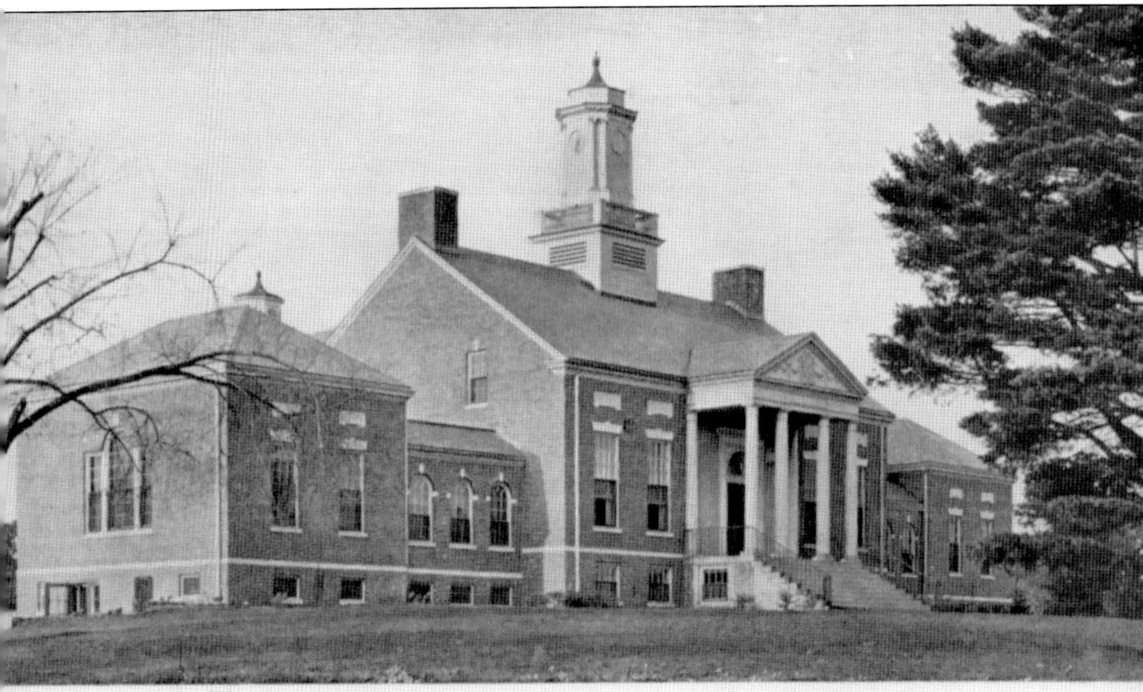

DOVER TOWN HOUSE AND LIBRARY
KILHAM, HOPKINS & GREELEY :: ARCHITECTS

Built in 1922. Cost $80,000. Hall to seat 450. Town offices in right wing. Public Library in left. Community rooms front centre. Banquet Hall to seat 300, with kitchen, etc. Boys' Club Room, etc.

On November 11, 1922, the new Dover Town House and Dover Town Library was dedicated and the "Legion Room" was presented to the Dover American Legion, Post No. 209. One of the speakers was Boston mayor James Michael Curley. In 1999, an interior renovation of the building was done. (Hope Hynes scrapbook.)

The Dover Church has stood on Meetinghouse Hill since 1839 on the site of a previous meetinghouse that had been built in 1811. The church had its beginnings on November 10, 1762, when Benjamin Caryl was ordained the first minister of the Springfield Parish in the meetinghouse across the street. A parish building was added in 1986. (Hope Hynes scrapbook.)

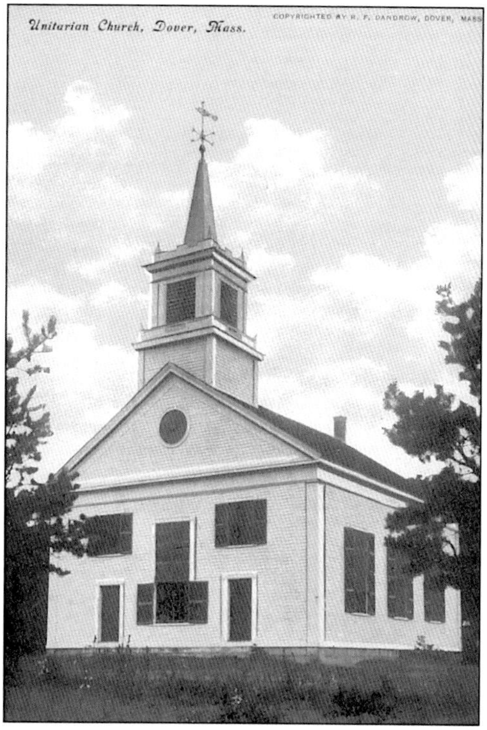

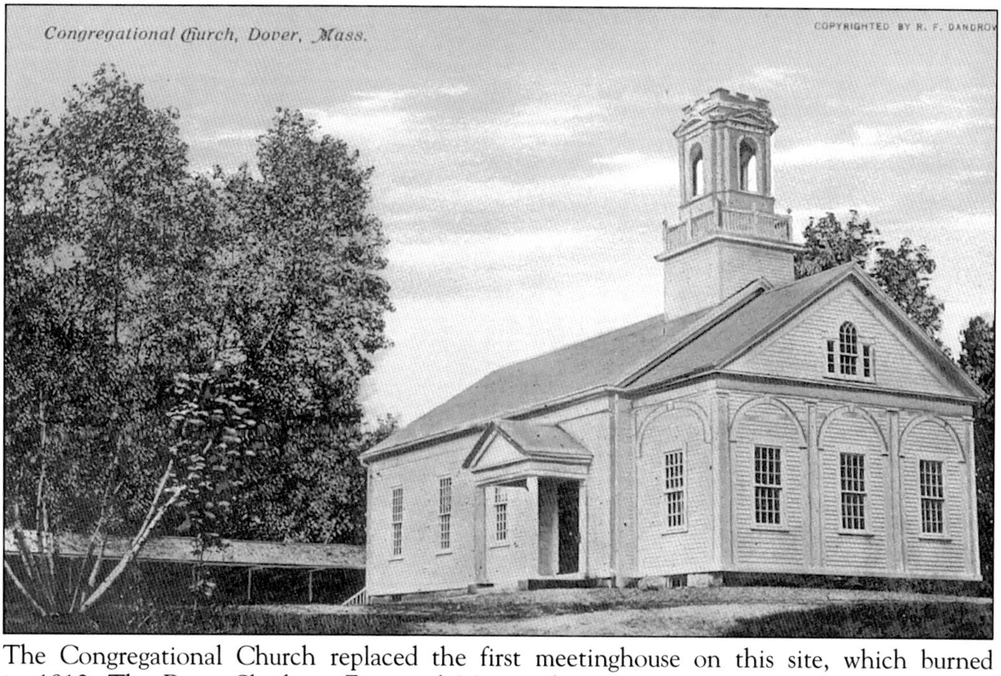

The Congregational Church replaced the first meetinghouse on this site, which burned in 1810. The Dover-Sherborn Episcopal Mission began activities in Dover on September 27, 1967; originally, they shared the Dover Church. In 1969, the name was changed to St. Dunstan's Episcopal Mission. St. Dunstan's became a parish and appointed a rector in 1975. Once the home of the Dover Grange, this building most recently has been renovated to become St. Dunstan's Episcopal Church. (Hope Hynes scrapbook.)

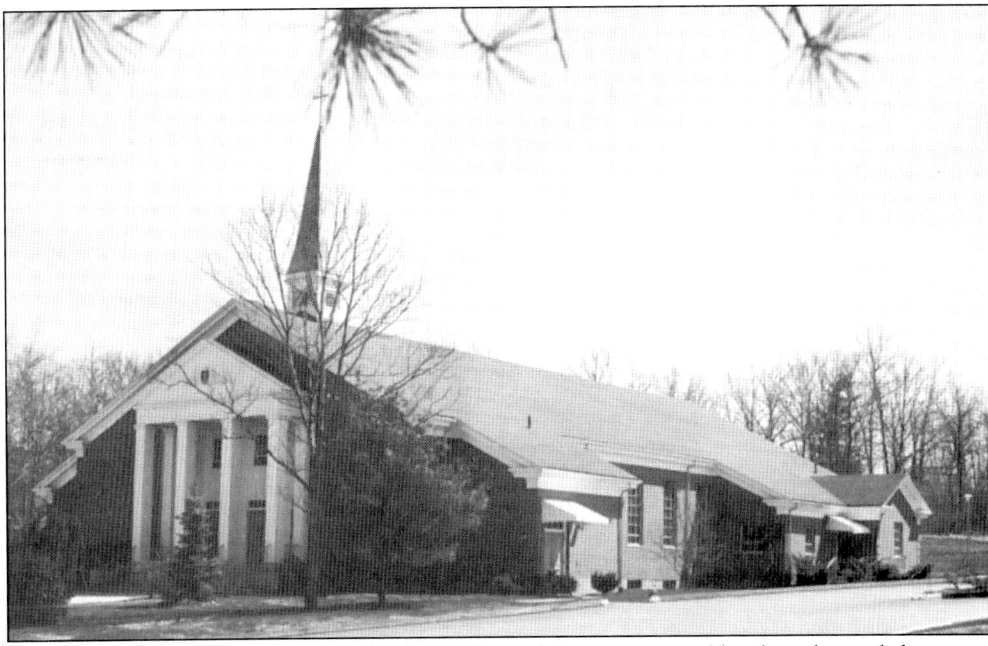

In 1937, the Coughlan family on Walpole Street left two acres of land to the archdiocese of Boston. Catholics in the community began ten years of raising money. The Church of the Most Precious Blood on Centre Street was established on September 15, 1959, and construction began. The church was completed for Easter services on April 2, 1961, and was dedicated by Richard Cardinal Cushing on April 19, 1961.

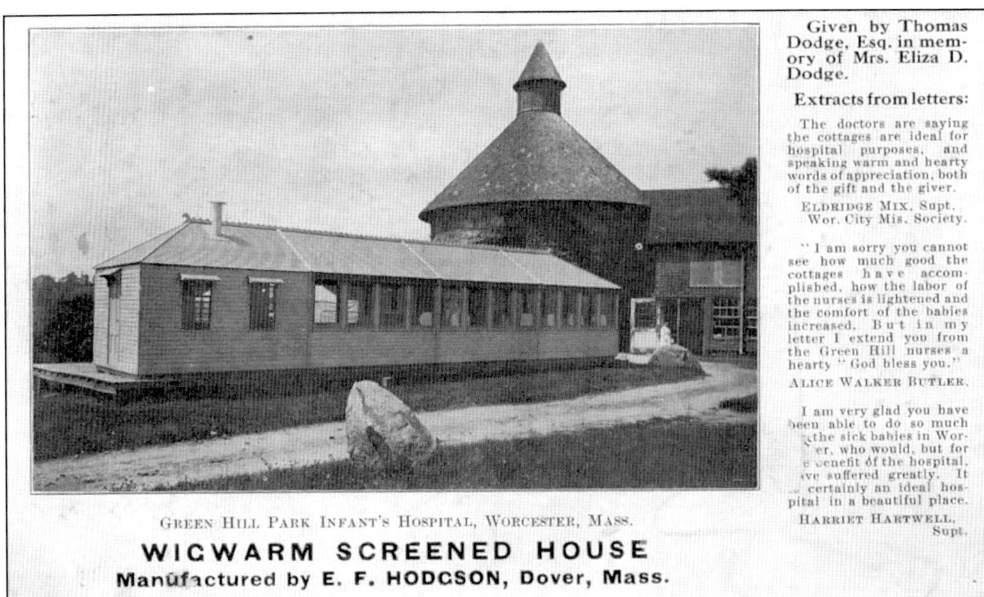

This example of E.F. Hodgson's portable houses demonstrates the versatility of his product. Note the four prefabricated sections of the long building in the foreground. These sections could easily be configured to satisfy a wide variety of needs. (Hope Hynes scrapbook.)

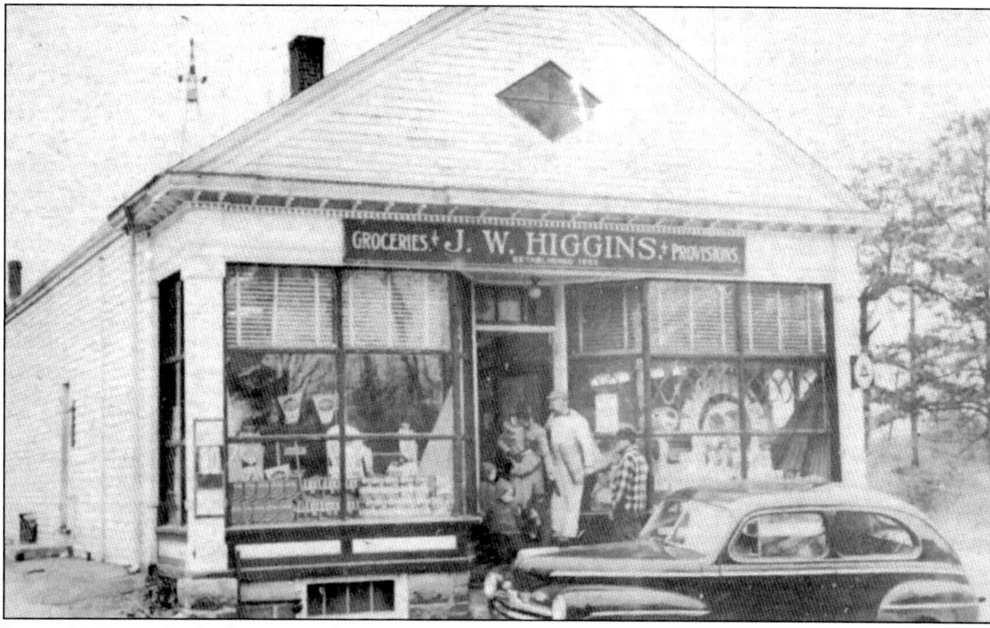

Lewis B. Paine built the original store in 1879 that J.W. Higgins bought in 1883. The store was struck by lightning and completely destroyed in 1901. Jedediah Higgins rebuilt and reopened the store for business on the same site in 1902. This 1930s view of the much changed store captures a certain flavor of the times. (Hope Hynes scrapbook.)

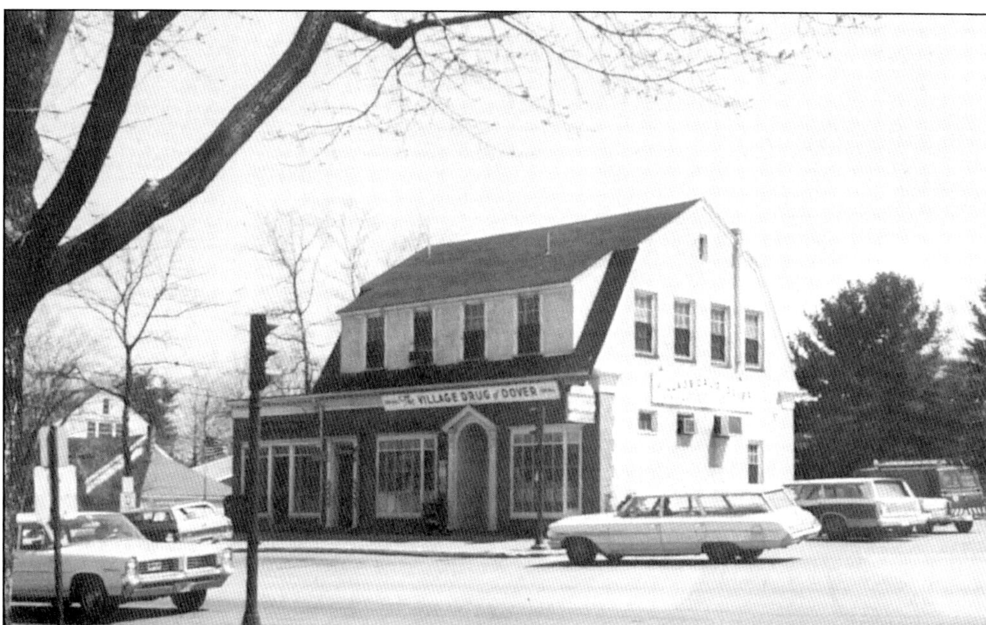

This 1968 postcard of the Dover Center business district reminds us what those gas-guzzlers looked like back then. There is no doubt that the automobile has taken over our lives. The post office was still in the left wing at the time. The Charles River School can be seen to the left of the post office wing.

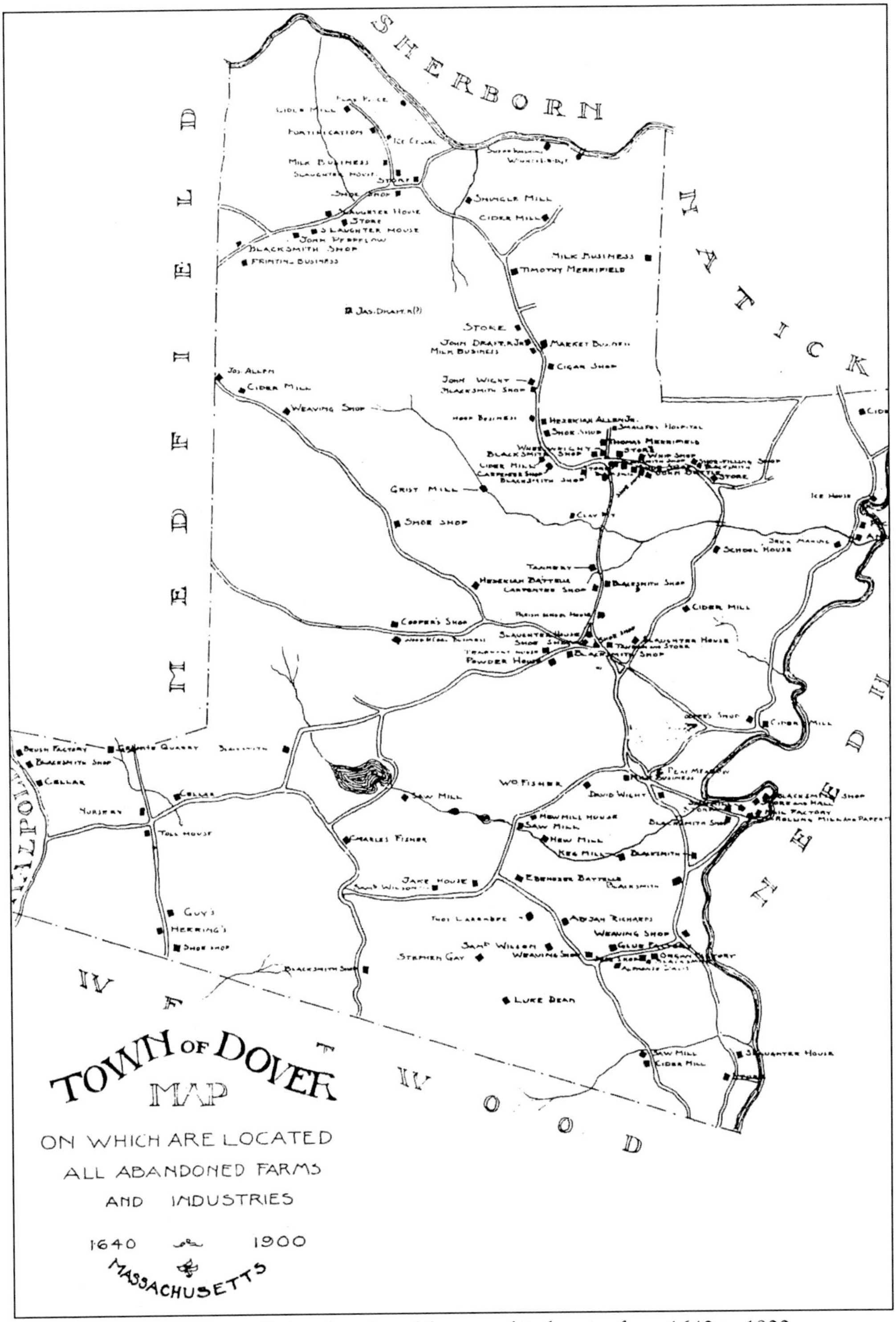

This map of Dover shows all the abandoned farms and industries from 1640 to 1900.

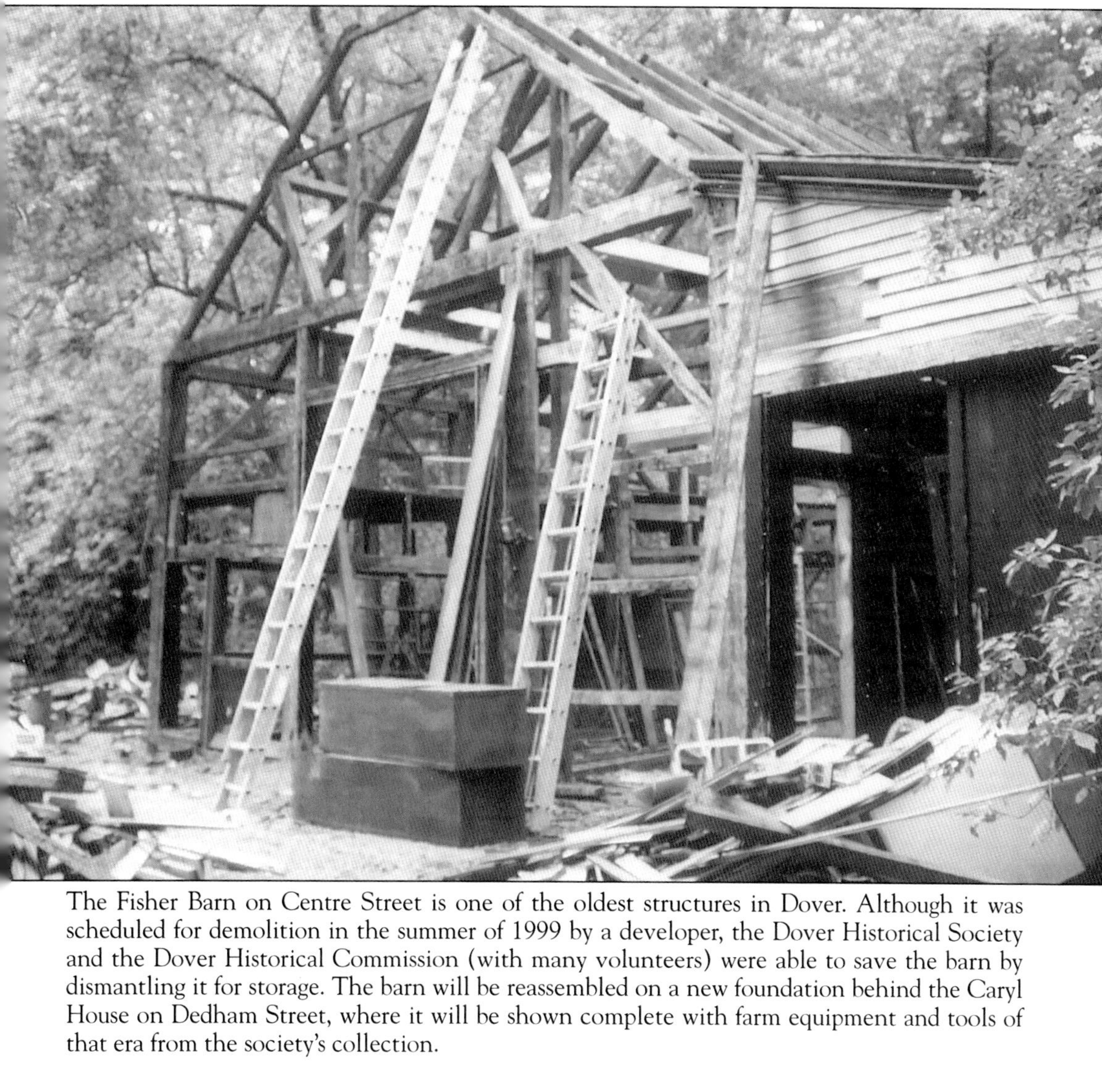

The Fisher Barn on Centre Street is one of the oldest structures in Dover. Although it was scheduled for demolition in the summer of 1999 by a developer, the Dover Historical Society and the Dover Historical Commission (with many volunteers) were able to save the barn by dismantling it for storage. The barn will be reassembled on a new foundation behind the Caryl House on Dedham Street, where it will be shown complete with farm equipment and tools of that era from the society's collection.

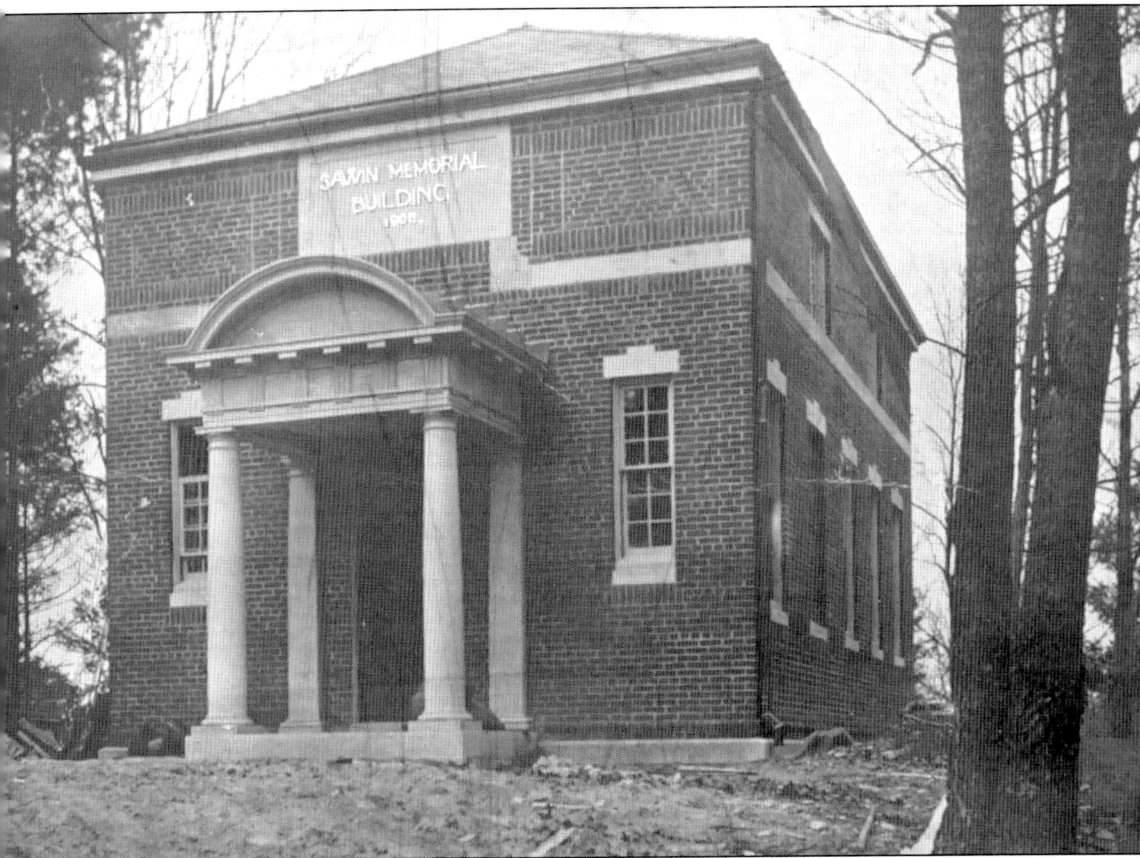

The Sawin Memorial Building, dedicated on May 14, 1907, houses the Dover Historical Society. Benjamin Sawin left his estate to the society to give the group a proper home. The 1960s saw renewed interest in the society and the town's historical resources. With the recent addition of modern climate controls to protect the collection and proper cataloging, the society continues to be an active and integral part of the community.

ACKNOWLEDGMENTS

In putting together a pictorial history, one owes much to others, especially those who furnish the images. In particular, the Dover Historical Society has supported this venture from the beginning. All of the photographs, unless otherwise indicated, come from the society's collection.

I would like to thank the following members of the society and the Dover community for their assistance in the photograph collecting, the photograph copying, and the photograph identification: Donald R. Ball, Sandra J. Ball, Robert F. Comiskey, Marion J. Gerrity, Eleanor A. Greim, Kenneth J. Jones, Priscilla Pitt Jones, Pamela S. Kunkemueller, Ellen A. Little, Janet L. MacKenzie, Glenda Garrelts Mattes, Shirley B. McGill, George W. Newcomb, Cornelia Clark Roberts, Marvin Rosenkrantz, Eleanor Hollis Tedesco, and Richard H. Vara.

For help in collecting and processing the maps, I am grateful for the assistance of the director of operations Craig S. Hughes and Robert Homer, Dover Highway Department; the Dover Historical Commission; and the Harvard Map Collection at the Nathan Marsh Pusey Library, Harvard University.

The following organizations also were kind enough to assist me in answering questions, finding references, and assisting with finding photographs: the Dedham Historical Society, the *Dover Hometown Weekly*, the Dover Town Library, the *Dover-Sherborn Press*, the Needham Historical Society, and the Norfolk Hunt Club.

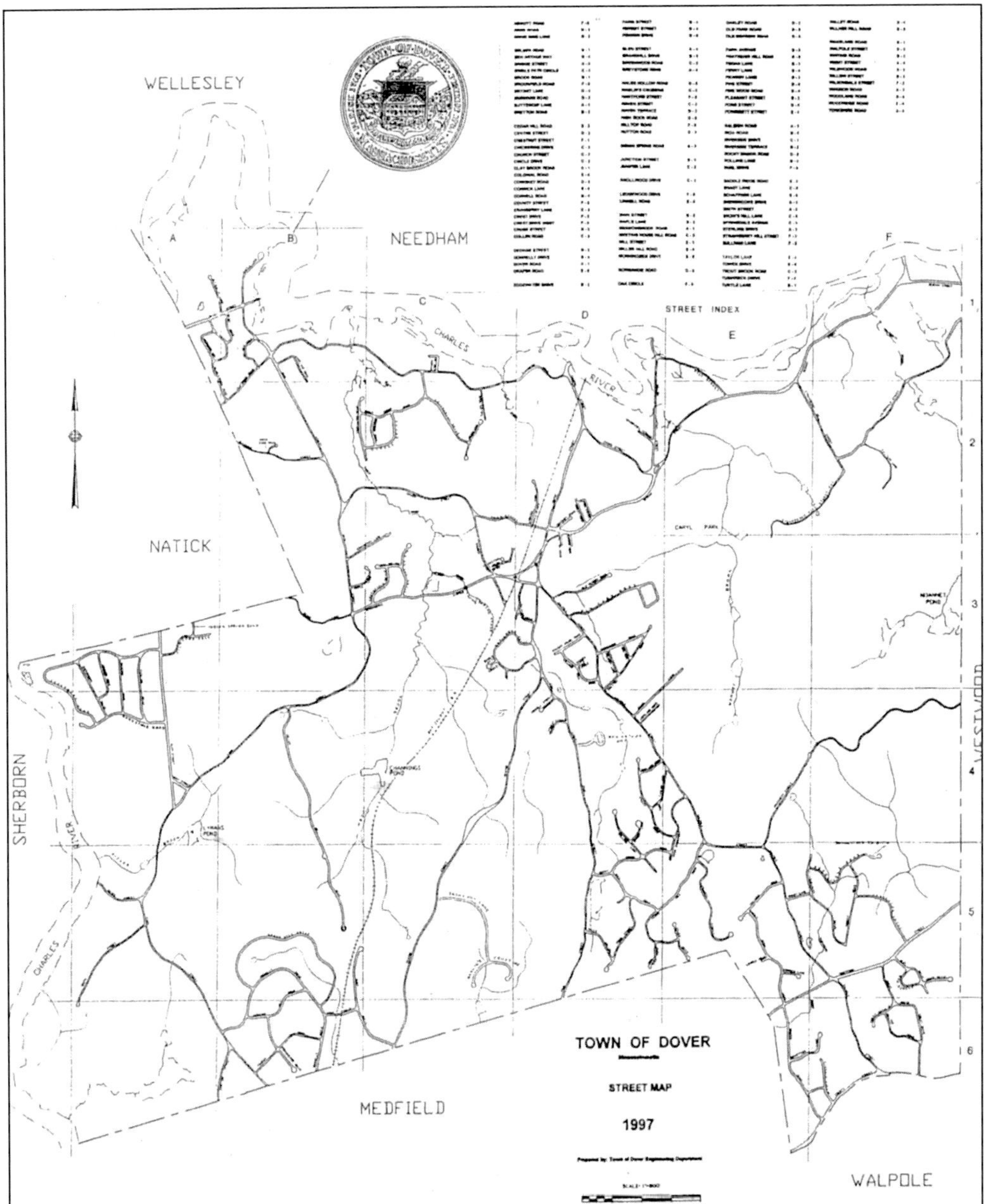

This street map of Dover shows the town at the end of the 20th century.